ENCHANTED GROUND

ENCHANTED GROUND

GARDENING WITH NATURE IN THE SUBTROPICS

GEORGIA B. TASKER

of *The Miami Herald*

Photographs by Georgia B. Tasker

ANDREWS AND McMEEL

A Universal Press Syndicate Company

KANSAS CITY

Library of Congress Cataloging-in-Publication Data

Tasker, Georgia B.
    Enchanted ground: gardening with nature in the subtropics / by Georgia B. Tasker

        p.   cm.
    Includes bibliographic references (p.   ) and index.
    ISBN: 0-8362-8056-3
    1. Natural landscaping—Florida. 2. Landscape plants—Florida. 3. Native plants for cultivation—Florida. 4. Tropical plants—Florida. 5. Native plant gardening—Florida. I. Title.
SB439.24.F6T38   1994
635.9'51759—dc20   93-40952   CIP

ATTENTION: SCHOOLS AND BUSINESSES

Andrews and McMeel books are available at quantity discounts with bulk purchase for educational, business, or sales promotional use. For information, please write to: Special Sales Department, Andrews and McMeel, 4900 Main Street, Kansas City, Missouri 64112.

TO MY MOTHER AND FATHER

"In my attempts to unravel [nature's] mysteries, I have a sense of reverence and devotion, I feel as if I were on enchanted ground. And whenever any of its mysteries are revealed to me, I have a feeling of elation—I was about to say exaltation, just as though the birds or the trees had told me their secrets and I had understood their language—and Nature herself has made me a confidant."

CHARLES TORREY SIMPSON

In Lower Florida Wilds

CONTENTS

Introduction . . . . *xi*

1 NATURAL AREAS AND THEIR SEASONS *1*
A New Outlook on Wildscapes and City Gardens 8

2 GARDENS AND THEIR SEASONS 13

3 TOOLS AND TECHNIQUES: HOW TO WORK IN THE GARDEN 19
Tools for Gardeners 19
Building Flower Beds 20
Planting 21
Pruning 22
Propagating 25
    Planting Seeds 25
    Taking Cuttings 26
    Air Layering 28
    Making Divisions 29
Fertilizing 30
    Nutrient Deficiencies 34
Composting 34

4 ADVERSITY: WHAT TO WORK AROUND IN THE GARDEN 37
Hurricanes 37

Trees with Shallow Roots and Brittle Wood 38
Freezes 42
Drought 44
Insects and Small Forms of Wildlife 44
    When Turning to Chemicals 49
Diseases 50

5 BUILDING A FRAMEWORK: TREES FOR THE GARDEN 53
Energy Conservation with Landscaping 54
Selected Trees 56
    Native Trees for Use on Fill 63
    Native Trees for Wet Areas 64
    Fast-growing Native Trees 64
Adding to the Scaffold 64
    Useful Small Trees 64
    Choice Flowering Trees 68
    Flowering Trees and Their Seasons 71

6 CONSTRUCTING THE WALLS AND THE FLOOR 73
What Works as a Shrub 73
    Native Shrubs 74
    Shrubs for Barriers 77
    Shrubs for Fragrance 77
    Shrubs for Color 78
    Shrubs for Seaside 79

Shrubs for Flowers. 79
Exotic Shrubs 81
Ground Covers 85
Vines 88

7 SAVING WATER 91
Drought-Tolerant Plants 95
Drought-Tolerant Shrubs 97
Drought-Tolerant Ground Covers 97

**8 TROPICAL PLANTS: THE FINISHING
TOUCHES** 99
Bromeliads 100
Aroids 102
Ferns 104
Heliconias 106
Orchids 109
Repotting Orchids 114

9 PALMS AND CYCADS 117
Native Palms 117
Common Landscape Palms 119
Palm Care 122
Cycads 124

**10 TOUCH, TASTE, AND SMELL IN
THE GARDEN** 127
Fragrant Plants 128

Roses 129
Fruit Trees 130

11 CREATURE FEATURES 139
Butterfly Gardens 140
A Pineland Planting for Butterflies 141
Wildflowers 142
Nectar Plants 143
Larval Plants 144
A Native Garden for Butterflies and Birds 145
Food for Birds 146
Trees 146
Shrubs 146
Vines 147

12 RESTORING THE SOUL 149
Building a Hammock 155
A Keys Hammock 156
A Pineland and a Hammock 156
Water for Wildlife 156

Appendix: Invasive Plants 159

Selected Bibliography 162

Gardens to Visit 164

Index 165

ACKNOWLEDGMENTS

As a JOURNALIST, one learns by working. This is especially true when covering a subject such as gardening and one goes into it untutored, as I did.

My education in gardening began with a Master Gardening course, at which I met Seymour Goldweber, now University of Florida extension agent emeritus. He has been entirely generous with his vast knowledge then and now. Dr. David Lee at Florida International University is responsible for sparking my love of tropical botany by inviting me to audit one of his courses in the early 1980s. I then signed up for the certificate program in commercial tropical botany, and have continued to learn from him.

Sandy Dayhoff, park ranger extraordinaire at Everglades National Park, graciously and lovingly showed me many of the mysteries of the Everglades.

Don Evans, chief of horticulture at Fairchild Tropical Garden, has helped unstintingly at each and every turn. Dr. Carl Campbell, University of Florida emeritus professor, has answered many tropical fruit and native plant questions over the years; he and his family have shared knowledge, Becky's delicious tropical foods, and warm friendship.

Other teachers include Chuck Hubbuch, Mary Collins, Cathy Ryan, and the entire staff at Fairchild Tropical Garden; Fred Berry, David Bar-Zvi, Margarita Calvet, Doris Rosebraugh, Susan Hall, Lester Pancoast, Joan Green, Bill Lessard, David McLean, Kathryn O'Leary Richards, Jill Sidran, Bob Scully, Bob Fuchs, the Fennell family, Peter Strelkow, Tim Anderson, Bob Knight, Jr., Way Hoyt; Jack Parker, at Florida International University's department of environmental studies; Chris Rollins at the Fruit and Spice Park; Larry Schokman at The Kampong; Gene Joyner at the Palm Beach extension office.

Joyce and Don Gann have been especially kind, answering all questions about native plants, sharing their appreciation of South Florida and their home in a hammock. George Gann-Matzen has helped me understand the intricacies of habitat restoration, which he continues to pioneer. Roger Hammer, naturalist and humorist, has led wonderful field trips to North Key Largo, the Everglades, Elliott Key, Castellow Hammock.

I'm grateful to Dr. Derek Burch for his many patient explanations through the years, as well as his expertise and suggestions in reading over the manuscript. Any mistakes or omissions, however, are entirely my own.

And as this project has proceeded, I am indebted to friends who listened, encouraged, and nudged, to the gardeners who have welcomed me into their gardens, and to my department colleagues at *The Herald* who have been understanding and supportive through the ordeal.

INTRODUCTION

OUR SUBTROPICAL LANDSCAPE is a subtle and vital one. It has to do more with green than gaudy, more with function and interaction than exhibition, and as a consequence it seems to invite elaboration.

Juan Ponce de León called Florida *Pascua florida,* or "flowering Easter," when he sailed here in 1513. Ever since, we have felt obligated to add to the scenery. Citrus groves and coconut palms swaying on the beaches have become synonymous with Florida, even though they came from elsewhere.

A generally pleasant state of affairs climate-wise has allowed the introduction of all sorts of plants and all manner of gardens.

Population pressures, however, have changed the rules of gardening. There are far more people than natural areas; agriculture and housing developments have pushed into woodlands and wetlands, polluting them, plowing them under or filling them in, pushing out plants and animals. The plants we once thought would help drain the swamps have very nearly done so. The trees we cut have not grown back because there is no place left to grow back into. Things, generally, are a mess.

As gardeners, we have a responsibility to change the way we do things. Water cannot be used wantonly in the dry season; chemicals no longer can be dumped mindlessly in the backyard; plants that might escape to remnant natural areas cannot be planted with impunity.

While this means a different and more cautious approach to gardening, it does not mean our gardens must be any less beautiful. Rather, it means that by being better stewards we will be better gardeners.

We still can find delight in the sensual attractions of the garden, in the leaves of *Costus barbatus* that feel like velvety ears of mastiffs, in the clovey nighttime perfume of *Brunfelsia nitida,* in the lemony scent of sweet bay magnolia, in the elegant green architecture of the triangle and thatch palms.

These gifts of the garden are ours for the asking, provided we bring to them a little know-how.

That know-how begins with using native plants more often. It means building a framework of the natives that survive best under our conditions, adding the flourish of exotics with care. It means working with the seasonal fluctuations of rain and drought, bugs and diseases. It means increasing our tolerance of chewed leaves and fungus on the mangoes. It means allowing the snakes and lizards to be allies, not enemies, and allowing a few aphids to survive in order to build up the population of aphid predators.

I have lived in South Florida since the late 1960s, and written about gardens, landscapes, and the environment since 1980. During that time, I've watched natural areas become fragments of a once beautiful land. Half a century ago, naturalists Thomas Barbour and Charles Torrey Simpson lamented the ruin of Florida. They surely would not recognize it today. Yet gardeners, I believe, care deeply about the land, and can lead the way in allowing a healing process to occur.

This is a book that I hope will encourage healing. Its lists of trees and other plants are those I know or like, and are not meant to be all encompassing. Certain ways of doing things are those I have found work for me; you may develop your own. But the basic premise is one I hope you will adopt: live lightly here; work with the land and not against it.

Unlike the built environment, gardens are living and therefore, always changing. They are exciting because of change, and they hold our interest in ways nonliving things cannot. That we are heading into a new millennium in a world that demands change as never before ought to bring out the best in gardens as well as gardeners.

ENCHANTED GROUND

Cypress being entangled by a strangler fig in the Corkscrew Swamp Sanctuary. Boston ferns surround them.

1

NATURAL AREAS AND THEIR SEASONS

LITTLE ELSE speaks as eloquently of our primitive ties to the earth as a swamp. The blurred and indistinct boundaries between water and land, the wetness on the plants and thickness of the air seem to wrap us in protoplasm not yet bound by membrane.

Discovering the beauty of Florida's swamps gives any subtropical gardener a touchstone of nature's grace and haunting images: the glory of guzmanias on the pond apple trees, cascades of peperomias on floating logs, graceful strap ferns on cypress knees. Royal palms deep within the swamp are often surrounded by billowing green fountains of Boston ferns; resurrection ferns creep along pop ash branches; tiny orchids cling to the pond apples, dangling their pouches of seeds on tenuous stems; alligator flags mark the deeper water while the lizards' tails and the wild iris skirt the shallows.

Some years ago, I followed the changes in a swamp, a hammock, and a pineland over a year's time, recording differences where none was said to exist. A swamp, many thought, was always a murky, dank place that, just as the other ecosystems in our flat landscape, varied little in elevation, much less seasonal charm.

The changes proved to be many and often dramatic, and I found out firsthand how to see and interpret the seasons in our ever-so-subtle subtropics.

I found that violence and beauty freely roam over the flatness of the land. Threatening storms move in and out quickly, sweeping across the marshes and plundering the mangroves and hammocks with fury, as do the spring and summer wildfires. Periodic hurricanes can be massively destructive and regenerative at once, while winters can bring killing frosts or merely a gentle hiatus of rampant growth. These are changes everyone can notice, but beneath those obvious, urgent manifestations there are quiet and often quite wonderful ones. As a gardener, I learned to understand the way things work here and the expressions of those workings.

Worlds away from neatly cut St. Augustine lawns and precisely pruned cherry hedges, the woods full of lancewoods and blollies, dodoneas and cassias grow in what seems to be a bewildering mishmash of disarray, but in fact are finely honed, dynamic systems. If we watch these systems over time, we learn how the seasons affect whole communities of plants; we also learn what adversities we may encounter and what balms to expect when we transplant these systems to our gardens.

This is not to say that gardens have to mimic the local woods. But the woods tell us a lot about what will work, and the survival skills plants have developed that we can exploit in our gardens. We can even garner ideas for landscaping, as they are freely available to anyone.

Sunup in Taylor Slough of Everglades National Park.

Because the native landscape is a subtle one, with look-alike hardwoods, expanses of slender-boled pines, and vast stretches of beach and marsh, we have tried to improve on it, to embolden it with more color, more drama, more exotic vistas. Some of these efforts have worked well: the palms and bromeliads, orchids, calatheas, and many other tropical plants add a benign elegance to the native palette. Others have been robust to a fault, escaping and smothering vast tracts of our heritage in melaleucas, Australian pines, and Brazilian peppers, in pothos and downy rosemyrtle.

Then there's the human stress on the land. The demand for water has lowered the water table, riven the marshes and flow-ways, withered the periphyton, dried the solution holes, and killed off the birds—threatened within heartbeats the very life of the place.

As gardeners, as people who work with the land and on the land, we have a special responsibility to exert care. Moreover, we must work to reinvigorate and heal what once was given. While biology explores the science and art of restoring natural landscapes, as it is doing in tallgrass prairies and deserts and rain forests, we can take action on our front.

What I'm proposing is thoughtful gardening: gardening with the knowledge that what we do to this piece of land impacts uncounted creatures and things, from millions of microorganisms to earthworms, anoles, snakes, pillbugs, sowbugs, orange dog cater-

Paurotis palms stand as sentinels, looking over the prairie of sawgrass in the Everglades.

pillars, fritillaries and flycatchers, cardinals, marsh hares, golden orb spiders, other gardeners, other generations, and whole ecosystems.

Use fewer chemicals. Mulch. Plant butterfly gardens and keep sanctuaries for the birds and critters. Restore, if possible, a niche with what was there naturally. Work to protect natural areas, to revitalize parks, to replant and maintain, to have street trees and streetscapes. Foster among everyone a sense of pride in this place. It is yours, mine, ours, theirs.

It's not hard as a gardener to do this. Get to know the lay of the land, learn from it, and work with it. You'll find that you sink your own roots as you do so.

WINTER

Winter is the best time to meet the scenery—the mosquitoes are at a minimum, the breezes are usually balmy, and the sun is warm.

Winter is our dry season, summer the wet one. Drying down—sometimes at a rate of half an inch a day in Corkscrew Sanctuary and Big Cypress Swamp—is the main event of the winter cycle as it slowly progresses toward the droughty spring. Freshwater prairies are golden brown as the tri-cornered sawgrass sighs in the warm, lazy light of winter afternoons. Willows—having shed their leaves in fall and formed smoky halos around the deeply dug alligator holes—bear wintry spikes of yellow flowers, called catkins, and begin leafing out again by January. Silvery cypress trees, which stay leafless all winter, mingle with the red-leaved maples, while the dark green of the wax myrtles stands in bold contrast among them.

Egrets, anhingas, woodstorks, and blue and green herons are highly visible in the winter landscape, gathering on the edges of the water holes along with the ebony and mossy alligators that heave themselves ashore to sun in lethal torpor.

The roseate spoonbills nest around Florida Bay in November and December, and are gone again by March. Ten different wading birds, from herons to pelicans, nest in cacophonous colonies in the mangroves, staining leaves white with their droppings, enriching the water and the silt, literally surviving on the fringes.

Dahoon holly is laden with red berries, while the saltbush is covered with fuzzy white seeds. Alligator flags have flowered and hang their seed pods on fragile stalks. Mahoganies bear plumlike fruit that gradually harden, split, and release winged seeds in the spring.

SPRING

By late winter and early spring the thick mat of algae on the floor of the marsh, called periphyton, begins to dry and in some places to crack. This mat is at the base of the food chain. In the dry season, seeds and microorganisms are sheltered beneath this protective layer, to reemerge with the coming rains in dazzling numbers. In times of severe drought, periphyton can be killed back, meaning a long delay in the swamp's return to fecundity.

Waterholes—generally alligator-made but including the man-made canals that slice through South Florida—are gathering spots for wildlife in winter as the drying continues. Fish collect in these pools, as do the fish-eating birds, followed by bird-eating mam-

Pinelands once covered thousands of acres in South Florida, but now only a handful remain outside of Everglades National Park. Yellow-flowering *Bahama cassia* is a resident of the pines ecosystem.

mals and reptiles. When drought threatens and the water sinks lower and lower, oxygen depletion will kill off the larger fish. Still, the tiny killifish and gambusias are able to siphon oxygen from the surface by virtue of their upward-turned mouths. Garfish, those cigar-shaped primitives, have elemental lungs, and they, too, can breathe as the water gets nastier.

The water may drop below ground level by the time spring arrives, and there is, in this season, a sharply drawn battle between life and death. The struggle to survive with little water and the urge to mate and reproduce at the same time color everyday events with a compelling sense of drama.

Endangered woodstorks fish for their nestlings in remaining pools that threaten to dry; should too many fish die, the adult storks will abandon their young to starve as they disperse to keep themselves alive. Even plants reproduce in the face of drought: red maple, royal palm, and cypress seedlings will root and grow in the dryness, racing to gain height so they don't drown when the water returns.

Eastern diamondback rattlesnakes may venture into dry sloughs during spring searching for food; alligator hatchlings will thrive unless unseasonal rains drown them; swallow-tail kites will arrive from South America and begin their mating flights. Sweet bay magnolias flower, giving off a lemony scent described by Marjorie Kinnan Rawlings in *Cross Creek* as "the fragrance of a rare perfume." The oaks, red bay, lignum vitae, and wax myrtles flower; gumbo-limbos lose their leaves, flower, and flush out again.

After the vernal equinox and the spring tides, the open sea is highest around our peninsula. Water rises in Florida Bay, scattering the wading birds into the black mangroves and the intertidal zones to feed. The white-crowned pigeon returns from the Bahamas and Cuba in April, nests in the mangroves, and feeds in the hammocks on poisonwood, blolly, mastic, and pigeon plum. Like the swallow-tail kite, some pigeons stay until October. Along the beach, oyster

North Key Largo's tropical hardwood hammocks are filled with dappled light. Here are the red-barked gumbo-limbos and splotched poisonwood trees so characteristic of the tropical woods.

Bringing the wildscapes into the garden can mean building carefully among the trees in their natural setting. This home was constructed in the middle of 15 acres of pines in far South Dade County.

catchers, marbled godwits, whimbrels, sandpipers, willets, and other shore birds appear in April and May in large numbers, stopping to feed on isopods and small invertebrates as they return from the tropics and head north. The sea oats green up, flower, and begin forming their tall spikes of seed heads, while the beach sunflower, the oxeye daisy, and the succulent-leaved scaevola shrubs flower.

By the end of May or early June, the rains normally begin, bringing back life-giving waters. The light begins to change as the sun moves directly overhead. As humidity builds, winter's clarity fades; the sky changes from deep blue to lighter blue; the clouds begin their daily cycle of accumulating, building, and darkening; and afternoon storms become a part of the sultry diurnal routine.

In the early spring, when the earth responds to the longer, warmer days with a surge of growth, a curious thing normally happens in these mangroves: larval forms of shrimp, tiny and unseen, migrate into them to feed at night and hide securely among the prop roots during the day. Over summer, they feast in the waters enriched by the falling leaves broken down into usable specks by bacteria and fungi. By October or November, grown into adults, shrimp migrate back through the Keys to the Dry Tortugas.

By the late 1980s, however, the lack of fresh water flowing into Florida Bay had begun to change the ecology of the mangrove fringe, the water quality of the bay, and the functioning of the system. The bay became saltier, turtle grass began to die, and shrimp, fish, and birds became fewer. The outcome is uncertain.

SUMMER

Rain returns. Insects supply the white noise for summer's extraordinary show as growth takes center stage. Sawgrass is green again, almost magically changing the backdrop. Character actors are abundant: pig frogs, tree frogs, cicadas, dragonflies, and whining mosquitoes, food for chuck-will's-widow that calls out the return of the season.

Wildflowers provide the tints: marsh pinks, red swamp hibiscus, white and fragrant swamp lilies, delicate green butterfly orchids, violet lobelias, blue ageratum, yellow-tops. Others send up the perfume. Water lilies smell of almonds; liverworts give off clouds of licorice aroma when you touch them; wax myrtles, when crushed, smell of bay.

When you get to know them, these places have personalities all their own. The tropical woods of North Key Largo, with trees of blotchy bark and small leaves, have a sun-dappled look and feel to them. Mangroves take on a menacing verticality from all those prop roots and pneumatophores. Hammocks, from the Indian word *hummuck* or *hamaca* meaning "tree island," have a rocky substrate with dark, fern-splattered solution holes and a damp woodsiness. The pinelands sparkle with a misleading airiness—they often are hotter than any other ecosystem, except perhaps the scrub.

The scrub is a desertlike holdout of ancient Florida, with plants and animals adapted to hot, sun-soaked sand dunes. Robust rosemary shrubs and sand pines, scrub oaks, and ground-dwelling lichens thrive here, along with scrub lizards that have developed extra long legs for racing along the sand and gopher tortoises that burrow into it. Because of clearing by settlers and planting by citrus growers, only the tiniest remnants of this habitat still exist, but the scrub once flourished on the sandy backbone of the Florida peninsula, along the central ridge and on the high eastern coastal ridge among the pinelands. Some 35 plants and a dozen animals are endemic to this Florida-only habitat, including the scrub dayflower, *Commelina erecta*; seymeria, *Seymeria pectinata*; four kinds of mints; a lupine; pygmy fringe tree; pink-petaled *Cuthbertia ornata*; Curtis's milkweed; a sand skink; the Florida scrub jay; and the Florida mouse.

When the summer rains build and finally fall on the superheated scrub, the lichens and mosses turn green and become soft as velvet underfoot.

All summer the growth cycle continues. Water returns to the marsh, and from small lakes above Lake Okeechobee it flows southwest at its mile-a-day pace across the imperceptibly sloped peninsula. Along the mangrove fringe, the black mangroves bloom in June and July, attracting butterflies from everywhere, especially the whites and sulphurs. Trees and shrubs flower and fruit, tree snails browse up and down the lichen-covered lysilomas of the hammocks, and the sawgrass bends with heavy dew in the morning and rain in the afternoon. The sagittaria and pickerelweed in the sloughs send out beautiful smooth leaves, only to have them notched and chewed by countless insects. Bromeliads fill with rain and become home to wiggly larvae and frogs, while the water lettuce blooms unnoticed deep within its leaf axils as it floats across the lakes and ponds.

In the pinelands, the tetrazygia flowers are white with brilliant yellow stamens. The morinda forms its aggregate pineapple-like fruit that will turn the color of Swiss cheese when ripe. The coontie's grass-green new leaves darken and harden. Beautyberry opens flowers along its shrubby, viny stems, and soon the purple fruits will pull the stems low with their weight.

The hurricane season begins in earnest in late July, August, and September, as the ocean waters get hotter. The 1935 hurricane killed black mangroves around the Keys, while the 1964 storm, Donna, left a swath of mangled trees across the lowest part of the mainland and killed about half of the great white herons. The 1992 hurricane, Andrew, devastated the south end of the peninsula, but left the Keys intact.

AUTUMN

As autumn approaches, the wax myrtle, snowberry, smilax, baccharis, and myrsine will bear fruit in time for the fall bird migration. Warblers, vireos, buntings, and gnatcatchers *zzzt*, *spreet*, and *cheep* among the tree canopies, darting for beetles, spiders, and flies. The great white herons nest between November and July, sometimes twice in one year, congregating in colonies around Snake Bight, Cape Sabal, Sandy Key, and the lower Keys. Along with the spoonbills, they once were slaughtered and eaten by the local fishermen and spongers; their feathers were sold from Havana to France.

Wild petunias will flower violet. Wild coffee fruit blushes red, the redstarts flit through the hammocks, and the mushrooms appear and release their spores. A final spate of thunderstorms often marks the end of the rainy season, giving everything a last good soaking, and things settle down again.

These are the rhythms. They may vary by a month, they may be warmer or cooler, more or less rainy, but their cyclical regularity is what defines subtropical South Florida. We learn to live by the rhythms, wet and dry, changes in the light and humidity, flowering and fruiting, fires and storms, and we garden in their wake.

A NEW OUTLOOK ON WILDSCAPES AND CITY GARDENS

How do you learn from the wild landscapes? What changes can you make in your suburban or city yard that will bring wild landscapes closer?

In niches and nooks. Around corners and along perimeters. First, outline what you want to accomplish in your garden—a place to sit, a place to play, a visual buffer, energy conservation, or a butterfly garden.

If the totally natural area is not suited to your lifestyle, then a section or even a small corner of the yard can be planted in natives. This will go a long way toward providing berries, fruits, nuts, shelter, and nesting areas for birds and small animals. If you have a paucity of songbirds, if you have seen nothing wilder than opossums or gray squirrels in years, then you know how desperately these native areas are needed.

The fact that you want to design a yard to save energy does not conflict with creating habitat. Energy conservation is enhanced by natives. Plants that use less fertilizer and water are generally those most suited to the local growing conditions, and those, by default, are the natives. However, there are non-native plants that are equally useful and often more easily found in nurseries than some native plants. Use them in combination with the natives.

Additionally, such gardens lessen the risk of adding toxins to the water and create healthier soils and landscapes, which in turn become more valuable.

Provide a basic native backdrop, then add the tropical or temperate touches. For the tropicals that require protection from cold, you will have put in place a hardy ceiling and walls; for temperate plants that take cooler conditions or acid soils, you will have provided shade and lower summer temperatures; and for plants that require more water, you will have added humidity and less drying from winds.

Flowering trees, shrubs, fruit trees, annuals can be added. Even small townhome gardens can have a couple of native trees or shrubs to attract butterflies; a trellised or espaliered fruit tree; a containerized flowering tree.

Plant at the start of the rainy season. Even native plants must be watered regularly after planting in order to make the transition from field or container to landscape. Often, plants will take one or two growing seasons to develop a root system before beginning

Leather ferns, a red bay tree, and paurotis palms are natives that easily bring the natural feeling of South Florida into a suburban setting.

noticeable top growth. Water is the key to establishment and by planting at the start of the rainy season, you use a natural supply.

Don't grow plants you know are riddled with disease problems, such as mangoes prone to the fungus disease anthracnose. Vegetable gardeners know to select disease- and insect-resistant varieties. The same should hold true for landscape gardeners. Ask nurserymen, extension agents, and horticulturists about the suitability of plants you want for your yard, balcony, or patio.

Allow bugs their place in the garden. Every leaf does not have to be perfect. The snakes, lizards, spiders, birds, and other bugs will control many of them. Some bugs are there almost all the time. But they have natural cycles, so they may have disappeared by the time you see the damage, and chemicals you apply will be wasted anyway.

If you must take action against insects or diseases, reach first for organic solutions to your garden problems. Try oils, soaps, or naturally occurring bacteria, such as *Bacillus thuringiensis* (*Bt*). Don't spray the lawns for insects and diseases unless the lawn has insects and diseases, and then spray only the affected areas. The soil is a living substrate, full of such things as beetles, earthworms, and microorganisms as well as roots. Don't poison it.

Compost plant trimmings to recycle nutrients and keep valuable resources out of the landfill. Use compost to improve soil.

A strangler fig literally climbs over the wall at Villa Vizcaya Museum and Gardens in Miami.

Reduce chemical fertilization. Wait for plants to signal their need for nutrients; learn to read the signals plants are sending you.

Reduce water use. Water before sunup and not in midday. This reduces loss of water to wind and evaporation. Remember that the South Florida Water Management District prohibits running lawn sprinklers between 9 A.M. and 5 P.M. Above all, stop running the sprinklers when it's raining. Buy a rain control mechanism that automatically turns off the system when a hard rain begins. Use low-volume irrigation whenever possible.

Quit hatracking trees. Select trees for your landscape that will not get too big or grow into the power lines. Keep your trees pruned so they allow wind to pass through. Keep trees free of deadwood to reduce the chance of fungus finding an entrance.

Learn to make decent flower beds so you don't have to pour water and fertilizers on the annuals.

Mulch when possible and called for, but do so properly without stacking a thick layer of mulch against the trunks of trees, shrubs, and palms. If you pack moisture-holding mulch against trunks, fungal diseases can develop and invade.

Attach orchids, ferns, aroids, and bromeliads to trees if that's how they grow in nature. It adds depth to your garden.

Try to create more than one habitat type in your yard. Normally, a lot of butterfly-insect-animal activity takes place in the transitions between one type of habitat and another.

A single native yard in a desert of St. Augustine grass will help the environment in a small way; several together will help in larger ways. A corridor of natives can replace impenetrable fences and walls, provide barriers and habitats, and serve as living classrooms for the kids.

If we are to express concern about the Earth, this kind of gardening will go a long way toward inviting nature home again.

Summer's garden is vibrant green, with avocados and flowering bromeliads.

2

GARDENS AND THEIR SEASONS

THIS IS WHAT comes of living on the cusp between the temperate north and the tropical south: We grow winter tomatoes and summer malanga. We catch spring fever in March and again in October. Often our forecast is sunny and mild, but often it is not.

We have about five to six months of wet and six to seven months of dry weather, which approximates the tropical way of doing things. Key West is but 50 miles north of the Tropic of Cancer, the northern edge of the tropics, and we are influenced greatly by the Torrid Zone.

Indeed, the wet and dry seasons dictate our garden chores in the subtropics much more than the four temperate ones, but for many years, gardeners in South Florida seemed to believe it was summer here all year round. We now know that some things are better done during appropriate times, especially since our water supply has reached critically low levels within the last few years and all resources are stretched as thin as possible.

With sensitivity to what's beyond the garden wall as well as what's inside it, then, we chart our gardening course through the year, taking compass directions from the sun and stars, drawing a rhumb line through the tropical seasons as well as the temperate ones, doing our dead reckoning by careful logs.

Here's how it goes.

November is generally the transition month from rainy season to dry, when humidity takes a nosedive, and life becomes bearable, even for geraniums. It marks the end of the hurricane season, the beginning of days overseen by porcelain blue skies and peach morning light.

Fall often is no more than a final burst of growth before semi-dormancy, a last hurrah of rain followed by a sudden jump in the size of the trees and shrubs. The sun begins to throw longer shadows, and in the afternoons it slips in beneath the hurricane shutters.

Chorisias, also called floss-silk trees, bloom in the fall. These Brazilian trees have large pink or white flowers that can be the size of a softball when the petals are unfolded. They are so big they can fall with a *plop*.

The golden rain tree opens yellow flowers, but quickly they disappear and are replaced by copper-colored pods. The pods are the prettier of the displays, reminiscent of tiny Japanese lanterns.

Purple orchid tree, *Bauhinia purpurea*, blooms in the fall and again in the spring.

If you don't anticipate cool weather until Halloween, then you

The tropical floss-silk tree blooms in the fall. This one is a cross between the deep pink *Chorisia speciosa* and the white *Chorisia insignins*. Its flowers are larger, lighter pink, and the trunks and branches are thornier than either parent.

will be delighted if it arrives early. When it does, it is time to create flower beds for winter color. Besides impatiens, you may plant petunias, pansies, geraniums, salvia, gerbera daisies, ageratum, calendulas, nasturtiums, statice, sunflowers, wax begonias, kalanchoes, alyssum, dianthus, portulaca, snapdragons, and zinnias.

Vandas still will flower in the fall, and orchids will begin to settle back and harden off the growth they made during the hot, wet months. The pine trees will shed needles for the dry season. There are fewer flowers on the allamanda and the hibiscus, but the grapefruit will begin to ripen.

Come late November/early December, the poinsettia and its close relative, the white lace euphorbia, or pascuita, will begin coloring their bracts. When snowbirds begin to jam our highways, the white pelicans fly from Yellowstone National Park to Florida Bay, taking much the same route as the Arctic air masses. January is our coldest month. Back in January 1977, it snowed in Miami. In the 1980s, there were several freezes in late December and January. A windbreak in the northwest corner of your yard is a good idea.

Look for orange and red flowers on the Chinese hat plant, which appear to have brims and tassels, and watch, too, for the spikes of yellow flowers on the *Cassia alata*, the Christmas candle tree. *Brunfelsia americana* and other species in this group of shrubs add a lovely clovey smell to the winter air when they bloom.

Be prepared to move tender plants inside in late December and January, even February. Cover those cold-sensitive or small plants in the landscape that cannot be moved. Have old sheets set aside for use as outdoor covers, along with stakes to make tri-cornered frames or tepees. Don't use plastic or metal to cover plants because they conduct heat away from the leaves.

Take a lesson from Fairchild Tropical Garden, the largest tropical botanical garden in the continental United States and home of one of the world's premier palm collections. Before a freeze, horticulturists at the garden may use sheets of foam rubber to wrap

Wax begonias are among the annuals that grace winter beds.

the crown (growing point) of young, cold-tender palms. This keeps the new bud warm enough to continue growing even though the fronds may be damaged.

Have on hand a supply of Kocide, maneb, or mancozeb in case you need a fungicide and antibacterial treatment for palms after a freeze. These can be mixed together in water and poured into the growing points of palms to avoid bud rot.

It's best not to prune off frozen, dead branches on trees and shrubs until March. Brown and unattractive, the dead parts nonetheless will protect living ones should successive freezes occur. When new buds appear in spring, you will know exactly how far back to prune twigs or branches.

Water the lawn less in winter because it grows more slowly. Remember, however, that windy, bright days can dry plants quickly in winter, so do not abandon entirely the job of watering. When you do water, apply three-quarters of an inch to one inch of water

Each spring, long spikes of yellow flowers of *Oncidium altissimum,* an orchid from the West Indies, cascade from their roost in an avocado tree.

to wet roots to a depth of a foot. Watch for spider mite damage in dry weather, as well as powdery mildew. See Chapter 4 for more information on insects and diseases.

At the end of February, you can prune those shrubs that produce flowers on new growth, such as allamanda, hibiscus, and oleander. Frangipani, royal poinciana, and jacaranda, which are dormant in winter, can be pruned before the spring flush. When trees begin pushing out new growth, however, it's too late to prune without causing unwanted bushiness. So wait several weeks before pruning for shape. If bushiness is what you are aiming for, however, prune in early spring.

Spring is generally around March in South Florida and the subtropics. Roots stir. Fertilize in late February so the nutrients will be there when the plants require them. When orchids begin to show new growth, it's time to repot.

In the spring, the flowering tree *Butea monosperma* unfurls orange claws of flowers as bewitching as anything you've seen. The erythrinas hold up torches of flame-colored flowers; the shaving brush and the Guiana chestnut, both with staminate or brush-like flowers that are big and loopy looking, appear. The white bauhinias bloom.

Early March brings the Miami Orchid Show, where phalaenopsis orchids are at their peak with sprays of round, mothlike flowers hovering in the air. But also look for lady slippers, dancing ladies, miniature cattleyas, and outrageous vandaceous orchids that will send you home to repot those languishing in the shade house.

As new growth begins and winter doldrums are shed, the avocados put out new leaves after dropping their old ones, and the jacarandas and tabebuias flower. Cypresses and oaks respond to the spring impulse with new growth. The golden shower, *Cassia fistula,* will produce pendant clusters of beautiful yellow flowers, while *Cassia javanica,* the apple blossom cassia, blossoms in pink. Frangipani flowers white, pink, yellow, and, lately introduced from Hawaii, red.

Be alert to the vulnerability of new shoots and leaves in windy spring weather, and to spider mites that cause the leaves to look bronzed or stippled.

Change over annual beds to summer color. Grow such heat-tolerant plants as marigolds, shrimp plants, crossandra, coleus, portulaca, and pentas. Put caladium bulbs beneath the shade of trees. Watch for the incomparable aquamarine flowers on the jade vine, the upside-down yellow flowers on the chalice vine, and the beautiful purple and blue clusters of flowers on the queen's wreath vine.

May beetles, which appear in May or June and again in the fall, are attracted to many plants, including roses and floss-silk trees. To trap them, fill white buckets with water and shine light on the buckets at night. Beetles are attracted to white; they will fly to the buckets and drown.

At the beginning of the rainy season—normally late May or early June—begin planting or transplanting your garden and landscape. Spread mulch and step up the watering as light and temperature increase. Make cuttings, air layerings, and divisions of those plants you want to increase in your garden.

Life on our crest of the planet takes a decidedly exuberant turn in summer. The earth and its plants drink with unquenchable thirst, setting into motion the complexities of growth beneath the primary sky. You remember: prophase, metaphase, anaphase, telophase, cell division, enlargement, differentiation. The processes are proceeding furiously, but not randomly. They are extraordinarily exact, making sawgrass and sagittaria and *Swietenia*. Making hay.

Make way for the emergence of juvenile lubber grasshoppers that hatch from eggs in the soil, and for the glory of the royal poincianas that will help you through the heat by their dazzle.

During the summer, you'll have your hands full mowing the grass—which is reason enough to reduce the size of the lawn—but take walks before it gets too hot and discover the sensual perfume of the albizias hanging in the morning air. Tree frogs and cicadas sing in two-note harmony, tree snails descend from their lofty lysilomas where they have estivated, sealed in during dry weather. Early on a summer's morning, light shines through the palms and across the bromeliads in hazy shafts.

Before the hurricane season gets too far under way, do your hurricane pruning.

Rain may leach nutrients from the soil, so keep an eye out for yellowing leaves. When new growth appears on newly planted trees or shrubs, fertilize lightly.

Seasonal signs. *Heliconia caribaea* cv. Jacquinii is a bright light of summer.

Summer's rampant growth brings out hordes of insects: mosquitoes, slugs, snails, aphids, and whiteflies. It brings sweat, hives, blisters, and backaches. But those are a small price for the mangoes and avocados, bananas, heliconias, gingers, and the feeling of belonging to the place.

As August and September approach, the hurricane season builds and so should your survival supplies. One of the hurricane precautions you may wish to take is to photograph your landscape so you will have an adequate record for insurance purposes should a storm strike. September will remain surprisingly hot, and October will not be much better, but the cycle will complete itself before you know it.

3

TOOLS AND TECHNIQUES: HOW TO WORK IN THE GARDEN

LIKE A PAINTER, WRITER, or any other artist, a gardener must have a set of tools and learn to master them. Tools and techniques outlined in this chapter are basic and often used. By often using them, you will include them in your second sense of what can and must be done in the garden.

TOOLS FOR GARDENERS

It will not take you long to discover that a green thumb is not enough in the garden. You need a good set of tools.

✓ **Trowel.** Wide-bodied for small digging chores.

✓ **Transplant trowel.** Narrow for removing a single plant or getting into corners.

✓ **Shovel.** A long-handled, medium pointed shovel for general purpose work in rocky or sandy soils. Spades are good for sand, but not for rock. A spade with a solid socket, closed around the base of the handle, is stronger than one with the handle exposed to wear at the base.

✓ **Digging bar.** For rocky soils, this, in combination with a shovel, is essential. Use a digging bar with a chisel tip to break up limestone, then clean out the hole with a shovel. You will alternate between the two.

✓ **Rake.** A bow-head steel rake is stronger than a flat-head steel rake. You can make seed rows with it. Use a lawn rake with steel tines for the leaves of avocado, mango, oak, or mahogany trees.

✓ **Reel-type lawn mower.** You can purchase push or gas-powered reel mowers for a cleaner cut. Bur rotary mowers or power mowers make life easier with St. Augustine grass, and the blades are more easily sharpened at home.

✓ **String trimmer.** You can edge and trim with this, but do not use near the base of trees, palms, or shrubs. Telltale grooves at the base of trees from string trimmers indicate improper use. Palms can be weakened to the point of falling over; hardwood trees and shrubs may have the cambium destroyed beneath the bark. The cambium is the cell layer that produces conducting tissue: phloem on the outside and xylem on the inside.

✓ **Spreader.** A rotary spreader will fan out seeds or fertilizer, and a small, hand-held one works just as well as a push type.

✓ **Hand pruner.** Use a bypass blade pruner. This works like a half-scissors to cut rather than crush twigs and stems. Felco No. 2 is a lovely tool to own.

✓ **Lopper.** A bypass action is better than the anvil type, which crushes.

✓ **Pruning saw.** Felco makes a curved pruning saw that has replacement blades. Teeth angle back to cut on the pulling motion.

✓ **Pole pruner.** Try to find one with a wooden handle for overhead work so you can avoid accidental electrocution should you brush it against a wire. A pole pruner with saw combination can be tricky to use, as one side interferes with the other while you work.

✓ **Wooden ladder.** If you are standing on a metal ladder and accidentally hit a power line, you can be killed. Store a wooden ladder out of the weather. Don't paint it; you may not see any cracks that develop.

✓ **Hose.** A rubber hose is long-lasting. Plastic can kink and snap when cold. Vinyl deteriorates in the sun. An attachment that creates a showerlike stream of water is good for orchids, to reach plants in the middle of beds, and to water bromeliads or orchids attached to tree branches.

✓ **Watering can.** A can with an upward-pointing oval rose head is useful for seedlings. Use a can with a long spout for plants that don't like wet foliage, such as African violets.

✓ **Sprayers.** I have yet to find a hose-end sprayer that worked more than once, if at all. A wide-mouthed compression sprayer is best. If the capacity is greater than three gallons, it may be too heavy to carry easily. Wide-mouth types, while more expensive, are easier to clean.

✓ **Small siphon** that screws into the water spigot; the hose then screws into it. Enormously useful for fertilizing because the siphon adds soluble fertilizer as you water.

BUILDING FLOWER BEDS

Keeping color at the front door or near the entrance makes your work easier because you have to travel less when you want to clean off old flower heads or splash on a bit of liquid fertilizer.

By concentrating the color, you also can concentrate your watering needs. If you are apt to want to change that color seasonally, plan on building a good garden bed initially—or build a bed that will allow you to submerge the pots and mulch around them.

Raised beds for flowers help to overcome nematode problems, as they do for vegetables. Nematodes are microscopic worms that invade plant roots or feed on the outside of the roots, depending on the species. Those that invade roots cause the most damage, moving into the tissue and causing rot. Those feeding on the outside stunt the roots, cause swelling, and eat root hairs. Some plants are more susceptible to them than others. Annuals planted directly into Florida soils are vulnerable, as are bulbs. Wilting, lack of flowers, lesions in the stems, and reduced size are symptoms.

To avoid buildup of nematodes in the soil, use sterilized soil in your planting bed, or solarize the soil beneath the bed for four to six weeks in August and September. After you have turned and worked the soil, cover the bed (which should be located in full sun) with clear plastic that is between two and six mils thick. Sun shining through the plastic raises soil temperatures high enough to kill the nematodes, fungi, and other pathogens.

For an annual bed, use a 50-50 mixture of Canadian peat moss and sharp sand, with the addition of slow-release fertilizer such as Osmocote 14-14-14, following package directions.

As a potting mix, try a combination of peat, bark, perlite, and sand. Some nursery or garden centers package their own potting mixes, which are likely to be more suitable for subtropical conditions than mixes made and distributed on a national basis. Try lifting the various bags to feel the weight. A very heavy mix won't drain well. When you make cuttings or want an extra light soil mix, add perlite until it looks right, which is probably about half perlite, half mix.

Vermiculite is an additive that also will lighten your mix, but it breaks down over a long time and turns to mush, which can cause roots to rot.

When you shop for containers of small flower or vegetable transplants, avoid buying plants that are too big for their pots. If the flowering plants are large, full of flowers and tumbling over the sides, the roots may be a mess of constricted, brown, limp strings that won't function when you put them into the ground. Ease a small plant out of its pot to check the situation. Avoid buying plants with masses of roots squirming out of drainage holes.

When you get home, don't remove your new plants from their containers until you have prepared the bed, or the roots will dry. When the bed is ready (fertilizer thoroughly mixed into the soil), press on the sides of the container to loosen the root ball, slide the plant out and right into the hole, disturbing the root ball as little as possible. Trowel soil around the root ball and water well. Space plants about six to 24 inches apart, depending on size at maturity. Alyssum can be as close as six inches; nicotiana require 24 inches; asters need about 12 inches between plants.

Use a light liquid fertilizer solution (about one-quarter strength) to water in your new transplants, and again when new flower buds appear. Water the beds daily for the first few days, and then every two or three days.

Other sources of winter color are annually displayed at Flamingo Gardens and Arboretum in Davie, west of Fort Lauderdale. Flamingo Gardens is a botanical garden created from a citrus estate. It has favored perennial color in the Acanthaceae family, and the strolling garden beneath the protective canopy of large trees is planted with shrimp plant (a year-round bloomer), zebra plant, cardinal's guard, justicia, and Brazilian red cloak. The colors in this tropical plant group are bold yellow or scarlet, with copper and pink included in the family. Usually, the color is in spikes of bracts, but Brazilian plume or *Justicia carnea* has clusters of pink to reddish petals.

There are other sources of perennial color for winter, including bougainvillea, which is at its showiest in the dry season; Chinese hat plant, which comes alive with its intricate coolie-hat flowers that are red and orange when in full sun; Christmas candle, *Cassia alata*, with spikes of yellow flowers at the ends of its branches; and brunfelsias, which have cream-colored to lavender tubular flowers (turning to white with age).

Shrub beds can be a mix of muck and sand (30 percent muck to 70 percent coarse sand). Use a couple of inches of mulch around your shrubs, but keep the mulch away from the trunks to avoid rot or fungal diseases.

PLANTING

While planting can be done in every season, that done in early summer at the start of the rainy season will reduce the amount of irrigation necessary.

This is one of the most exciting of times for the gardener. All the palms and saplings bought over winter can go in the ground. All the plans made during the dry season can be executed.

Having gardened on solid rock for years, my recommended strategy for planting trees is this: dig as much as you can with a shovel, which will be in the neighborhood of two or three inches, and then alternately chip away at the limestone with a digging bar and the shovel. You gradually will get the hang of loosening hunks of rock with the bar by striking the rock at an angle, then plunging the bar straight down. The bar itself—indispensable on rocky soil—is heavy enough that just dropping it can cause limestone to chip.

Hole-digging in rock is a slow process, one that can throw your back out of whack if you overdo.

A planting hole ideally is three times as wide as the container in which the tree or shrub is purchased. Recent research indicates that most tree roots are in the top 12 to 18 inches of soil, and they spread out perhaps three times as far as the tree is tall. A broad, shallow planting hole loosens the soil in such a way as to prepare for rapid root growth over future months as the sapling/shrub seeks to become established.

Once the hole is dug, loosen the plant from the container. You may find it easier going if you lay the plant on its side and press on the plastic container, turning the plant until you have worked your way around the whole thing. With small shrubs, a long butcher knife can be wedged between the sides of the pot and the root ball.

Ease the container off the sapling (without tugging at the trunk of the plant) and lower the plant into the hole. As you backfill with the soil taken from the planting hole, water in well with the hose.

Make sure, also, that the top of the root ball is positioned at the same level in the ground as it was in the container. You may wish to build a basin to retain water over the root zone of the tree or shrub with leftover soil. This is a standard procedure. and it works well to keep water where it's needed as it seeps into the ground. However, if you mulch, this isn't necessary. By mulching over the wide hole—remember, it is three times the width of the root ball—you will help keep moisture levels high.

When planting palms, follow the same procedure.

I have not amended planting holes of trees or palms in my own yard. I simply backfill with soil taken from the ground, then add mulch. I find that watering conscientiously allows the newly planted palms and trees to do well. Even when water is restricted, new plantings are allowed to be watered by hand daily for 30 days.

PRUNING

Why prune? To ensure the health and strength of your trees and shrubs.

Occasionally, if a tree has a low-growing limb that interferes with walking a much-traveled route, or if it develops an out-of-proportion limb, you may want to remove those for your convenience and aesthetic considerations. Fruit trees may be brought down to size for easier harvesting. But primarily, pruning is for the benefit of the tree. Ultimately, healthy, strong trees will endure, and in that sense pruning will be beneficial to you.

To prune with skill requires knowledge of the shape of the tree you wish to prune. Look at the poetry of the tree first, listen to its rhyme and hear its music, study its architecture.

Trees must produce leaves, hold themselves upright, compete with other living plants in the landscape for water and nutrients and sunlight, and then, with leftover supplies of energy, produce flowers and fruit to pass on their special genetic codes. The forms trees most often take are the forms they have worked out over time, forms best suited for what they have to do.

When you really look at trees, you'll find a great diversity of forms. Live oaks have open, wide, rather low canopies held up on massive, horizontal branches. Pigeon plums have slender, narrow and upright crowns with a naturally formal look. Wax myrtles, which straddle the line between tree and shrub, have a many-branched, twiggy, round form. Avocados are rather boldly upright. If you try to reshape these forms into something other

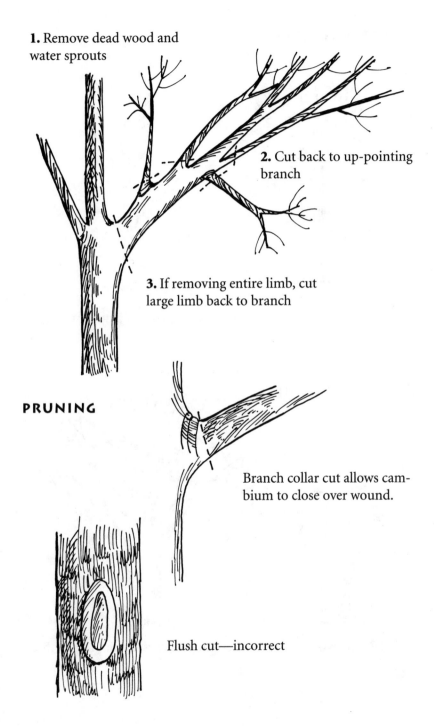

1. Remove dead wood and water sprouts

2. Cut back to up-pointing branch

3. If removing entire limb, cut large limb back to branch

PRUNING

Branch collar cut allows cambium to close over wound.

Flush cut—incorrect

than what they naturally are inclined to take, you're making more work for yourself than is reasonable and you're crippling the tree in its work, turning a sonnet to a haiku where full realization and not abbreviation was intended.

All of this means the first rule of pruning is to select the right tree with the right shape for the right spot.

As is true with most things tropical, botanical studies and understanding are less well known or amplified than equivalent studies and understanding of temperate plants. Many tropical trees don't have annual growth rings, but have several growth spurts a year. Work has begun in Miami on measuring and timing the growth of tropical trees, but it is just under way. Pruning guidelines have been developed, nonetheless.

Bushy growth results from pruning in the spring during the spring flush of growth. It also stresses the trees, asking them to cover over wounds and produce new leaves at once.

Pruning to shape is done later in the summer. After the new leaves have emerged and hardened off, they begin adding to the carbohydrate reserves, so subsequent pruning for shape is less stressful to the tree. Usually in early or mid-summer, prior to the peak of hurricane season, there's time to thin, shape, then compost the debris or have it picked up.

Flowering and fruit trees are pruned after they have flowered and fruited. Trees and shrubs that flower on new growth can be pruned while still inactive in late winter.

Ordinarily, pruning is not done between November and late February, when it could stimulate new growth susceptible to cold and freeze damage. Arborist Robin Luker says an exception may be the black olive. When pruned in spring or summer, light stimulates new sprouts on the interior of the black olive. The canopy becomes dense, making the tree an excellent target for wind damage. In Broward County, Hurricane Andrew toppled many black olives with thick canopies that resulted from bad pruning. To get around that, try pruning in the late fall/early winter when growth is slower.

Begin actual cutting by removing deadwood. When trees develop a full canopy, the interior branches receive less and less light and trees allow them to die, shedding what they cannot use. You should remove deadwood to prevent insects and diseases from invading. Mangoes and black olives tend to have a lot of deadwood in them, as do bottlebrushes and occasionally oaks. Remove branches that might grow straight up into the center of the tree. Citrus and black olives produce a lot of these branches, which are called water sprouts.

Next, look for crossing and rubbing branches. Remove the weaker of the two, or the one coming from an odd angle or a subservient position on the tree.

To do so, follow the branch to its fork. Generally keep the upward-pointing branch or the one that best maintains the canopy's balance by leading to one side or the other.

Assess the shape of your tree and determine whether light and air flow through the canopy with ease. Pick out the main scaffold branches—the ones that give the tree its basic shape. These are the branches to keep, and to keep in balance. A single leader is the most desirable habit of a landscape tree (exceptions are multi-trunked trees such as wax myrtle) and strong, well-placed branches coming off the central leader will produce a strong tree.

To thin the canopy, remove branches that are not needed for the scaffold. If this entails cutting branches larger than two or three inches in diameter, make three cuts to allow the branch to fall away cleanly without ripping off bark:

About 15 inches from the trunk, make an undercut a third of the way through the branch.

PROPER PRUNING

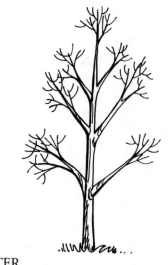

BEFORE
Unpruned

AFTER
Develop main scaffold branches, with clear central leader when possible

IMPROPER PRUNING

HATRACKING

Resulting witches' broom regrowth

Just beyond this, make a second cut on the top side of the branch. This takes off the branch.

Make the final cut just beyond the branch collar. That is the wrinkled, somewhat raised area where the branch emerges from the trunk. In this collar area, tissue develops that quickly grows over the wound, closing it to insect and disease invasion.

Do not use pruning paint, which is likely to seal in moisture and fungus.

However, another type of painting may be needed on trees prone to sunburn, such as avocados, mangoes, citrus, and black olives. If you have removed quite a large limb that will expose bark on these trees to strong sunlight for the first time in years, the bark could blister and peel. The branch or even whole portions of the canopy could then die. You may wish to protect the newly exposed area with a coat of diluted, water-based white latex paint.

Rejuvenating shrubs is an entirely different form of pruning. When crotons, hibiscus, ixora, cherry hedges, acalypha, or many other shrubs grow old, particularly if you trim them as a hedge, they have a tendency to have all their leaves on top with few at the base. Ixora, when sheared, will gradually reduce the size of its leaves; ligustrum will lose its spunk and vigor.

Rejuvenation pruning causes the plant to put out new, more vigorous wood and leaves.

With this kind of pruning, you take the shrub back to its base in thirds, which means dividing the work over three years. Cut a third of the main trunks back to the ground, then prune the rest normally. The next year, take the second third back to the ground and prune the rest, thinning the new shoots on the new growth. The last year, cut the remaining branches to the ground, thin the second year's twigs, and prune back the first year's. The fourth year, you will thin the third year's new branches and prune the rest for balance and shape.

PROPAGATING

Watching seeds sprout, rooting new plants from cuttings, or air layering the crotons are enormously satisfying activities for any gardener, especially if you want to increase your plant collection or fill in the garden without anything more costly than pots, peat, perlite, and patience. Early summer conditions are ideal for these undertakings, before the unrelieved heat of July or August.

Planting Seeds

Growing from seed is the most logical way to increase your plant collection because nature has done most of the work for you and packaged it in convenient bundles. However, you have to keep an eye out for ripening fruit. Sometimes, the packaging of fruit is beautiful because pollination is only half the job of making more plants; germination of the offspring completes the cycle. So fruit is often conspicuous or colorful to attract birds or animals that will disperse it.

You can wander around the neighborhood when the round, flat, jacaranda pods turn black or the long poinciana pods are brown and dangling from the trees, and simply collect them. Watch for the fruit on the white stoppers to turn purple, the green seeds of the Florida thatch palm to turn white, and the tiny citrus-like fruit of the limeberries to go from green to deep red. Collect them before they drop so they don't rot or become infested with fungus or bugs. Put them in an envelope and label immediately.

When you get home, clean them of fleshy pulp, which can chemically inhibit germination, and plant soon.

Tropical and subtropical seeds are viable for short periods of time because there is no overwintering in the tropics. The seeds ripen, they fall or are eaten, and germinate quickly—competition for light and space is always keen.

Because they're so perishable (lychee seeds last only a couple of weeks), don't put your seeds on the back bench and forget them. There are always exceptions: annonas and papayas can remain viable for years. However, your best strategy is to plant right away.

There's little advantage to soaking most tropical seeds, but some seeds, such as milkweed, like to be soaked overnight. Citrus seeds actually like to dry out first. Hard-coated seeds, such as those of the poinciana, need a nick to let in water. This nicking of the seed coat is called scarifying, and you can do it with a file or a sharp knife.

What do you plant them in? A 50-50 mix of Canadian peat moss and builder's sand make a good blend that will retain moisture while allowing drainage and oxygen circulation. Peat and perlite in equal measure are fine. Sphagnum that has been soaked in water and squeezed out is another good medium (though it may be hard later to tease out the seedling from this material).

Water your medium, then plant your seeds just deep enough to cover them so they won't dry out. Tiny seeds can be scattered on the surface of beds or soil in pots. Even big seeds, such as mangoes, should be planted no deeper than a couple of inches beneath the surface. Palm seeds, however, should be planted at or just beneath the surface.

An excellent guide to propagating Florida plants has been published by the Florida Cooperative Extension Service. It's Circular 579, "Propagation of Landscape Plants," by Dewayne Ingram and Thomas Yeager. In addition, daylong propagation workshops are given annually at the Fruit and Spice Park in Homestead.

What you do *not* plant from seed are plants that won't reproduce those characteristics of the parent plant you find desirable. For instance, mangoes and avocados will not "come true to seed"; that is, they won't give you fruit just like the parent tree. It may be better, or it may be worse. To remove the guesswork and to shorten the time it takes the tree to produce fruit, we grow grafted mangoes and avocados.

Orchid seeds, which require exacting conditions to germinate, are difficult for amateurs to grow successfully. In the wild, orchid seeds germinate in particular fungi. Decades ago, orchid enthusiasts discovered how to make an agar that would stimulate germination, but putting seeds into the agar and making the sugar/hormone mix require sterile conditions. I have tried a couple of times—these attempts require washing down bathrooms with Clorox and all manner of elaborate preparations—and failed miserably. I don't make my own orchid crosses, and am content to simply propagate the plants by division. What pods form in the shade house are fortuitous, and for this reason, they may one day sow themselves if that is meant to be.

Taking Cuttings

This technique involves snipping off a vigorous, tender part of the plant, allowing it to take root and ultimately become a new plant. You can take leaf or tip cuttings, twig cuttings, or even whole limbs from some plants such as gumbo-limbos and aralias.

Tip and stem cuttings are easy as pie. Pentas will serve as an example because these butterfly-attracting plants root quickly, and you can always find another little sunny spot in which to use them.

PROPAGATING FROM CUTTINGS

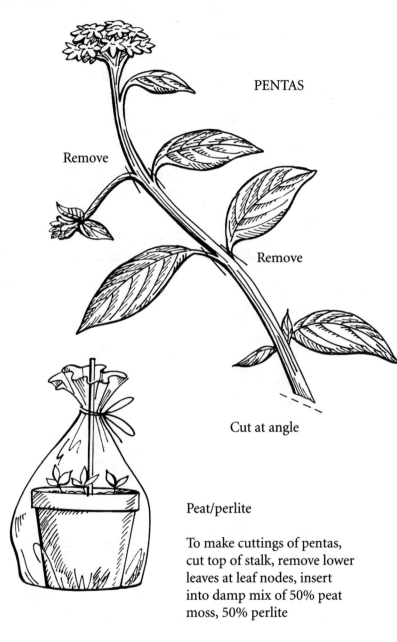

PENTAS

Remove

Remove

Cut at angle

Peat/perlite

To make cuttings of pentas, cut top of stalk, remove lower leaves at leaf nodes, insert into damp mix of 50% peat moss, 50% perlite

Cut off the tops of several pentas, each with three or four leaf nodes (the points on the stem where leaves are attached). Cut the stem at an angle. This exposes more root-producing tissue while it helps rain run off the part of the plant left in the ground.

Remove the several pairs of leaves on the bottom of the stem so you have only a couple of leaves remaining; insert the end in peat and perlite to cover the leafless nodes. Keep the plants moist, shaded, and protected from winds.

The cuttings will send carbohydrates from the leaves and stems to the cut end, where they'll be used to produce roots. Put them in a spot where they won't jiggle and wiggle, or the emerging roots will be broken off. Enough humidity has to be maintained around the leaves so they won't dry out.

A mist bed—a shallow planting tray of rooting medium watered by misting heads run on a timer—is what commercial nurserymen use to start cuttings. You can rig up a little tent from a plastic bag that will create mist-bed-like conditions. Insert three or four cuttings in a pot, along with a couple of bamboo sticks to keep plastic from falling on the cuttings. Place the pot in a plastic bag and tie it shut. Keep it in shade, or the sun will cook the cuttings. At night, as the temperature drops, beads of moisture will form on the inside of the bag. When droplets do not form, you should rewater the pot by setting it in a tray or container of water and allowing the water to be drawn up through the drain holes. For small two-inch pots, upend a plastic sandwich bag over the top.

After several days or weeks, you can begin acclimating the rooted cuttings by opening the plastic for an hour, then two, then more, until gradually the leaves are hardened off, or able to withstand the conditions outside.

Air Layering

Air layering is cutting away a band of bark and cambium from around a stem, then wrapping the area in damp sphagnum moss and plastic to force roots to form.

Try it on ficus or crotons, which layer readily, and then move on to hibiscus, azaleas, or annonas.

You will need a knife or shears; wet sphagnum moss; string; plastic and florist's tape; or aluminum foil.

Use a sharp knife or air layering shears to remove a section of bark—an inch or two wide—on a slender twig. The twig or branch should be straight and positioned so its leaves get plenty of sun, says tropical fruit expert Chris Rollins. Carefully avoid cutting into the wood and disrupting the flow of water to the leaves. In the spring and summer the cambium layer, although hard to see, will be slippery. Be sure to clean all the cambium off the wood, or it may create new bark tissue over the wound you have made. Squeeze out the sphagnum moss and mold it around the wound. Sugars from the leaves will gather at the end of the bark cut where the band begins, and roots will form.

The moss provides a medium into which new roots can grow. Wrap moss with plastic; the enveloping plastic keeps the whole thing moist. Use plastic from a cleaning bag or a sandwich bag. Tie each end securely with the green ribbonlike tape available at garden or nursery supply stores. Or use aluminum foil wrapped around the moss and tightly wrapped against the branch at both ends to keep water from running inside.

If you use clear plastic, you can see roots grow through the moss; if you use black plastic, you will have to feel the ball to check on root formation. In a few weeks, the moss should be full of new roots and it will be time to cut what is now a rooted sapling from the parent tree. After the rooted top is removed, the plant will pop new buds below the cut.

STEPS IN AIR LAYERING

1. Remove one-inch-wide band from stem of shrub to be air layered.

2. Clean off any cambium.

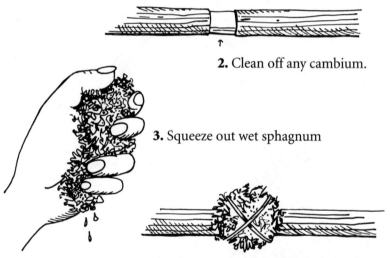

3. Squeeze out wet sphagnum

4. Apply moss around wound; tie in place.

5. Cover with foil or plastic; tie ends so water will not enter.

Have planting materials ready before removing the newly rooted top. Prepare a bucket containing a dilute mix of balanced soluble fertilizer and some chelated iron (one tablespoon of iron to five gallons of water). Soak the mossy root ball in the solution, then pot.

Work as gently as possible so tender roots don't break. Pack soil against the sides of the pot, then around the root ball.

Keep your new sapling in a protected area; gradually acclimate it to sun, and plant in the ground once roots fill the pot.

Making Divisions

Plants that grow on underground stems, such as begonias and heliconias, and those that form clumps, such as calatheas and some palms, can be increased in number by separating new plants from parent plants. A peat/perlite mix isn't necessary for divisions; they can go right into potting mixes or the ground. (A potting mix may be a combination of peat moss, bark, perlite, and sand. Some nursery or garden centers package their own mixes that are made especially light for subtropical conditions.)

Liriope, which is expensive, can be divided from a gallon pot once you get it home. Amaryllis bulbs can be divided, separating small bulbs from a large one.

Bromeliads will flower and then form small plants from their bases, called pups. When the pups are a third of the size of the mother plant, use pruning shears and cut the stem as close to the base of the mother plant as you can manage. Pot in an orchid mix, such as bark and tree fern.

Orchids that grow on rhizomes, such as cattleyas, are easily cut into smaller new plants. Those that grow monopodially, that is, on a single upright stem, will form keikis or babies along the sides of the main stem. These, too, can be cut off and potted.

DIVISION

Bromeliad pup emerges from the base of the mother plant. Cut stem close to mother plant when pup is one-third size of parent.

Footed ferns, which grow on rhizomes, may be divided by cutting sections of the rhizome. The sections can be attached to tree limbs or tree fern baskets, covered with sphagnum moss, and kept damp until new growth appears. Whenever new fronds appear on ferns, new roots will form, so you know when your transplant is successful.

I have a delicate rabbit's foot fern growing on an avocado limb that I started on some sphagnum moss in half of a coconut husk. I wired the husk to the tree. The husk is now rotting and the rhizomes of the fern are creeping like slender hairy feet around the tree limb.

FERTILIZING

The basic equation for the secret of life is this:

Six molecules of carbon dioxide combine with six molecules of water to form one molecule of glucose and six molecules of oxygen.

The glucose may be combined with nitrogen, sulfur, or phosphorus to form proteins. It may become part of a leaf, a root, a stem, or a flower. It can be stored for a rainy day. Because we ask plants to do so much, to grow abundantly and in unnatural combinations and on so many rainy days, we often have to supply them with the raw materials to do so. That's where fertilizers come in. Fertilizers are not plant food: they're minerals that plants combine to produce their food—and ours.

Nitrogen, phosphorus, and potassium are the three elements needed by plants in the largest amounts. Their chemical symbols are N, P, and K. They are called "macronutrients" and are represented by the three numbers on the front of a fertilizer bag.

Nitrogen is the material most needed. Even though the atmosphere is 79 percent nitrogen, it is not in the form used by plants. They must get it from soil as ammonium or nitrate. With it, they produce amino acids, protein, DNA, and RNA. Too much nitrogen will delay flowering and fruiting.

Phosphorus makes cell membranes and nucleic and amino acids (the components of proteins). It is needed for strong roots and stems.

Potassium moves from cell to cell causing various reactions, such as leaf movement and stomate opening. It helps move sugars and is needed for flowering. It also contributes to disease resistance and root development.

Carbon is made into sugar, tannins, vitamins, camphor, menthol, lignin, and cellulose, among other things. Hydrogen and oxygen are taken from air and water.

Sulfur is contained in all amino acids.

Magnesium is used for chemical reactions that produce ATP, the plant's energy. It is a component of the chlorophyll molecule.

Calcium activates enzymes in seeds so starch turns to sugar for embryo growth, and it cements cell walls.

Iron is a catalyst for the production of chlorophyll and is used in the light phase of photosynthesis.

Chlorine helps break down water in photosynthesis, releasing a spare electron that sets off the chain reaction converting solar energy to chemical energy.

Manganese works with chlorine in water breakdown, and it is used to synthesize fatty acids, enzymes, and chlorophyll.

Boron moves sugar inside plants; it helps synthesize substances that make up RNA and DNA.

APPLYING FERTILIZER

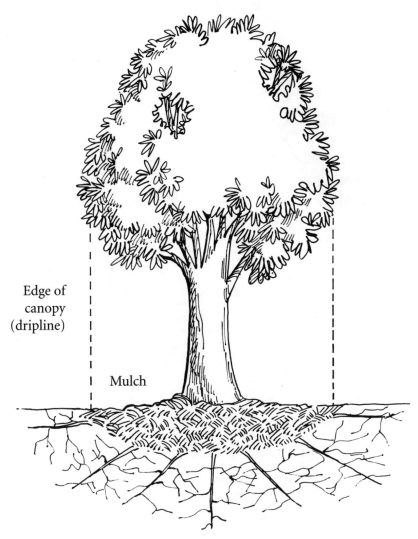

Edge of
canopy
(dripline)

Mulch

Actual extension of roots beyond dripline—broadcast fertilizer well beyond edge of canopy.

Zinc is used to synthesize hormones and enzymes.

Molybdenum is used in nitrate assimilation, making nitrogen usable.

In most cases, plants are able to take these minerals from soil. They do this best when soils are neutral or slightly acid. But soils in much of South Florida are generally alkaline, tying up chemically some or many of the minerals plants require. Another problem for mineral uptake is that some housing developments are built on filled land that previously was under water or seasonally flooded. By scraping off the muck and peat layers and scooping up rock to create fill, developers have been able to create whole new neighborhoods. These fill soils have special problems, however. They're alkaline, highly compacted, and do not drain well. Special planting techniques and micronutrient foliar sprays may be needed to maintain a healthy garden or landscape in these areas.

Compost, mulch, and fertilizers are part of gardening anywhere, but particularly in alkaline soils and infertile, sandy soils. Compost improves soil texture and its ability to hold onto minerals; mulch gradually decomposes, adding a small amount of acid to the soil. Fertilizers, added directly on top of mulch, begin to work soon after you apply them.

Broadcast granular fertilizers over the root zone of trees and shrubs, remembering that roots extend out from the trunk far beyond the edge of the canopy (called the dripline).

(Liquid or water-soluble fertilizers quickly run through sandy or rocky soil and are available to plants only briefly, sometimes just a matter of a few minutes. If you apply liquid fertilizers to potted plants such as orchids, do so on sunny days when the plants are metabolizing at optimal levels so they can absorb as much as possible. Also, add a spreader-sticker to help the solution adhere to the leaves. You can buy a commercially packaged version, or add a few drops of dish detergent to the fertilizer mix.)

When using granular fertilizer on landscape plants, water the ground around your plants the day before you fertilize, broadcast the fertilizer, then water it in. Since fertilizers are in the form of salts, if you allow material to stay on moist or dew-covered grass or roots, or even piled next to a young tree trunk, without watering in, you can burn or kill the plants.

Fertilizers with balanced ratios of N-P-K, such as 10-10-10 or 6-6-6, with micronutrients, are for general use. Low-phosphorus fertilizers, such as 7-3-7, are for long-term use on South Florida's alkaline soils that are high in phosphorus. There are pockets of acid sands in South Florida, and to double-check whether you have alkaline or acid soil, send a sample to the Florida Cooperative Extension Service. Check with your local extension office on how to do this.

Fertilizer labels identify the source of nitrogen as soluble organic or insoluble organic. In the summer rainy season, when microorganism activity in the soil is high, you may want to use an insoluble organic source of nitrogen; in winter, when microorganisms are less active, you could try a soluble organic. Natural organic sources of nitrogen include sewage sludge, manure, seed meal, blood, and fish meal. Organic fertilizers are slow-acting, have less potential for burning plants, and are good soil conditioners, but they often have small amounts of nitrogen, phosphorus, and potassium. Horse manure has only 2.8 percent nitrogen, 1 percent phosphorus, and 1.5 percent potassium.

Sewage sludge (now being called "biosolids") is not recommended for edible products because of trace amounts of heavy metals, although it is fine for ornamentals. It contains about 6 percent nitrogen, 2.2 percent phosphorus, and 0.5 percent potassium. Seaweed and fish emulsion are good as well.

Slow-release fertilizers are becoming more widely used because they provide some minerals on a steady basis to the plants over a period of time. Regular granular fertilizers create pulses of

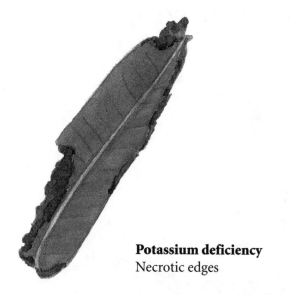

Potassium deficiency
Necrotic edges

Manganese deficiency
Mottled between veins on new leaves

SYMPTOMS OF NUTRIENT DEFICIENCIES

Sulfur deficiency
lack of green pigment—even veins

Nitrogen deficiency
Yellowing gradually overtakes entire
leaf on older leaves

Magnesium deficiencies
Yellowing on new leaves

Zinc deficiency
Malformed, wavy edges

Magnesium and iron deficiency
young leaves lack green pigment except in veins

mineral availability, surrounding plants with more nutrients than they can use at once, and then leaching away.

Nutrient Deficiencies

How do you know when plants need fertilizer? They will indicate it by changing color or developing smaller or deformed leaves. In generally, macronutrient (N, P, K) deficiency is seen in older foliage, while micronutrient deficiency appears in new growth. Here's a guide, put together with help from Cathy Ryan at Fairchild Tropical Garden:

Nitrogen. Pale yellow, all leaves. The entire leaf will change color, often from the edges inward, and gradually the leaves will die back from the tip.

Phosphorus. On older leaves, look for darkening, a purplish cast. Does not occur in South Florida soils.

Potassium. Drying, dying edges on leaves and leaf tips. On palms, the older fronds can appear checkered with orange, or dried and brown.

Calcium. Young leaves remain folded or wrinkled; older ones become thick or brittle. This does not occur in South Florida's soils.

Magnesium. Older leaves show yellow mottling between veins, starting at the tip and edge of the leaf; margins curl.

Sulfur. Younger leaves, including veins, turn yellow; some dead spots.

Iron. Yellowing between the veins on new leaves. Eventually, the chlorosis can include bleaching of the veins.

Manganese. New leaves will show yellow blotches, mottling, and yellowing, but not as severely as with iron shortage. Skimpy

blooms. Often, this deficiency occurs together with iron deficiency; the two mimic each other.

Zinc. Leaf margins become wavy; leaves appear deformed.

Copper. Death of the terminal bud and formation of multiple buds; witch's broom. Not a problem in South Florida soils.

Boron. Dwarfing of leaves.

Molybdenum. Crinkled leaves; leaves narrower than normal. Not a problem in South Florida soils.

Chlorine. Not deficient in South Florida soils, but can be a tip burn or leaf browning. Excess chlorine in the water also can cause tip burning on sensitive plants, such as spider plants.

Macro- and micronutrient foliar sprays will treat nutritional deficiencies. When one element becomes severely deficient, you can purchase it separately in a dry form and add it to the ground around the plant. There are caveats here, however. You may apply too much, or by adding one, you may cause deficiency of another. Potassium deficiency in palms, which is discussed in Chapter 9, requires both potassium and magnesium.

COMPOSTING

Compost is decomposed waste, animal and plant, that conditions soil, returns nutrients to the earth, allows plants to absorb nutrients more readily, and enables the microflora to flourish.

If you can find four or five square feet behind a shrub or in some out-of-the-way place in your backyard, build a compost bin or start a compost pile.

Ideally, you should be able to reach it with a hose in order to keep up the moisture level. The site should be somewhat blocked from wind to avoid drying, and water should drain from the pile. It should be accessible for turning the yard waste in it.

Leaves, clippings, fruit peelings and cores, table scraps, sawdust, and twigs can be added. Shred or chip twigs and big or tough leaves to hasten decomposition.

Do not add diseased plants or plant parts, or matter treated with herbicides, since the life of the herbicide may extend past the time the material is in the compost pile and adversely affect the plants on which you use the compost.

My compost pile is nothing more than a hidden heap. I simply add leaves and cuttings to it without worrying about making layers of enzymes, soil, and manure. From time to time in the dry season, I shoot some water from the hose onto it. It gradually produces a soil-like material at the bottom.

If you are inclined to recipes, the Broward County Cooperative Extension Service says a compost pile should have successive layers of three kinds of materials: something rich in bacteria and natural enzymes, such as garden soil or already-composted soil; nitrogen-containing materials, such as manure, grass clippings, or kitchen waste; chipped leaves, twigs, straw, or sawdust. These will provide a good carbon-to-nitrogen balance that allows other nutrient elements to stay in the compost.

Mix the compost pile occasionally—a month or so after starting it, say—as the interior starts to heat. The center should heat to 140 degrees, killing off weed seeds and harmful bacteria. (Not every place in the pile will get that hot, which is why you want to avoid adding weed seeds that could survive.)

It will take weeks or months for good, crumbly, black soil-like compost to form, depending on how you turn, water, and manage the material. You can then use it as potting soil, a soil amendment, mulch, or starter for the next compost pile.

If the compost begins to stink, it may be too wet (anaerobic decomposition without oxygen is taking place), and you should stir or mix it more frequently, adding some dry organic material. If it smells like ammonia, add wood chips, sawdust, straw, or dry leaves.

If it is just sitting there, the components may be too big. You didn't chip or shred, right? Or you may have the opposite problem, and the particles are too small to allow air and water to start their work. You may have to add more moisture if it is dry, or aerate it.

If the compost attracts rats or roaches, you may have too many table scraps not thoroughly mixed into the center of the pile.

Hurricane damage in August 1992 left much of South Florida looking like this section of Fairchild Tropical Garden. Vortices of high-speed winds spun off the main storm, many of them exceeding 200 miles per hour.

4

ADVERSITY: WHAT TO WORK AROUND IN THE GARDEN

UNFAVORABLE conditions in the garden include bad weather, diseases, and insects. In the subtropics, these come in spades: hurricanes, droughts, occasional freezes dipping in from the Arctic, diseases that can sweep through crops or gardens with wind or rain, insects that never stop breeding in the heat and humidity.

There are ways to cope with these adversities, beginning with the premise that sooner or later cope you must.

Planting a variety of different plants—including cold-hardy, wind-tolerant, and insect- and disease-resistant choices—will protect your landscape and garden against mass destruction from one particular adverse event.

Careful monitoring for insects and diseases will help you keep ahead of the game. A respect for the cycles of nature will go a long way toward your tolerance of imperfect leaves in a healthy and functioning garden.

Here are some of the trials to expect in your subtropical garden.

HURRICANES

On clear and mild days, it's possible to think of our subtropics and tropics as Eden found again. Yet east of Eden lies the African coast where summer storms are born, growing as they cross the Atlantic until they are cyclonic and terrifying. Hurricane season runs from May through October. Southern Florida had not been hit by a hurricane for more than 20 years when Hurricane Andrew struck on August 24, 1992, though a storm of that intensity strikes Florida about every 15 years on average.

If there is one thing hurricanes and gardens have in common, it is that they are the essence of change. Hurricanes play a large role in the evolution of tropical ecosystems: casting seeds about, stirring up new life, pruning, pushing out the weak and leveling the sick and aged. When a hurricane plunders your neighborhood, it's hard to remember to take the overview, yet birth, growth, and death are cycles every gardener knows intimately, and these are strewn in the hurricane's wake.

That we live where hurricanes occur means taking precautions. "Candles, nails, a sudden increase in the faithful, and a mark-up on matches and bread," wrote Derek Walcott in *Omeros*. For homeowners and gardeners, plant selection and pruning are keys to keeping trees up and damage down. Avoid trees that have shallow roots or are brittle (see box). Keep trees thinned so wind can rush through the canopies rather than topple trees. Pruning to thin trees is outlined in Chapter 3.

TREES WITH SHALLOW ROOTS AND BRITTLE WOOD

Trees most easily toppled or split apart in hurricanes are those with shallow roots and brittle wood. Derek Burch, horticultural consultant and former associate professor of horticulture at the University of Florida, has written that the ideal way to avoid storm damage begins with proper tree selection.

Trees with shallow roots prone to toppling in high wind include:

Albizia lebbeck, woman's tongue
Casuarina species, Australian pine
Grevilla robusta, silk oak (dense canopy on medium tree)
Thespesia populnea, seaside mahoe

Trees with brittle limbs survive hurricanes by shedding those limbs. Some trees, such as the avocado and the earleaf acacia, may split. Trees with brittle wood include:

Acacia auriculiformis, earleaf acacia
Bischofia javanica, bischofia
Enterolobium cyclocarpum, ear tree
Eucalyptus species, (70-plus feet, too tall for most sites)
Persea americana, avocado
Spathodea campanulata, African tulip tree (another 70-footer)
Terminalia catappa, tropical almond (80 feet; many withstood 90- to 100-mile-an-hour winds during Hurricane Andrew)

After the storm, there are things to be done immediately, particularly if you live close to the shore, where a storm surge can drench everything with salt water.

If water pressure is still high and you can run the hose, wash the landscape with fresh water to rinse off salt. The more thorough this rinsing, the better. If there are days of enduring rain, as happened after Andrew, salt will leach from the soil, but expect many plants to be killed.

Trees will be the main problem in dealing with a storm-struck garden, but trees can stay down several weeks and still be righted, providing their roots are protected. Cover root masses with old sheets or blankets and keep the material damp. Otherwise the sun will scald and singe already damaged roots. Don't use plastic, as it can cook the roots.

Next, clean up the debris that has been spilled into your yard. This will keep the grass, ground covers, palms, and shrubs from being suffocated. It will give you some perspective on the work to be done, as well as some elbow room. The mess left by the storm will make things appear worse than they may be. If trees left standing were stripped of their leaves, you may feel a sense of hopelessness that will lift once the yard is organized and the leaves begin to shoot out again.

✓ **Assess the damage carefully.** If you have trees with more than 50 to 60 percent of their canopies gone, you may want to eliminate them from the garden. With major canopy losses, remaining trunks may be cracked and split. Examine the limbs and trunks, looking for vertical cracks in the bark—these indicate dangerously weakened trees.

If badly damaged trees include rare or beloved specimens, then you may want to do only minor pruning. Temporarily clean up stumps, but understand that eventually bad trees will have to be removed. The branches will sprout epicormal shoots—that is, shoots

Before Hurricane Andrew. This garden was photographed two days before the storm hit. It was a plant collector's garden, full of aroids, heliconias, and other tropical plants and palms.

that develop on the surface of the limbs—and as they put out leaves, the photosynthesis process will increase the sugars in the tree and encourage root growth. In the interim, propagate the tree either from seed (out-of-season flowering will occur after the storm on many trees and shrubs) or by air layering. You can keep a venerable but damaged tree in place while growing its replacement.

✓ **Remedial pruning:** Save as much green as possible. If you have to prune off major branches to reset trees, cut each back to the nearest sound wood V-crotch, the joint where the branch forks. If 50 percent of that joint still has bark intact, arborists consider it sound.

Clean off ragged branch ends if possible, but don't leave flat surfaces sticking up like end tables to collect water and rot.

A few days after Hurricane Andrew, the same garden looked like this. The garden had been built into limestone terraces of an old rock pit, and trees surrounding it, such as the royal poinciana in the center, were toppled onto the ledges below.

Follow good pruning practices: cut to branch collars and create a rough balance. Worry about fine pruning and shaping later. If the top was blown out of a tree, try to lighten the load of branches that remain. Where bark has been ripped and torn, smooth the edges with a chisel or knife, cutting away loose bark only as necessary. Do not carve a perfectly elliptical or round wound edge, enlarging the site of injury.

Do not hatrack the damaged tree. Hatracking is cutting back so severely that only stumps of the main scaffold branches remain, sticking out like hooks for hats. If you must remove a lot of canopy to reset the tree, whitewash the exposed bark to prevent sunburn. Trunks and branches that had been shaded for years can be killed by sun. Whitewash helps reflect light.

✓ **Staking righted trees:** Three stakes equally spaced around the tree are needed to brace reset trees. The farther out from the tree you can put them, the stronger they'll be. The National Arborist Association recommends driving the stakes into the ground toward the tree instead of angling them away from the tree, the traditional method. Angling the stakes toward the tree gives them more flexibility, allowing them to move slightly with the tree rather than pulling against it and possibly damaging the bark with too much pressure.

A section of wire or rope through the end of the stake should be run around the tree. Put pieces of old hose around the guy rope or wire where it wraps around the tree to cushion the pull and protect the bark. Stakes should remain in place for at least six months.

To stake palms, wrap sections of two-by-fours with burlap and wire these around the trunk. Nail long wooden braces into these. Never drive nails directly into palm trunks; these wounds will not close over, but act as entry points for insects and disease.

✓ **Watering:** Once you have reset trees, treat them as if they were newly planted. Water every day for two to four weeks, depending on rain. Gradually taper off from every day to every other day for another two to four weeks, possibly longer if the dry season begins. Then, reduce watering to every three or four days so the root zone stays moist for several months. Build a saucer of soil around the roots to direct water into the root zone. As winter approaches and the weather cools, the need for water will be somewhat reduced because trees will give off less water through their leaves.

✓ **Fertilization:** After Hurricane Andrew, many of South Florida's horticultural experts debated whether to fertilize damaged trees before spring. At issue was the need to supply vital nutrients to trees versus the ability of the roots to recover and absorb them, with an eye to the upcoming cold season. Root regrowth after the storm was debated; even trees not knocked over had been badly shaken so their roots were affected.

Many felt it was unwise to apply fertilizer before spring; what roots were left, as well as those struggling to develop, could be burned. Others felt water-soluble 20-20-20 applied at one-half or one-quarter the recommended rate would be helpful. October is the normal time to apply fertilizer to young trees to enable them to withstand cold. Experts feared stimulating new growth in the face of cold or even freezing weather. Yet new growth began to burst forth from many landscape plants, stimulated by the storm.

A middle-of-the-road position was to apply a small amount of 4-6-8, which adds potassium but doesn't push foliar growth, to trees or palms that were damaged but not toppled. When reset trees renewed growing, a light solution of 20-20-20 was then applied to the side of the root system that stayed in the ground.

✓ **Shrubs:** Few shrubs were killed by toppling in Andrew; most that were damaged outside the hurricane's eye zone were injured by falling limbs or trees. Many, however, were stripped of foliage. Post-storm treatment included light shaping once the leaves resprout, and light fertilization in October.

✓ **Herbaceous plants** such as heliconias and gingers, and shade- loving understory plants such as bromeliads, aroids, and ferns, may be severely affected by sunburn. Rig up temporary shade cloth over tree stumps and transplant or relocate pots beneath it. Or, allow old, sunburned leaves to remain on the plants, protecting new growth.

Heliconias, gingers, rhizomatous begonias, ferns, monsteras, and other aroids with underground stems or tubers will resprout. Many gardeners found that sun-loving plants such as these came back vigorously after the storm because more sunlight was available to them.

✓ **Palms** were survivors in 1992. Sabal palms, pygmy date palms, slender veitchias, and ptychospermas were able to flex in the wind. Heavy-headed palms, such as coconuts, were pushed over. Royals stood up well except in the worst-hit areas.

Because palms have only one growing point, the experts at

Fairchild Tropical Garden, overseeing damage to one of the world's greatest palm collections, treated survivors with fungicide and antibacterial compounds. Chuck Hubbuch, palm and cycad curator, used a combination of Kocide, a copper fungicide, and Manzate, a mancozeb fungicide that contains zinc with antibacterial action (one tablespoon each per gallon of water). Don't use copper around bromeliads; it will kill them. It also will damage orchids, ferns, and gesneriads.

A complementary treatment is the fungicide Aliette, which works against water molds and bud rot. Aliette is a systemic that travels throughout the plant and offers some protection to roots as well. The product can adversely react with copper or zinc, and must not be used in combination with any metal-containing fungicide.

When applying a spray of fungicide, water-soluble fertilizer can be added to the mix and applied to damaged palms. Leaves will take in the soluble fertilizer and transport it internally. Palms are slow growers and often produce no more than a single frond every month or two. Palms may take a year or more to recover from a hurricane, or decline and die over this same period.

Should tattered fronds be cut off palms after a storm? Not unless they are physically twisted to prevent the new spear from emerging, or unless they're so heavy they prevent securing and stabilizing reset palms. Palms are able to transport potassium and other nutrients out of old fronds into new ones, so removal of lower fronds robs the plant of vital nutrients. Only when the fronds turn brown should they be removed.

Queen palms throughout South Florida, as well as many palms that suffered cold damage in the 1980s, were showing signs of butt rot when the hurricane struck. Butt rot, or ganoderma, is a major disease that has no known treatment or cure. Large shell fungi develop near the base of the palms as an outward symptom, but the disease moves through the soil or through the air and can affect palms without showing outward signs for some time. It attacks many palm genera, including coconuts, phoenix, ptychospermas, royals, and washingtonias. Ganoderma kills roots, leaving palms weakly rooted. When Hurricane Andrew toppled palms at Fairchild, many were discovered to have only a halo or petticoat of roots around the outer rim of the trunk. Such palms were righted, but experts expected some would be lost.

For palms without evidence of ganoderma, the palm experts recommended using Aliette or Subdue, a fungicide, as a root drench. Subdue is quite expensive, but small amounts are required, and, as with other expensive horticultural aids, it can be shared among neighbors.

FREEZES

The freeze of 1983 was preceded by a day of gray, bleak clouds and some rain. Until late December, the weather had been especially balmy, with no cool snaps to harden the plants. Other freezes in that decade followed, including a bad one in 1989 when temperatures fell below freezing and into the 20s for more than 20 hours, even in South Dade County.

Keeping plants healthy and supplied with a full complement of minerals, particularly potassium, is a first step in helping them survive cold. When plant cells freeze and thaw, they burst their membranes and the internal protoplasm oozes out. Certain nutrients can act as a kind of antifreeze, and potassium is one of these. Plants' tissues, which are about 90 percent water, are usually about 1 percent potassium. In addition to activating enzymes, potassium moves mineral compounds throughout the plant and is important in maintaining the shape and resiliency of cells.

An application of low-nitrogen fertilizer in October may be required.

Many palm growers use a special palm fertilizer year-round. For the rest of your landscape plants, a 4-6-8 fertilizer will supply needed potassium without high nitrogen to push succulent new growth.

As cold fronts advance into the state, they generally are preceded by rain or thunderstorms. If rain is scant, or if you have ample warning that a front is on its way, water the ground around your landscape plants the morning before the front arrives. (Don't water whole plants so leaves stay wet; this will cause tissue damage.) Moist soil transmits heat better than cool soil, and one secret to plant protection during cold is to move mulch away from plants, allowing soil heat to rise.

Many orchids need protection when the temperature reaches 55 degrees. While phalaenopsis orchids are stimulated to bloom when the temperature drops to 60 degrees, they do not like to stay chilly. Phalaenopsis usually are developing flower spikes in winter, and should be brought inside. Vandas do not take cold and should be protected at 50 to 55 degrees, particularly if in bud or flower. Cattleyas can survive short periods in the upper 30s, but to be safe, bring them in when the temperature hits the 40s. Fertilize orchids once or twice in October with a high potassium liquid fertilizer to harden them in preparation for winter.

Bromeliads need to be protected from dessication by wind as well as low temperatures. Potted bromeliads can be put in boxes, moved under trees, or brought inside. Cover those in the ground with newspapers or burlap.

Aroids that take cold include *Philodendron selloum,* one of the most commonly used landscape plants. *Philodendron hastatum, P. x evansii, P. lacerum, P. pinnatifidum, Monstera deliciosa,* and the bird's-nest anthurium, *Anthurium hookeri* types, can endure cold weather. Others, such as aglaonema and dieffenbachia, must be protected, along with heliconias, gingers, and mussaendas.

How? The best way is to cover tender plants, small trees, and shrubs with sheets or blankets. Newly planted or transplanted trees and shrubs are particularly susceptible to cold damage. Ideally, try to create a tripod or tepee of stakes and drape the sheets over that. This will keep the cold from touching the leaves. Like your fingers and toes, leaves get cold first. Very tender plants may benefit from an incandescent bulb being turned on beneath the propped-up covering. The tepee will trap the heat that rises from the ground and the lightbulb. I have flung sheets directly over young plants in a pinch and this has worked. Be sure to use terra cotta pots, stones, or other weights to keep the covers from blowing away.

On really big plants, such as *Heliconia caribaea* or bananas, a sheet tied around the foliage may help protect leaves. If burned back to the ground, however, these plants will probably recover, sending out new growth from their tubers or rhizomes.

Small palms at Fairchild Tropical Garden have been protected with sheets of foam rubber wrapped around the terminal bud. Freezing will affect the fronds but not the growing point.

Shade houses can be covered with plastic. You can buy plastic in large rolls from nursery, hardware, or building supply stores. Attach it so at night you can seal it to keep the interior of the shade house cozy, and roll up the sides during the day to prevent heat buildup.

After a freeze, South Florida turns a discouraging brown. Yet, the best thing to do is nothing. Freezes generally occur in late December or January, but also can occur as late as February. Any dead leaves should be left on trees and shrubs to provide protection in successive cold snaps.

Wait to prune until after new leaves appear. The plants will tell you how far back their twigs and branches have been killed. As a precaution against distorted growth, prune back past the second viable bud.

Commercial nurserymen and fruit growers begin a weekly spray program immediately after freezes using fungicides such as

Daconil, Manzate, or copper. Commercial orchid growers also use a preventive fungicide spray on orchids before and after freezes and hard cold snaps. Damaged tissue is an open door to infection. I have never sprayed my trees or shrubs after a freeze, although I have applied copper fungicide to vulnerable palms, since they have only one growing point. If that becomes infected, the whole plant will be lost.

Do not fertilize until roots become active again, usually around late March. Do not try to water the lawn out of its off color. When chilled, lawns turn reddish because the chlorophyll has been killed and red pigments are showing. Water won't change the color, and too much may lead to fungus.

In 1989, impatiens were turned to mush by a freeze and most people replaced them. Tender plants can resprout at the ground if quickly cut back so they do not rot.

Cumulative damage from freezes throughout the 1980s left many tropical fruit trees with loosening, bubbling, splitting bark. The Cooperative Extension Service recommended doing nothing to the trees, allowing them time to heal themselves.

DROUGHT

From 1988 to 1991, drought gripped the South Florida region normally cushioned against it by virtue of geography. During that time, several water-saving gardening techniques helped save the landscape. They can be used in normal times, too.

✓ **Water before sunup.** When irrigation systems are run during midday, as much as 30 percent of the water evaporates before hitting the ground.

✓ **Group potted plants together** so they can create their own microclimate, sharing in the humidity that results from evapotranspiration.

✓ **Fertilize at reduced rates,** providing necessary nutrients without pushing thirsty new growth.

✓ **Plant only at the onset of the rainy season.** What rain occurs will help reduce the amount of water drawn from the aquifer.

✓ **Mulch, mulch, mulch.**

✓ **Reduce chemical use.**

✓ **Let the shrubs get shrubby.** You may find they'll bloom more often. This reduces the need for the plant to continually push out new growth.

✓ **Plant drought-tolerant and native** trees, shrubs, and ground covers.

INSECTS AND SMALL FORMS OF WILDLIFE

When new growth is translucent and fragile as moonlight, certain things begin happening in the garden. Cricket calls and frog trills play to a half moon dissolving in haze left over from rain. A lady night spider emerges and begins to spin and weave a web.

About the size of a quarter, or maybe a half-dollar, a night spider is brown and unremarkable, neither fierce nor fragile looking. She drops on a single silken thread from her hiding place in a leaf and balloons to an anchoring spot below. Pulling herself back up to the starting point, she drops repeatedly until the scaffolding is strung. Then, deftly and without wasted motion, she fills in the intricate, strong interior of her trap. And she waits.

As the moon moves, the nighttime breezes jostle the web, and stars spin in the heavens, twinkling. A night-flying moth happens unwarily by and becomes entangled. The spider springs. Her night has been a success, and she feasts. At dawn, she carefully scoops up the web by pulling it back into her body, hoisting herself back to her crinkled leaf to hide through the day and wait for the next night, when she will spin and weave again.

Years ago, I discovered a lady night spider and went out each August night to watch her work. Sometimes I took my flashlight to see her spin. One morning, I saw her draw up her web. I don't know how many weeks she remained in her spot, but as faithfully as the evening star she appeared for as long as I watched.

You will discover small wonders in your garden if you become a spider, snake, and insect watcher.

Not long ago, poking among the bromeliads, I interrupted a tiny snake, brown with a faint black pattern just visible down its back, grabbing an equally tiny snail. Frightened, the snake released the little snail and squiggled into the ferns as the snail oozed away.

For several years, a pair of Everglades racers has lived in my front yard, sunning on fine days in the hairy thatch of the old man palm. They watch me, and I them. We converse on occasion; I verbally, they flicking slender tongues.

Geckos live in my garage. Spider eggs hang in strings from the porch eaves. Ancient dragonflies cling on cloudy mornings to the footed ferns.

Not every creepy crawly in the yard is good. Slugs and snails, great destroyers of bromeliads and begonias, are a constant bedevilment. The grasshoppers of spring and summer are an equal menace. Aphids periodically curl the aralia and gumbo-limbo leaves, and once an infestation of hand grenade scale withered the hibiscus.

Yet, for the most part, we live in harmony, these creatures and I. I have pitched my share of snails over the fence, and even, from time to time, crunched them into the mulch. These days, I put out diatomaceous earth; they seldom drag their soft bellies over its razor-sharp edges.

Without qualm, I try to step on all the baby lubber grasshoppers I can find when they emerge in the spring. Those I miss grow up and eat the lilies. The skippers that dance around the pentas lay eggs in the nearby heliconias (I don't have cannas, which they love), and those turn into leaf rollers that eat windows in the leaves. Yet, we do all right despite them.

Basically, I advocate a light hand on the pest and pesticide front unless and until a plague descends. Then reach for the soap and water spray, but go easy on the soap or you'll knock off the leaves.

By the 1990s, scientists were finding insects developing resistance to *Bacillus thuringiensis,* or *Bt,* the organic natural toxin that kills worms and caterpillars. The reason: wholesale and indiscriminate use of the stuff, which is the same way we have used chemicals of greater potency and danger in the past. It's the way we take aspirin: if two are good, four are better.

A dozen years ago, entomologists teaching my Master Gardening class said arthropods (insects) make up about 75 percent of all animals on Earth, that one million insects have been identified, and only about 1 percent of those is harmful. In the interim, with the discovery of perhaps as many as 30 million new species in tropical rain forest canopies and the gradual realization that ecosystems require these forms of life to survive, we have begun to respect them a little more. Still, garden stores and home building supply stores carry an appalling array of poisons to do them in.

To know the bugs may not be to love them, but it surely is to be amazed by their comings and goings and their earth-working roles. Here are some notes from those gardening classes.

Insects: Three body parts make up the basic creature. They are the head, thorax, and abdomen. The thorax is the chest area, and all adult insects have three pairs of legs that grow from the thorax. Insects usually have two pairs of wings. Cockroaches and grasshoppers have leathery front wings; butterflies and moths have wings covered with scales. Some insects, such as the ant and termite, lose their wings, while others, such as springtails and silverfish, are wingless.

Most insects have compound eyes. Thrips, aphids, and whiteflies are highly attracted to yellow. Scientists tell us, however, that insects generally see blue.

While some insects, such as wingless silverfish, do not go through metamorphosis, most progress through a range of changes. Grasshoppers begin as eggs with no wings; they molt, gradually getting larger. Dragonflies start out as eggs, change to naiads with gills, then shed their skin and emerge as flies. Beetles, moths, wasps, and fleas start as eggs, turn to larvae such as grubs or maggots, pupate, then emerge as adults.

There are ways of dealing with insects without resorting to chemicals: grow things they don't like, such as chives among the roses; grow things they do like, as we do with butterfly gardens, and assign that area to them. Pulverize garlic and spray it in water on plants to fend off insects; pulverize insects themselves. Grow plants resistant to insects (nematode-resistant rootstock for roses, annonas, gardenias, and so forth). Keep the landscape free of weeds—though you'll eliminate some first-rate butterfly plants this way. Grow a diversity of plants.

Having many different plants may mean that something at nearly all times will be eaten up, but not everything all at once. Geiger trees in groups are magnets for beetles; mahoganies, too, seem to get webworms when there are several in close proximity. The bigger the feast, the more the feastees.

Aside from snails and grasshoppers, sucking pests are the peskiest. Aphids, mealy bugs, whiteflies, and scales stick needle-like mouthparts into tender leaves and suck out the protoplasm. Then they excrete droplets of sugary liquid called honeydew onto the leaves below them. Mold grows on the honeydew, turns black, and, as it spreads, covers the leaf surface. Photosynthesis can be shut down in severe cases.

Ants love aphids. Ants farm them, carrying the insects around and protecting them from predators because they lap up the sugary juice. The next time you notice curling new leaves on the aphe-

landra or citrus or gumbo-limbo, take a close look and watch aphids (they come in green, purple, yellow, orange, or black) and their ants. Ants even gently massage aphids to get them to excrete the sugar.

Aphids also carry viruses around with them, and when they inject their snouts into the leaves, they can inject and spread disease from plant to plant.

Soap and water or insecticidal soap will knock off the ants, kill the aphids, and loosen the sooty mold from the leaves. Here's something else: aphids always collect on new growth, and heavy doses of high nitrogen fertilizer push new growth. Slow-release nitrogen may help spread out the new growth rather than pushing a huge burst of foliage at once. Of course, there are natural growth flushes in spring and fall, and these are the seasons to be on the alert.

Whiteflies are a nuisance indoors, where it's hard to spray. I don't often find them outside (they are more common on food crops and in ornamental nurseries than in the home landscape). Even after I find telltale signs of white, flying insects, it's hard to see the nymphs, which suck plant juices. I did get a big infestation of whiteflies once on plants in a small shade house where air circulation was poor. I read that they are attracted to yellow and put out sticky yellow strips intended to trap them. The strips proved to be death traps for tiny lizards called anoles, so I never again used them. Instead, I try to provide good air circulation.

Mealybugs hide in leaf bases, in the axils, and in tight spots on plants. They look like cotton swabs. They go through a nearly invisible crawler stage, when they are vulnerable to death by soapy water, but overall they can be tough to eliminate.

Scale insects come in two forms: hard- and soft-shelled. Hard-shelled or armored scale look like pimples on leaves, stems, and twigs. Florida red scale, banana-shaped scale, terrapin scale, and nigra scale are armored and look like what their names imply. Soft scale include hibiscus snow-scale, false oleander scale, and cot-

Lacewing larvae, which will become part of the army of good bugs that eat other bugs in the garden, are easy to recognize because they are propped up on little pedestals along leaves.

tony cushiony scale. Soft-shelled scale are mushy when you poke them, hemispherical, oblong, weird. Horticultural oil can be used in winter months on scale, but not in summer, as heat will cause the oil to damage plants. Horticultural oil has to cover the insects to either choke them or dissolve fatty acid in their armor.

Thornbugs and stinkbugs also are sucking insects. Thornbugs resemble precisely what their name says, only they appear on normally thornless plants such as tamarind, hibiscus, and bottlebrush.

Biological controls for these sucking pests are the good bugs: the ladybug beetles, praying mantises, lacewings, and wasps. A number of biocontrol firms sell these through the mail, and you can find listings in gardening mail order catalogs. Remember that lady beetles are likely to fly away, and that their larvae are the real eating machines, so learn to recognize them, too. The Florida Cooperative Extension Service has compiled a set of insect identification cards for good and harmful bugs. Ask your cooperative extension office.

Thrips are tiny black insects that wedge themselves inside flower buds, including orchids and gardenias, preventing them from opening. *Ficus microcarpa* leaves close in half from thrips (don't spray; the leaves will drop off) and avocado and mango leaves will show damage on the undersides of leaves. Thrips have what's called rasping mouth parts. They rasp at the surface to cause sap to come out

A Canary Island date palm dying from a fungus called butt rot, *Ganoderma zonatum*. An air- and soil-borne disease, ganoderma attacks older palms and rots the bottoms of the trunks.

with one part of their mouth and lap up the sap with another part, leaving a stippled effect. They also cause leaves to look lacquered from excretions. Lacewings and damsel bugs feed on thrips, as do lady beetles and frogs. Use insecticidal soaps or, in cool weather, horticultural oils.

Spider mites also leave a peculiar look to the surface of leaves. The eight-footed creatures with sucking mouth parts appear in the dry months and cause a bronzed or stippled look to foliage on roses, orchids, and African violets. In severe cases, they will build fine webs among the branches. Rust mites attack citrus and hit not only the leaves, but the fruit. Blister mites cause blisters on black olives and galls on the edges of satin leaf trees. Norfolk Island pines have notoriously bad mite problems. The lower branches turn brown and die. Italian cypresses also are vulnerable. Use a hard spray of water to knock mites off—be careful to spray the undersides.

The leaf-chewers comprise a different group: caterpillars and cutworms, which are the larval forms of moths and are active at night; beetles and their larval forms, the grubs; the grasshoppers. Slugs and snails leave telltale holes and often eat only the succulent part of the leaf, not the veins.

Orange-dog caterpillars are the larvae of the giant swallowtails. You'll find them on citrus. They look for all the world like long puddles of bird droppings. When you touch them or an enemy threatens them, they poke up two bright orange horns. Zebra longwing larvae are white with black hairs; the gulf fritillary caterpillar is orange and black; and the queen caterpillar is black with white bands and yellow marks. The more you learn, the less you want to destroy.

Caution: the saddleback, pussmoth, and io caterpillars have vicious stings from hooked and toxic hairs. Work with garden gloves.

Beetles begin as grubs and go on to bigger things. The Cuban

May beetle, which appears in May or June and again in September or October, spends part of its life as a grass-munching grub. When it changes to a beetle, it flies at night, often quite far, to feed on such delectables as roses, lychees, mamey sapotes, and cassias, consuming flower pollen. White and light pink roses are magnets for these and euphoria beetles, which burrow into the opening buds. Euphoria beetles are small and black with silver markings. They also eat sap. Set out a white bucket filled with water and aim a light on it at night. Because these beetles are attracted to white, they'll fly into it and drown.

Often beetles will invade wood, feeding on cambium or sap. The pine bark beetle is particularly harmful to South Florida's pines when they are stressed and damaged, as most in Dade and Broward counties are because of development and the lowered water table. Many pines were stricken after Hurricane Andrew.

One of the best resources on pests is *Common-Sense Pest Control* by William Olkowski, Sheila Daar, and Helag Olkowski, published by The Taunton Press.

When Turning to Chemicals

First, identify the insect. Good insects need bad ones to exist. Nature can work for you.

Physically killing insects may be distasteful, but it is ecologically sound.

A hard spray from the hose works to remove many insects, such as scale, from an emerging palm spear.

Choose the method least harmful to you and the environment. Sevin kills bees and wasps. If you must use it, do so at night rather than in the morning, when bees are working.

Know the best application method. If you mix the chemical with water, should you add a spreader-sticker so the liquid will adhere to the foliage and be effective? Should you use a dust or spray? (Dusting is far more dangerous.)

Malathion is a chemical that is quick to disappear once used, and it can be sprayed on sucking insects such as aphids, whiteflies, mealybugs, scale, and thrips. Sprays may have to be repeated depending on the life cycle of the insects. Whiteflies, for instance, are not affected by Malathion when adults but only in their egg stage. Therefore, you don't spray when you first see the flies but a couple of weeks later, and then repeat the spray in seven to 10 days. Be sure to spray the undersides of the leaves, since that's where they live. Mealybugs and scale may need a second application two weeks after the first. Scale may require three or four treatments. Aphids, on the other hand, usually require only one chemical spray.

Cygon, another insecticide, is a systemic that puts poison into the plant, killing insects when they take a bite. This will get the armored scale, which is covered over with a waxy, impervious coating. Malathion affects the crawlers.

Dipel is one of the organics that attacks the stomachs of caterpillars.

Mites are controlled by a good strong spray from the hose. You also can buy predatory mites to fight spider mites. Mites quickly build up a resistance to miticides; rose growers often alternate such chemicals when they use them.

Read labels carefully to avoid killing your favorite plants. Hibiscus, for instance, should not be sprayed with Malathion.

Pine bark beetles can be treated with Metasystox R, an insecticide injected directly into the tree. The insecticide should be injected when the first white or red extrusions are seen on the bark. That treatment can be followed with a fertilizer-growth regulator, called Bayleton, injected when pines begin to put out new needles. Bayleton promotes production of hormones in trees that stimulate root growth over top growth. Mobay Corp. produces it; a licensed applicator must use it for you.

DISEASES

Just look around, and you probably can find black spots, streaks, dots, and dashes that are symptomatic of some disease or other lurking in your garden.

There are few natural predators available to combat plant diseases. Instead, sanitation, disease-resistant varieties, good air circulation, and good cultural practices are your main preventive weapons.

Sometimes, given the weather or extremely susceptible plants, you have to use a chemical. Before reaching for one, however, you have to know what it is you're going to treat, so you have to become an amateur plant pathologist, which is no easy task.

You start by noting conditions. What time of year is it, and is the symptom a seasonal change or is it really a disease? Avocados shed their leaves in late winter or early spring. Crape myrtles shed leaves in the fall. These are naturally occurring events, not signs that something is wrong.

Has there been a recent cold spell, drought, heavy rain, or extreme heat? These climatic conditions can stress plants. Dry winds may cause brown leaves or leaf drop. Was a tree struck by lightning? Physical damage, such as bark wounding by string trimmers or lawn mowers, can cut off the flow of water or nutrients, causing leaves to drop and branches to die. Check the trunks and branches for wounds, cracks, or breaks.

When plants wilt in the afternoon but come back and are turgid again in the morning, that's a normal response to water stress. But when they wilt and don't plump up again, even after watering, it may be root injury. Dig around the plant and find some roots. Are there swollen nodules on them? If so, nematodes are interfering with water uptake.

Are you looking at spots on leaves? Are the spots black, surrounded by a yellow halo, or tiny and white so the leaf looks off-color? If the first, you're looking at a fungus or bacterial attack; if the second, you're seeing the results of mites (turn the leaf over and use a hand lens to find the culprits).

Fungal spores are spread by wind; they germinate in water. Since they depend on plants for energy, they begin stealing from the host. The result is disease, and symptoms are a variety of spots, some circular, some long and angular, some streaks and teardrops. Usually, however, the center is black, indicating dead tissue, and the edges brown or yellow.

Rust is an exception. Rust disease is a fungus that forms rusty-colored pustules or pimples on the undersides of leaves and yellow spots on the tops. Frangipani is extremely prone to rust, as are figs and some grasses.

Because fungal spores germinate in water, they are most prevalent in the rainy season—or in hot, humid spells in winter and the close conditions of greenhouses that lack air circulation. Leaf spot diseases proliferate in the summer, and these are fungal diseases.

There is one exception: powdery mildew. It likes a dry season. It doesn't need water to germinate. It shows up in midwinter on mangoes, avocados, and papayas. The leaves appear to have a coating of light dust on them, and they become distorted. Since this usually happens before avocados shed their leaves, there's nothing to worry about or to be done on this tree. Sulfur is a treatment for powdery mildew.

Fungi also can cause root rot. Citrus foot rot, mushroom root rot, and a similar palm butt rot, or ganoderma, are diseases caused by air- and soil-borne fungi. If plants sit in water, these diseases can get started. You'll notice severe wilting and yellowing of the leaves from the base to the top. Citrus and avocados need well-drained soil.

Get rid of diseased plants and monitor your watering habits

closely. Don't reuse potting soil. Water before sunup. These are ways to avoid conditions favorable to the root diseases.

Make sure there's good air circulation around your plants so leaves dry after a rain or irrigation. A fungus needs eight hours of wet to become established. So a spot that stays wet all the time encourages disease.

If the spots you're looking at are slimy, the disease probably is caused by bacteria. These diseases love high humidity; they sweep through a plant fast, entering through wounds or leaf stomata, which are the natural pores for gas exchange. Air circulation is vital, as are clean tools (a 10 percent Clorox solution cleans shears and pruners) in preventing the spread of diseases.

Viruses cause bizarre patterns on flowers and leaves. Color breaks are often the result of viruses: colors are streaked and flowers distorted and small on orchids, tulips, and gladioli. Orchid leaves show viral symptoms in long black streaks, usually on the lower, older leaves. Mosaic virus on rose leaves causes an irregular, white spotting.

Insects are the transmitters, or vectors, of viruses. Aphids inject enzymes into plants when they suck out juices, and these enzymes can contain bits of virus. But dirty tools also can spread viruses. When repotting orchids, never use your shears on two different orchids without disinfecting them to avoid the risk of transmitting a virus, even if you do not see any symptoms.

Basically, there is little you can do for a viral disease but destroy the plant.

Lethal yellowing, a mycoplasma-like organism resembling a virus, was spread by plant hoppers that decimated coconut palms in South Florida in the 1970s. Although the palms were treated with antibiotics for a number of years, the treatment did not cure the palms, but only delayed the final demise.

The action on your part comes at the front end of the deal: buy clean, disease-free plants and discard sick ones if you do not want disease to spread. Sterilize containers or discard them. Never use diseased plants for mulch.

Select the right chemicals if you choose chemical treatment, and don't overspray. Keep chemical spray bottles just for chemicals, and don't use them for anything else. Get rid of excess chemical sprays by using them. Wash the spray tanks three times. Be sure to read the labels of the pesticides and fungicides you use, and apply them only to those plants listed.

A live oak covered with bromeliads and orchids is among the most venerable of South Florida's trees.

5

BUILDING A FRAMEWORK: TREES FOR THE GARDEN

PERHAPS AS LONG AS seven hundred years ago, two centuries before Columbus set sail, seeds from a few cypress cones were released in winter and germinated in the clean brown water of the swamp. They grew there, shedding their fine needles every year, standing smoky gray until spring, when they put out shoots so soft as to be unrivaled in their innocent greenness. They stand there now, in what we call Corkscrew Swamp Sanctuary. Their crowns have been sheared by the storms of eons, but they retain the girths of giants. It is these cypress trees, massive ancients, that show us the grandeur of the place.

A few months after the 1992 hurricane, an ancient oak steadfastly held its branches over a ferny sinkhole as white light from a full moon enveloped it like gossamer. The stature of that tree was apparent in the day, but at night—shorn of its twigs, stripped of viney growth, and outlined by moonlight—its unadorned architecture was a revelation of sinewy strength: irregular and rough to the touch, noble, and absolutely venerable.

That trees can attain and embody such solidity and produce tender new foliage from water and minerals is one of the marvels of the planet, alongside lichens that dissolve rock and orchids that mimic bees.

Trees also produce oxygen and breezes, shade and comfort.

They sough, they sway, they shelter. They provide hollows for nests, branches for song, and furrows for epiphytes. They produce resins, rubber, dyes, oils, syrup, quinine, fruits, flowers, and nuts. From trees we make paper and pencils, houses, fences, poetry, song, and once, it is told, a fundamental explanation of a law of physics.

Even our families have trees.

Our trees have evolved, migrated, become established, invaded, and disappeared on the landscape, all the while unable to move from the sites in which they are rooted.

In the subtropics, the tree flora is dazzling if only for its myriad look-alikes. We have trees we call sweet bay, buttonwood, poisonwood, inkwood, ironwood, torchwood, dogwood, soapberry, sugarberry, bitterbush, saltbush, graytwig, varnish leaf, satin leaf, milkbark, and paradise.

Yet we also are graced with trees from other parts of the world that share our sun, space, and water. The citrus trees and the tropical fruit trees, the fabulous flowering trees, the nut trees and nitrogen-fixing trees. And alas, the land-eating trees from Australia that threaten to devour the peninsula.

We can grow trees that disguise their new leaves by coloring them brown so they won't be eaten by insects; trees that provide homes for ant colonies, luring them with packets of protein on their leaves; trees fertilized by bats and trees fertilized by hummingbirds; trees that start their lives in the crotches of other trees, then send down long roots that breathe and strangle at once; trees that exude saltwater and trees that exclude saltwater; trees that aren't trees at all, but are in the same broad plant grouping as corn and grass—we call these palm trees.

So how, from among all of these, do you select trees for your yard?

There are two basic approaches. Plant what you love. Plant what makes sense. Hopefully, the two will jibe. But if the trees you love are too grand and your space for them too small, then find the trees you love planted elsewhere and visit them often.

You must consider size. A townhouse patio won't hold an oak, but it will be comfortably shaded by a citrus.

Consider soil. Acid-loving plants, such as magnolia, may not do their best here unless you happen to have a pocket of acid sand.

Consider the lay of the land, whether you are high or low, and consequently whether the planting area is wet or dry. Trees from wet conditions will grow in drier soils, but trees from dry soils will not grow in wet areas.

Consider temperatures. Areas in the center part of the peninsula, between the coasts, are often 10 degrees colder in cold snaps and several degrees hotter in summer than areas bathed in mitigating sea breezes near the shore.

Consider salt. Saltwater spray is more difficult to survive than salt breezes farther back from the dunes, and salt tolerance is a necessity if trees are to be exposed to them.

Consider exposure. Not only to sunlight, but the daily amount of sunlight, wind, and reflected light from buildings.

Consider existing plants. Will you retain what's already there? If so, will your new plants be able to grow in competition with the roots and shade of the established plants?

Consider also the sidewalk and septic tank that may be sinks for roots; the children, the neighbors; the pool; leaves staining automobile finishes; wildlife, wildlife, wildlife; birds, birds, birds.

What would happen if blocks of neighborhoods were organized to plant corridors of trees in backyards, running like narrow parks, to replace walls and fences? What if foxes and opossums and snakes and lizards and cardinals and warblers had shelter and safe places?

All of these questions will influence tree selection. Give long thought to the answers. Planting a tree is a public act of private courage and optimism. Even if you are planting in your backyard, your trees may last for generations. They can help maintain the health of the ecosystem, pass along vital genes, inspire, comfort, and countenance. Plant them with care.

ENERGY CONSERVATION WITH LANDSCAPING

If you are lucky enough to have a wide overhanging roof, a wraparound veranda or porch, or a natural hammock for a lawn, you know firsthand the value of these design and landscape features for saving energy. But more than likely, you have a concrete block house in the suburbs with a hip roof, a couple of trees in the front yard, and grass. So selecting the right trees and the right planting sites are your main weapons in the battle of the energy bill—and in the effort to reduce resource wastefulness.

There are a couple of ways to approach energy savings: reduce the use overall and/or reduce peak load use. Overall energy consumption can be cut by design elements, such as wide overhangs, windows that capture prevailing breezes, radiant barriers in ceilings that will insulate your house, ceiling fans, and white roofs to reflect heat rather than absorb it. (A 70-degree difference between

In the heart of Matheson Hammock, a ficus tree has stretched its enormous roots and worked them into the pitted surface of the oolitic limestone.

white and black surfaces has been measured by researchers from the Lawrence Berkeley Lab in Berkeley, California.)

Peak-load reduction is augmented by landscaping that allows use of air conditioning, but not all the time. It is designed to subvert the summertime peak electrical demand from 6 to 9 P.M.

Jack Parker, head of environmental studies at Florida International University, has gained an international reputation for documenting energy savings with landscape design. He and the Lawrence Berkeley researchers have gathered data on the energy savings of trees planted on the east, south, and west sides of the house; on white roofs; and on the use of shrubs to shield walls from heat buildup.

Here's how it works.

Because air conditioners become less efficient as temperatures rise, plant trees or shrubs around the exterior air conditioning unit to lower air temperature by six or seven degrees. This will increase the unit's efficiency by about 10 percent. Place them around the unit so that within five years, the canopy will completely shade the unit and the adjacent area, but not so close that they block air flow.

Next, plant trees on the east and west sides of the house (and in the subtropics, on the south side as well), to keep walls shaded. A tree planted 10 feet from a wall will shade that wall four times as long as a tree planted 20 feet from it. Subtropical summers often last through October, and the southerly, but still intense, sun will cause heat buildup in the fall and spring. Concrete walls begin gaining heat as soon as the sun strikes them. By 11 A.M., the east walls are hot, and they will stay hot until 6 P.M. in the summer. West walls retain heat until late in the evening.

Preventing this heat gain will reduce your need for air conditioning, particularly during late afternoons and early evenings when everyone comes home from school and work, turns on the television, and cooks dinner, turning up the air conditioning. Both trees and shrubs are needed for the job—trees protecting and shading the tops of the walls and roof as well as shrubs blocking sun on lower portions of the walls.

Additionally, you can plant shrubs to funnel breezes into or away from windows. At the southeast windows, which catch prevailing breezes in the summer, prune shrubs so they are just above window height and sloping into the window. In winter, prune the same shrubs a little higher, and angle the tops away from the window to keep air out.

When trees mature, prune the lower limbs so they don't block breezes passing beneath them toward the windows. Until they are several feet tall, however, allow lower limbs to remain as they contribute to the development of the trunk.

The use of water-conserving plants, mulch, and compost also contributes to energy savings. Creating a drive of mulch or rock allows rain percolation and reduces reflected heat and heat buildup. Ground covers reduce the need to mow; they also collect fallen leaves and hide them as if by magic.

All of these landscaping and gardening devices and techniques will allow you to leave less of a footprint on the land and live more in harmony with it. The Florida Solar Energy Center provides information on radiant heat barriers, energy saving appliances and house designs, solar heaters, and other energy saving practices. Write: Public Information Office, Florida Solar Energy Center, 300 State Road 401, Cape Canaveral, FL 32920.

SELECTED TREES

✓ **Red maple,** *Acer rubrum.* A temperate tree that ventures into South Florida's Everglades, this tree forms an upright, narrow crown. Quite tall, possibly to 70 feet. The leaves are lobed and turn red and then yellow in fall. Flowers usually begin to form in December and January, and fruit in February. The fruit occur in pairs and are winged (a winged fruit is called a samara). Tomlinson, in *The Biology of Trees Native to Tropical Florida*, says the race of red maples that occurs in wet woodlands has no need for chilling before setting buds.

Good for low swales or in transitions to lake-front plantings, red maples can be mixed with cypresses for an effective native grouping. The wood of this fast-growing tree can be brittle.

✓ **Crabwood,** *Ateramnus lucidus* (*Gymnanthes lucida*). 20 to 30 feet. A pretty native tree that ought to be used more often, the crabwood is a coastal hammock tree: drought tolerant, salt tolerant, and sturdy.

When young, the leaves are notched and have small glands in these notches that eventually fall off. The leaf tips vary from pointed to blunt, and if you look very closely, you'll see what botanists call shoulders at the base of the leaf where the stalk or petiole is attached.

Use this in shade, beneath the canopy of a big tree, or as a specimen. It has reddish new growth at the end of the dry season. Flower branches form one spring and sit there until the next year, when rain nudges them open. A single female flower among many males appears on each branchlet. Tomlinson suggests that the flowers are wind pollinated. Fruits ripen over summer, hanging on long stalks.

✓ **Black olive,** *Bucida buceras*. To 40 or 50 feet. A densely crowned tree with the leaves in whorls at the ends of twigs. This is a fast-growing, robust tree that often is hatracked and as a result becomes even denser. Many black olives that were toppled by the 1992 hurricane had thick, massive crowns as a result of bad pruning.

Because the trees are fast growing, they were frequently planted in the 1970s and 1980s in South Florida developments, which caused a reaction against using them by the late 1980s. Still, they are salt tolerant and grow well in alkaline soils.

The black olive was once commonly called oxhorn Bucida be-cause of the long galls that developed from fruits attacked by mites. Sapsuckers leave patterns of holes in the bark.

✓ **Gumbo-limbo,** *Bursera simaruba*. 50 feet. After the oaks and the Florida trema, the poisonwood and the myrsine, next come the gumbo-limbos and the stoppers, building the hammocks and giving them character, earthy smells, and interesting barks.

Red, peeling bark is the hallmark of the gumbo-limbo, which is said to be a Bantu name for the tree from the days when the gummy resin was spread on tree limbs to serve as bird traps. Birds that became stuck in the glue were caught and sold to the Spanish cigar-makers in Cuba and Key West to be caged in cigar factories.

Salt tolerant, of soft wood and often large-trunked, the gumbo-limbo was once carved into carousel horses, and its sap was used to make glue. The color of the trunks varies from copper and orange to silvery red. The trunks and major branches are massive and quite beautiful in a mixed planting, often catching the slanted rays of morning or afternoon light as no other tree in the forest can. Gumbo-limbo flowers in late winter or early spring. Its clusters of red fruit are eaten by macaws and other parrots that have naturalized in South Florida.

Leaves are compound, with seven to nine leaflets, each with a prominent yellow central vein and a driptip. Pioneers used the leaves to treat snake bites and rash, as well as for tea. The canopy of the gumbo-limbo is sparse, with new growth appearing in March or April. Old leaves drop first, and the tree can be leafless for two or three weeks.

✓ **Satin leaf,** *Chrysophyllum oliviforme*. To 30 feet. Dense, copper-colored hairs on the bottom of the leaves make this one of the coastal hammock's most beautiful trees. It takes full sun to partial shade and dry conditions. It's tolerant of salt breezes. The native tree has a narrow, upright crown with long, arching, loppy branches that, when young, come out on a plane. This is a beautiful tree to have in a hammock or as a specimen, where its leaves can be ruffled by the wind.

Some trees are more pubescent (hairier) than others, and those on Elliott Key are said, by native tree aficionados, to be "outrageous" in their luxuriance of rusty hair. When leaves age, the normally deep green leathery tops turn a pretty red and lose their pubescence.

The species name, oliviforme, is for the fruit—berries that look like olives and turn dark purple.

✓ **Pigeon plum,** *Coccoloba diversifolia.* 50 feet. Large leaves and a narrow, upright crown. The species name, *diversifolia,* indicates a diversity of leaf shapes, changing from broad to narrow, large to small, as the tree ages. The common name came about because the white crowned pigeons feed on the astringent fruits of the female trees in summer and fall. (They also feed on poisonwood fruit.)

These native trees also could be called "coon-scratched trees" due to the characteristic marks left on the female fruit-bearing pigeon plums by hungry raccoons. Another characteristic is the gold of the leaves after they fall in the autumn.

As the tree becomes better known, it is being used in formal plantings, regularly spaced to march along swales and in front of walls. But it can just as easily be used as a specimen tree, standing alone, framing a house, or even as a background tree. It grows in sun, partial or full shade, and likes well-drained soils, but tolerates moisture.

The bark is a lovely feature of this tree, as it is on the sea-grape, its close relative. Gray, beige, and brown, the thin bark falls off in patches and is quite smooth to the touch. The trunks are narrow, often slightly fluted at the base if the trees are growing in rocky coastal hammocks. The Vizcaya Museum hammock in Miami is full of these trees growing as close as two feet from each other.

✓ **Sea-grape,** *Coccoloba uvifera.* 25 feet. As sprawly and round as the pigeon plum is upright, the sea-grape is a seaside citizen: salt tolerant, drought tolerant, and generally useful in many ways. This native can be allowed to take its own shape or be shaped into a hedge.

While many sea-grapes broke apart under the onslaught of Hurricane Andrew, the trees have resprouted. They do drop leaves if singed by cold, and female trees drop ripe fruit in the fall.

Leathery round leaves, some as big as dinner plates, are attractive shades of bronze and red before they fall, a tropical signal of spring and summer growth, not autumn. Both the pigeon plum and sea-grape somnolently endure winter, reserving their growing spurts for the warm season. The fruit makes a wonderful jelly, but individual "grapes" ripen one at a time, and require patience when collected.

Grow these in full sun, well-draining soil. You'll get better growth in better soils. Since they do most of their growing in summer, a springtime application of fertilizer will boost them along.

✓ **Geiger tree,** *Cordia sebestena.* 25 feet. A dozen years ago, few Geigers were seen outside their native far south Dade County and scattered parks. Now, they're being used as street trees in downtown Miami, and showing off their bright orange, tubular flowers with aplomb.

Salt tolerant but cold sensitive (leaves will drop after a severe cold but quickly come back), the Geiger has leaves rough to the touch. Dried, as they are in my plant files, they are like fine sandpaper. It is said that the leaves were once used for polishing wood.

The Geiger will bloom off and on throughout the year in full sun and dry conditions. Beetles will chew at the leaves in the spring, though solitary trees aren't as bothered as several together. The trees are somewhat brittle and will break up in storms, but endure. It is their way in seaside and windy conditions.

✓ **Inkwood,** *Exothea paniculata.* 35 feet. Ink-colored fruit and sap that turns black when dried characterize this native tree. When the tree is young, the compound leaves are in pairs; when more mature, the leaves occur in fours and sixes.

Starting life as a shrub, inkwood eventually develops a canopy of dense, dark green leaves. In the spring, they flush out lettuce-green. The fragrant white flowers occur in late winter or early spring. Fruit, which turn from orange to purple by mid-summer, are savored by birds. There are male and female trees.

Use in dappled shade and well-drained soil. Prune the lower branches once the tree gains some height so you can better see the reddish-brown bark.

✓ **Short-leaf fig,** *Ficus citrifolia.* 60 feet. There are more than 700 species of ficus, which are in the mulberry family and related to the tropical breadfruit and jackfruit. One of two native fig trees, the short-leaf fig is distinguished by the long stalks on the leaves and fruit and by its pink stipules (protective, leaf-like structures that enfold new leaves). The native strangler fig has green stipules and stalkless fruit. Plant the short-leaf fig in full sun and well-draining soil, and use it as a specimen tree. Ferns, palms, and anthuriums, as well as St. Augustine grass, will grow beneath it.

The many fruits are produced three times a year, and birds love them, especially migrating cedar waxwings. The flowers are contained inside a round fruit that technically is a multiple fruit, with little fruits inside an outer part called the syconium. All but one are female flowers, and all are pollinated inside by a minute wasp that enters through a cavity at one end. As it squeezes into the fig, the wasp loses its wings but proceeds to fertilize each female flower, laying an egg within each as she does. Then she dies. Some of the eggs hatch into grubs and eat the flowers; some of the flowers develop seeds.

As the male flower matures and opens, the grubs hatch and become wasps. Male wasps are wingless, but they can impregnate the females and then eat holes in the fruit through which females escape. (Should the male wasps escape, they merely fall to the ground and die.) Before the females leave, they load up on the pollen of the male flower. Then they fly out of the fig, bore into another newly developing fruit, and start the whole cycle over.

For years, non-native figs planted here, such as the Bo tree, rubber tree, weeping fig, and a host of others, were thought to have unfertilized fruit because their specific wasps were missing. Now, however, many of those wasps have found their way to the state and fertile ficus seeds are sprouting throughout the urban area.

The short-leaf fig is not particularly resistant to hurricane winds, but drops limbs, thereby retaining its trunk.

Plant in full sun and well-draining soil as a specimen tree. It does not develop a significant number of aerial roots, but it has an aggressive root system and will invade a septic tank. A lot of leaves fall over winter.

✓ **Dahoon holly,** *Ilex cassine.* 40 feet. A true holly, the female matures red berries over winter. The dahoon is a wetlands tree, so it likes to have moist soil or a layer of mulch. While it will take full sun to partial shade, the tree will bear more fruit in sun.

An evergreen, the dahoon has a flush of new leaves and flowers in late spring. Berries then form, but do not ripen until winter. Spines on the leaves occur on saplings, but also occasionally on adult trees.

✓ **Krug's holly,** *Ilex krugiana.* A rarer holly; also called the tawnyberry holly. It likes more shade and somewhat drier conditions than the dahoon. If you come upon a tree with a white trunk surrounded by distinctly black fallen leaves, it's this one. Krug's holly doesn't like soil that compacts, such as fill; it will yellow.

Both hollies have shallow surface roots, and require mulch. The Krug's holly is sensitive to cold (it's a tropical tree at the northernmost limit of its range), while the dahoon is not.

✓ **Wild tamarind,** *Lysiloma latisiliqua.* 60 feet. Light bark and bipinnate leaves on zigzagging branches. This native is evergreen to semideciduous. Sometimes cold knocks off the tiny leaves; in warm winters, they may fall just before the new growth appears, or gradually drop. Tree snails browse the lichens that grow on lysilomas; gnat-cathers, warblers, and flycatchers flit in and out among the branches.

Flowers begin to open in March. They are staminate, fluffy round balls, greenish-white with purplish throats and a soft perfume. Seed pods develop over summer, and are somewhat flat and twisted. When they ripen, they're mottled black and white, as if charred. And they get thorn bugs, which are sucking insects.

Light filtered through this feathery tree is wonderful for ferns and orchids in the branches, and, beneath them, wild coffee, randia, marlberry, and myrsine of the hammocks, or ground-covering ferns. Roots will come to the surface as the tree ages. A pioneer that initiates the take-over of a pineland, the lysiloma takes tough conditions (except cold when young).

✓ **Sweet bay magnolia,** *Magnolia virginiana.* to 70 feet. When the wind sails across Shark Valley in the Everglades, the silvery undersides of the sweet bay appear and sparkle across and above the sweeps of sawgrass. When you go there in spring, stop and smell the fleshy white flowers. They are laden with a citrus-spicy perfume.

During summer, the fruits form, taking their distinctive, cone-like shape, but the seeds aren't released until winter, when they dangle on a slender stalk like the seeds of black-bead, which are suspended on bright pink and elastic seed stalks. Sweet bay seeds germinate in wet conditions.

Use the sweet bay in wet or damp areas (if too dry, you'll lose it)

A female Dahoon holly, with its characteristic white bark, is laden with berries in winter. This is the native Florida holly.

in sun or dappled shade, where it will be a little greener and lusher. An irregular crown casts a light shade and dances in wind.

✓ **Sapodilla,** *Manilkara zapota.* 35 to 50 feet. A wind-resistant tree. Mabel Dorn wrote in *Under the Coconuts in Florida* in the 1940s that the sapodilla was among those trees that "have withstood several hurricanes and seem worthy of mention." The sapodilla proved its strength again in 1992.

A semi-naturalized tree from Central America and Mexico, it is cultivated for shade and fruit. The leaves are pointed and long, whereas the leaves of the native wild dilly (*Manilkara bahamensis*) in the Florida Keys and very southern tip of the peninsula are blunt and often notched at the tips.

Chicle, the natural base of chewing gum, is the milky latex that is taken from the sapodilla. In *Costa Rican Natural History*, Gary Hartshorn says that before synthetic chicle, most of the natural product came from the Yucatan Peninsula of Mexico and the Peten of Guatemala. It is thought that the Mayans cultivated the sapodilla. Chicle was harvested by making zigzag cuts in the trunk and allowing the sap to collect in cups, just as rubber trees are tapped.

In South Florida, the scurfy fruit is sometimes eaten fresh; in the West Indies, it's boiled to make a syrup. The tree begins to fruit at about five years. It flowers in the spring with solitary white flowers in the axils of the leaves.

The tree thrives in sandy and limestone soils and requires little other care than removing deadwood. Scale insects sometimes infest the trees, causing sooty mold to form on the leaves. Use insecticidal soap or soap and water spray (one tablespoon of liquid soap to a gallon of water). Caribbean fruit fly has attacked sapodilla. Cultivated varieties include 'Prolific,' 'Brown Sugar,' 'Russell,' and 'Modello.'

✓ **Lancewood,** *Nectandra coriacea.* 25 to 40 feet. In sun, it becomes quite bushy; in shade, it's a full-fledged tree. From and for native hammocks, the lancewood has noticeably long, pointed leaves in its narrow crown. It grows well beneath gumbo-limbo, mastic, lysiloma, or in a confined area.

It likes dry to moist soils, but won't endure flooding. It is cold tolerant.

Thrushes and mockingbirds nest in this tree. The fruit looks like little purple-turning-black avocados. Cinnamon, allspice, and camphor trees also are in this family, the laurel family, along with avocados. Leaves of these trees are aromatic. The lancewood has a bay-like smell.

Flowers occur all summer, and like avocados they open twice, first as female, then male flowers.

✓ **Slash pine,** *Pinus elliotti* var. *densa.* 50-plus feet. Set aside an area for several of South Florida's native conifers to create a special grove where the trees' sensitive roots will be protected. Choose a sunny, fast-draining site; plant at least 10 feet apart; mulch with pine needles. Male and female cones are in separate clusters on the same tree. Pollen is shed in spring by small male cones and carried on wind to the female cones. New needles appear in spring and are in twos and threes. The trees develop what Tomlinson calls tiers of branches over the growing season.

✓ **Jamaica dogwood,** *Piscidia piscipula.* 40 feet. The dogwood has big, compound leaves with an odd number of gray-green leaflets; it is without leaves for one or two months during winter if the weather is cold. You'll have to do some raking. It has a distinctive bark, with horizontal markings of white against a dark gray background.

In full sun, the tree will grow on rocky soils. It has showy flowers that are dusty pink, followed by pods that are lettuce green turning to gold, winged, and ruffled. It will take a few years to flower.

Once economically important for ship building, the hardwood is embedded with silica. Limbs were used as curved braces, called dogs, for joining the hull and decking.

✓ **West Indian cherry,** *Prunus myrtifolia.* 45 feet. For full sun and dry soil, this beautiful tree is blessed with the addition of a prussic acid aroma when leaves are crushed. The glossy leaves are shiny and wavy, a pretty green with a hint of yellow in the new growth.

Small starbursts of flowers form in winter, usually November or December, and green to black plums or cherries develop by early summer. The bitter fruit will stain your hands, but birds are not at all put off by this quality.

Use this lovely native as a single specimen; put several together as a screen or a barrier.

✓ **Live oak,** *Quercus virginiana.* At 60 feet, the matriarch of South Florida trees. It is a favorite among tree experts for use as a shade tree, street tree, and native tree planting. Its openness, small leaves, rough bark, strong wood, and round to spreading shape are attractive to wildlife, epiphytes, birds, and people. Charles Torrey Simpson wrote in 1919: "It is found always in the very front of the firing line, a determined and courageous fighter. One of the most rapid growers of our native trees, if spared a few years from fire, it reaches a height of several feet and displays a goodly spread of branches."

Leaves are usually a couple of inches long, cupped, dark green and leathery on top, and hairy below. When young, they can be somewhat toothed.

A member of the beech family, the live oak grows all over the south and into Texas, where in the hill country it is dwarfed and gnarled. It does not grow in the Florida Keys naturally. Male and female flowers occur on separate small spikes in March, and acorns ripen in the fall, with good acorn years occurring once every two or three years.

Some oaks produce masses of root suckers and form thickets around the base of the parent tree.

✓ **Turkey oak,** *Quercus laevis.* Stays out of southeastern Florida, but ventures somewhat into southwest Florida and the rest of the state on sandy soils. It has what are more commonly thought of as oak-like leaves, deeply lobed and toothed. Of smaller stature, the turkey oak grows to about 30 feet.

✓ **Laurel oak,** *Quercus laurifolia.* This oak grows as far south as Broward County, but not Dade. It is a taller tree than the live oak, faster growing with slightly larger leaves. It also splits apart more readily and is shorter-lived.

✓ **Paradise tree,** *Simaruba glauca.* 25 to 40 feet. As a sapling, this is one of the hammock's jewels, positioning its young pinkish to yellow-green leaves on reddish twigs around a central trunk. North Key Largo has some fine paradise trees in its hammocks, protected by the buttonwoods and pigeon plums. This is, in fact, a clue to using it, because the tree can break up in wind and suffers from cold. Protect it in a mixed planting.

There are male and female trees, with flowers appearing from February to April and olive-like fruits, called drupes, following within a month. The fruits turn from yellow to purple when they ripen, attracting birds. They have been used as a source of oil, and the roots, containing a glycoside, have been used to treat dysentery. Simpson says every part of the tree is bitter.

Because it grows in the middle of a hammock, it tends to be sparingly branched, using its energy, instead, to rapidly reach light at the top of the canopy. Once there, it fills out. In cultivation, the trees are fuller. In full sun, they can be bushy.

✓ **West Indies mahogany,** *Swietenia mahagoni.* 60 feet. This densely crowned tree has beautiful red-brown wood that has made it a valuable timber tree. (Barry Tomlinson, in *The Biology of Trees*

Native to Tropical Florida, says the Honduran mahogany, *S. macrophylla,* is the more desired species because it has a larger trunk.) The leaves are compound with off-center veins, and they drop before the new ones emerge in late winter to early spring.

The trees are monoecious, meaning that both male and female flowers are on the same tree (*oikos* is Greek for house, and monoecious means "in one house"; dioecious means "in separate or two houses"). While the flowers are not conspicuous, the fruit are. Fruit are shaped like big plums that harden over summer and gradually break open, allowing winged seeds, called samaras, to flutter to the ground.

Buy mahoganies without V-crotches. The trees often have multiple leaders emerging from a single crotch, and this can weaken them in storms. A stem-boring insect attacks young mahoganies and kills the tips, causing the development of many shoots from one point, which results in poor structure in the mature tree.

Webworms feed on succulent young leaves. These little caterpillars, the immature stage of certain moths, build their webs to protect themselves while feeding in the spring. They will drop off within a couple of weeks. Fertilize to help the tree recover and put out new growth. A single tree will not attract insects as readily as many trees of the same species.

✓ **Tamarind,** *Tamarindus indica.* 30 to 40 feet (80 in its native habitat, India). Often confused with the lysiloma, the tamarind is wind resistant and a useful shade or background tree. In summer, it has small, pale, pinkish-yellow flowers, rather orchid-like in shape, and hard pods that develop thereafter. The brittle pods contain tart, pulpy seeds that are thirst-quenching when chewed or sucked. The pulp is an ingredient of Worcestershire sauce, chutney, and tamarind butter. Wilson Popenoe's classic book, *Manual of Tropical and Subtropical Fruits,* says the tamarind was known in Europe in the Middle Ages; Marco Polo mentioned it in 1298; New England sea captains brought preserved fruit from Jamaica to Boston in the eighteenth and nineteenth centuries.

✓ **Cypress trees.** *Taxodium* species. Bald cypress and pond cypress. The issue of whether these are separate species has not been finally resolved, although Tomlinson lists bald cypress as *Taxodium distichum* and pond cypress as *T. ascendens.* Pond cypress has more needle-like leaves than the feathery bald cypress, and it has a more rounded crown. Pond cypress heartwood is said to be stronger than bald cypress.

These trees can be planted on a lake shore or actually in the water. There are several planted in Lake Eola, in downtown Orlando. Wet feet is an optimal condition, but cypress will grow on sandy soil. They don't flourish on high, rocky soil, but will endure. Male cones are developed in the fall and overwinter on the trees; female cones appear in spring.

Cypress knees are formations on the roots that allow oxygen and gas exchange to occur. Often fluted at the base, cypress trunks can reach enormous sizes. The trees are in the redwood family. They resist disease and bugs, but many of the ancient cypresses in Corkscrew Swamp Sanctuary in Collier County long ago lost towering tops to storm and age.

Native Trees for Use on Fill

Gumbo-limbo
Pigeon plum
Sea-grape
Strangler fig
Wild lime
Inkwood

Mastic
Lancewood

Native Trees for Wet Areas

Bald cypress
Pond cypress
Red maple
Dahoon holly
Pond apple
Royal palm
Paurotis palm

Fast-growing Native Trees

Jamaica dogwood
Gumbo-limbo
Short-leaf fig
Strangler fig
Wild tamarind

ADDING TO THE SCAFFOLD

Useful Small Trees

"Stoppers" is the name given a group of small native trees that grow in the shady understory of the hammock. Ideal for small yards, they range between 15 and 35 feet. They often are fragrant, bear bird-attracting fruit, and have pinkish-red new growth. They will do well in sun or shade, and you can use them to create a small woods if you plant them in a group.

Several of these lovely small trees are in the myrtle family, the Myrtaceae. Aromatic leaves are characteristic of many stoppers as well as other family members, including allspice, eucalyptus, bot-

tle brush, melaleuca, and guava. An infusion brewed from the leaves of these trees was once said to stop diarrhea.

✓ **Spicewood,** *Calyptranthes pallens.* Leaves are opposite, leathery, and unfold pink or light red. They have a spicy fragrance. Flowers are little balls of many stamens with a lidlike structure encircling them; a second common name is pale lid flower. Purple fruit attracts a range of birds in the fall.

✓ **Myrtle-of-the-river,** *Calyptranthes zuzygium.* Each shoot ends in a pair of leaves, and branches are regularly forked; this is technically called dichotomous branching.

✓ **White stopper,** *Eugenia axillaris.* Has gray bark and leathery, non-glossy, large leaves that occur in pairs on red petioles. This is the source of the distinctive musky smell of the hammocks, described by early botanist Thomas Barbour as a "curious, spicy smell of a tropical jungle [that] is unmistakable, and is as characteristic to the nostrils as the smoke drifting downward at evening from a village in India." Well, perhaps. But earthy and refreshing it is, indeed.

✓ **Redberry stopper,** *Eugenia confusa.* Tallest of the group, a slow and durable tree with glossy leaves ending in a distinct drip tip.

✓ **Spanish stopper,** *Eugenia foetida,* with small, inrolled leaves closely spaced on slender branches, is columnar and ideal for town house gardens or patio plantings. A woodsy smell.

✓ **Red stopper,** *Eugenia rhombea.* Confined in the wild to North Key Largo, this is one of Florida's rarest trees. The roundish leaves have long driptips, the bark is gray, and the fragrance is menthol. It's grown by native nurseries.

✓ **Simpson stopper,** *Myrcianthes fragrans,* has reddish flaking bark and leaves that are darker on top than the undersurface. It flowers in May or June and produces showy red berries.

✓ **Carambola,** *Averrhoa carambola*. 30 feet. Full sun. The carambola has a nice, dense crown with small, pointy leaflets on compound leaves. The flowers are tiny but fragrant and appear two to four times a year; the fruit, commonly called star fruit, follows about a month after each flush of bloom. Because the canopy lets little light through to the ground, mulch beneath this tree and don't try grass.

✓ **Caesalpinia** species. 6 to 10 feet. Quite small and useful for suburban lots, even tub plants. Drought tolerant when established, but somewhat cold sensitive. The pride of Barbados, *Caesalpinia pulcherrima,* has yellow and red flowers, while the dwarf poinciana, *C. mexicana,* has yellow flowers. A cultivar of *C. mexicana,* 'Compton,' has pink flowers. The gnarled trunk and crooked shape make it an excellent accent tree.

✓ **Jamaica caper,** *Capparis cynophallophora*. 20 feet. From the salty zone right behind the buttonwoods in the mangrove fringe, this beautiful small tree has olive green leaves with rusty or silvery undersides. The leaves have a small notch at the tip. Full sun, excellent drainage. In shade, its branches elongate and leaves become sparse. Spring-to-summer flowers have long stamens and look a little like spider mums.

✓ **Papaya,** *Carica papaya*. About 10 feet. Male and female plants, so you need both, or a plant with bisexual flowers. Plant several to be sure. The fast-growing plants from Central America with deeply lobed leaves produce fruit in a single season. They are such rapid growers, you can use them as shade for tender plants until other trees take hold. The fruit is a melon full of seeds in a central cavity, and delicious eaten fresh. Fruit flies are a problem (as well as virus) and many homeowners will put brown paper bags on young fruit to keep the flies from laying eggs in the developing crop.

✓ **Key lime,** *Citrus aurantiifolia*. 12 to 15 feet. Bushy and thorny. Fruit are quite small, round, and thin-skinned; they are greenish-yellow when mature, quite tart, and fragrant. They mature year-round, but are most abundant in summer. They grow well on rock, better in sandy soil, requiring excellent drainage. Fertilize less than other citrus: scant amounts in winter, late spring, and fall. Too much fertilizer can cause luxuriant growth and fungus diseases.

✓ **Citrus** species. Orange (*Citrus sinensis*), Persian lime (*C. latifolia*), grapefruit (*C. x paradisi*), tangerine (*C. reticulata*) and tangelo (*C. x tangelo* [*C. reticulata* x *C. paradisii*]). The secret to citrus growing in South Florida is well drained soil and full sun. Keep weeds and grass away from beneath the trees, and prune only deadwood or to shape. Citrus fertilizer, 8-2-10-3, is recommended by citrus experts.

Cool weather in winter will add color to oranges. Tangerines begin producing around Thanksgiving and last through January or February (they don't store on trees well as do oranges and grapefruit); grapefruit ripen December to May. Depending on variety, oranges can be harvested in fall, winter, and spring, October to March. The fragrant flowers merit placement of the tree near a window or door. Very small citrus, calamondin and kumquat, can be kept in pots on the patio or in quite small spaces, since they grow only about six to eight feet. Citrus will flower when the last season's crop still is on the tree.

✓ **Green buttonwood,** *Conocarpus erectus*. 25 to 40 feet. Along the shoreline (far enough inland so they don't stand in water), buttonwoods often take a beating from storms and constant winds, and they assume twisted, grotesque shapes—which has made them prized by bonsai enthusiasts. The leaves are pointed and have two characteristics that make this tree easy to identify: domatia, which are small holes on the lower sides where the veins meet the midribs; and a pair of glands on the petiole which, like

Lignum vitae is a native of the southern tip of Florida and the Florida Keys. It flowers off and on through the warm season with small blue flowers.

those on the leaves of white mangroves, are probably nectar glands. Male and female trees produce flowers in March forming in the axils of the endmost twigs. Don't use in dense shade. The green buttonwood has a long period of inactivity in winter, but has weedy tendencies when it grows in the warm season. It once was the major source of charcoal in the Keys and South Florida.

✓ **Silver buttonwood,** *Conocarpus erectus* var. *sericeus*. A genetic sport of the green, this lovely small tree or large shrub has covered its leaves with downy-soft silver hairs, a protection against dessication. It flowers all year. While drought tolerant, it is more cold sensitive than the green.

✓ **White Geiger** or **Texas wild olive,** *Cordia boissieri*. 20 feet. A Tex-Mex, cold-tolerant small tree that blooms all year; white flowers with yellow throats. Leaves are rough-textured, like the Florida orange Geiger, *Cordia sebestena*. And like the orange Geiger, this drought-tolerant tree can be used as a street tree or for median plantings. *Cordia lutea* is the yellow-flowering species. Its bell-shaped flowers are sun colored.

✓ **Lignum vitae,** *Guaiacum sanctum*. 15 to 20 feet. Once believed by Europeans to be a cure for many diseases, including syphilis—particularly when used as a drinking vessel—this "tree of life" was even held to be fashioned into the Holy Grail. The bipinnate leaves are rounded, the flowers dawn blue with yellow stamens, and the wood is denser than any other. The Navy collected it in World War II for shipbuilding. The inky-colored heartwood is difficult to work but dearly prized if fashioned into a cup or mortar. A slow-growing tree, lignum vitae will respond to fertilizer and mulch, forming a naturally rounded canopy. Needs good drainage and full sun.

✓ **Jaboticaba,** *Myrciaria cauliflora*. 15 to 20 feet in South Florida. Native to southern Brazil. The species name, *cauliflora*, tells of the tree's habit of producing flowers and fruit directly on the stems. Cauliflory is the term used for this, and in many cases botanists believe it allows for easier pollination of the flowers or dispersal of the fruit. The fruit, in this case, is a grapelike, purple-skinned pulpy fruit that is eaten fresh. The tree takes many years to produce unless it is grafted. Since it likes a deep rich soil, the tree isn't particularly well adapted to our rocky, infertile, sandy soils, but will do well if you're willing to work at it.

✓ **Wax myrtle,** *Myrica cerifera*. 25 feet. Multi-trunked and sprawling, with many-twigged crown. Takes wet or dry conditions and sun or shade. Leaves and berries smell of bay, and once berries were used to make bay candles. Swallows, warblers, vireos, kinglets, quail, and other wildlife are fond of fruit. Can root-sucker.

✓ **Kopsia,** *Ochrosia elliptica*. 20 feet. Evergreen and glossy leaves on this stately small tree. In the Apocynaceae, the same family as oleander, allamanda, and tabernaemontana, the fragrant white flowers also have twisted petals, as if twirling, and the beautiful fruit is poisonous. Pairs of scarlet one-seeded fruit, called drupes, are joined at one end like Siamese twins. On the list of invasive trees compiled by the Exotic Pest Plant Council.

✓ **Allspice,** *Pimenta dioica*. 40 feet. Light green, long leaves emerge shiny, quilted, and light pink to faintly mahogany. In the myrtle family. Leaves are aromatic and can be used to make tea. The tree has an upright, oval shape. The bark is attractive and flakes off. The flowers are in terminal clusters; that is, they occur on the ends of the new growth, and the fruits are the commercial spice. While found here and there in South Florida, it is from Jamaica and Central America. Gordon Courtright's *Tropicals* says it does best in a hot, dry climate. Grow in sun or dappled shade.

✓ **Cattley guava,** *Psidium littorale*, 15 to 25 feet. Two or three narrow, crooked trunks with flaking, mottled bark. Prune to show off this feature. The leaves are leathery, glossy, and thick. Use as small accent tree in sunny courtyard, patio area. Prefers rich soil, but adaptable. Mulch. Drought tolerant when established.

Choice Flowering Trees

✓ **Hong Kong orchid,** *Bauhinia* x *blakeana.* 25 to 30 feet. Winter-flowering orchid tree that adds fragrance and purple-and-crimson flowers to the winter skyscape, this is a good tree for hummingbirds. It's a sterile hybrid that won't develop messy seed pods or escape. *Bauhinia monandra* is a summer-blooming species with pink flowers from April to October. It is leafless in the dry season. *Bauhinia purpurea* has pink to rosy flowers that are fragrant in late summer and fall, September to November. Hummingbirds like this, too. *Bauhinia variegata,* the winter-flowering species, is considered invasive by the Exotic Pest Plant Council. You can find seedlings coming up around telephone poles and fence posts in the city. *Bauhinia galpinii* is called nasturtium bauhinia. It is a sprawling bush that produces salmon-colored flowers in the warm season. It is quite lovely but unruly and needs constant pruning or a pergola of its own.

✓ **Red kapok,** *Bombax ceiba,* a big tree (it grows to 90 feet in India), has crimson, waxy flowers in mid-winter when bare of leaves. It's called the red kapok tree. In Jamaica, the kapoks are said to be home to departed spirits called duppies.

Another bombax, the baobab, *Adansonia digitata,* is sometimes home to humans in Africa because the trunks are so big. The trunk swells with water in wet season rains and elephants have learned to puncture the trunks for water. The fruit, a large fuzzy pod, hangs in such a way as to give the baobab the common nickname "dead rat tree." A few specimens grow in South Florida.

✓ *Bulnesia arborea.* 25 or 30 feet. Dark green compound foliage sets off the chrome yellow five-petaled flowers in the warm season. David Fairchild introduced this from Venezuela, and it has proved to be drought resistant and salt tolerant.

✓ **Flame-of-the-forest,** *Butea monosperma.* 40 feet. Searing flames of orange lick up from brown cups on these rare Asian trees, lighting the landscape in scattered backfires of color. Irregular trunks and weak roots are handicaps, but the trees grow well in alkaline soils. Tip borers can reduce the flowering; freezes can reduce tip borers, as can insecticides.

✓ **Powder-puff,** *Calliandra haematocephala.* 15 feet. This lovely, sprawling little tree holds up its puffs of staminate flowers as if they were ornaments. The puffs are in red, pink, or white during the warm months. They have compound leaves. Full sun; water well until it becomes established, then it is drought tolerant. *C. emarginata* is the miniature powder-puff.

✓ **Bottlebrush,** *Callistemon citrinus.* 20 feet. There are two forms: upright and weeping (*C. viminalis*). Both have red staminate brushes of flowers in the spring. *C. citrinus* has leaves that smell of citrus if crushed. They are twiggy and sometimes get virus-induced galls called witch's broom. They need water and nutrients to look best. Nematodes may cause them to languish, becoming puny and hungry-looking. Fertilize and mulch to keep nematodes down.

✓ **Ylang-ylang,** *Cananga odorata,* the perfume tree. Of medium stature (35 feet) with long, limp-looking branches holding big leaves, the ylang-ylang is not a strong tree and many were lost in the 1992 hurricane. But the flowers are so perfumed that they are a component of Chanel No. 5. A few flowers in a bucket of water once were used in Cuba to sweeten the newly mopped floors, even though the tree is from Southeast Asia. The flowers are as limp as the limbs, and somewhat hidden by them. They are green-yellow to yellow, and their petals are long, twisting, and ribbonlike.

✓ **Cassias.** There are several ornamental species of these tropical trees. *Cassia fistula* is the golden shower tree from India, where pods are used in traditional medicines. It reaches 30 feet. A short-lived tree, it has problems with alkaline soils, and leaves can turn quite yellow from lack of iron and other micronutrients. The lemon-yellow flowers are in long clusters in June and July. Apple blossom cassia, *Cassia javanica*, grows to 30 feet or more. An open, spreading crown that lets clouds of pink and white blossoms tumble over the foliage in May and June, often lasting throughout summer. Gorgeous tree. *Cassia alata,* the candlestick tree, is a winter-blooming shrubby tree with spikes of golden yellow flowers that open from the bottom up. The tops of the spikes are rounded and curious until the individual flowers open.

Any number of cassias are being introduced into cultivation from around the tropics. Botanical name changes afflict many with uncertain identifications—some are called Cassia, some Senna, and some names go back and forth between the two genera.

✓ **Floss-silk,** *Chorisia speciosa*. 45 feet. To say these trees have thorns is to say it may rain in the tropics. Apple-green trunks are elaborately decorated with dangerously sharp studs of thorns that often disappear on old trees but are quite prominent on juveniles. Hormones, one supposes. Big, palmately compound leaves, toothed, are dropped in the fall or early winter. Flower buds open gradually around the canopy. Floppy petaled flowers with long stamens have a nice fragrance. Trees are leafless throughout winter. The hybrid between *C. speciosa* and the white flowering *C. insignis* has vast numbers of thorns and grows with great vigor. Flowers are light pink. This tree needs a lot of space. Roots will surface with age.

Monrovia Nursery in California has patented 'Majestic Beauty,'

The apple blossom cassia is among the most beautiful of tropical flowering trees that grace the landscape.

a thornless version. 'Fuchsia' is a cultivar with fuchsia blooms. Another has been bred at The Kampong, the National Tropical Botanical Garden outpost in Coconut Grove. It is a cross between a hot pink hybrid and a large white bombax from Ghana with the unwieldy name 'Sugar Loaf x Rhodognaphalon.'

✓ **Royal poinciana**, *Delonix regia.* 40 feet by 40 feet or greater, a sprawling tree with bark that gathers at the crotches like folds of skin. Its clawed petals in shades of vermillion or yellow color the landscape all summer, adding great glory and majesty. From Madagascar, this tree has been carried throughout the tropical world, so admired is it for its fabulous color. It is the official flowering tree of Miami.

The wood is said to be brittle, but many held up well in the last hurricane. Twice compound leaves, long and brittle brown seed pods, and aggressive roots that can lift the asphalt of a suburban street also characterize the tree.

✓ **Erythrina** species. The native *Erythrina herbacea* is the loll-about of the hammock, languidly bending its head of scarlet into the sun here and there with no great conviction. It needs something else to lean on; use it in sheltered areas with light shade and watch as hummingbirds find it. *Erythrina caffra,* the coral tree, is a 60-footer with spikes of tube-shaped vermillion-colored flowers. *Erythrina crista-galli,* 25 feet, is a spreading Brazilian tree which offers its red flowers from late summer to early fall. Erythrism is a condition of blushing and erythrite is a hydrous arsenate of cobalt, usually rosy red. So now you know.

✓ **Jacaranda**, *Jacaranda mimosifolia.* To 40 feet, although shorter in South Florida. A Brazilian tree with panicles of blue flowers washed with purple from April to June. In the pea family, the jacaranda has the legume's spreading form, fast growth, and bipinnately compound leaves. The jacarandas of South Florida seem begrudging bloomers; those in Central Florida fare better flowerwise. Yet the trees can be frozen back and killed by Central Florida freezes. May be leafless before flowering.

✓ **Sausage tree**, *Kigelia pinnata.* 25 to 45 feet. A tree once so unusual in South Florida that people gave directions by well known specimens. The big flowers are produced on long cords that hang down from the canopy. When big, nectar-filled flowers are held out from the trees, that's a sign that they usually are pollinated by bats. Orioles now are said to pollinate some trees in Dade County. Fruits are in long cylinders that hang from the tree like individual sausage links.

✓ **Queen's crape myrtle**, *Lagerstroemia speciosa.* 60 feet. Mauve or pink flowers in big, loose panicles or branching flower stalks are held on the ends of the branches. Watkins and Sheehan, in *Florida Landscape Plants,* advise planting this in fertile acid soils, yet the tree flowers and thrives in many difficult spots in South Florida's limestone. When hit by cold, the big leaves turn deep red before dropping.

✓ **Lance-pod**, *Lonchocarpus violaceus.* 20 to 30 feet. From Trinidad, Tobago, with coarse compound leaves, the chief attraction of this tree is the glorious two-week burst of lavender-rosy flowers in the fall. The racemes (spikes of flowers with individual flowers held on stalks) are at the ends of the branches and held in V-shaped ranks above the canopy. Leaves are shed before flowering occurs. The flowers attract butterflies.

✓ **Shaving brush**, *Pseudobombax ellipticum.* A relative of the chorisia, this has olive-green bark. It flowers while leafless in the early spring. Flower buds stand erect, closed by brownish petals that burst open at night to free a mass of stamens that are rose-pink or white. Stamens are topped with fresh powdery pollen. While bees are madly attracted to the flowers, the true pollinators (probably bats) do not occur in Florida and the trees don't set seed.

✓ **Copper-pod** or **yellow poinciana** or **yellow flame,** *Peltophorum pterocarpum.* Grows to 40 feet. From Malaysia. Another legume. Rusty buds open to yellow flowers above the foliage in spring and summer that appear in terminal clusters. The tree is wide and spreading, a fast grower that tolerates dryness but defoliates in cold.

✓ **Trumpet trees,** *Tabebuia* species. Commonly planted yellow tab, or silver trumpet tree, *Tabebuia caraiba,* flowers profusely in early spring with clusters of clear yellow bell-shaped flowers. Has gray-green leaves and silver, furrowed bark. It was brittle in hurricane winds. It has only half a dozen strong roots. One suggestion: create an arrangement of cap rocks or limestone boulders over the root area to literally hold it down. *Tabebuia chrysotricha* is a late winter bloomer with golden yellow flowers. Has an open canopy and ridged, rough bark good for tillandsias. The pink tab, *Tabebuia heterophylla,* is an upright, pyramidal tree, more densely crowned than the yellow. Delicate flowers appear in late winter and early spring. The pinks stood up better in Hurricane Andrew than the yellow.

Flowering Trees and Their Seasons

Spring
Apple blossom cassia
Bottlebrush
Coral bean
Geiger tree
Jacaranda
Jamaica caper
Jerusalem thorn
Sweet bay magnolia
Tabebuia

Summer
Bauhinia monandra
Crape myrtle
Geiger tree
Golden shower
Jacaranda
Lignum vitae
Royal poinciana

Fall
Annatto
Bauhinia purpurea
Cassia bahamensis
Golden rain tree
Lance-pod
Ylang-ylang

Winter
African tulip tree
Bauhinia variegata
Bombax ceiba
Hong Kong orchid
White cordia (all year)

Wild coffee is among the most beautiful of the native shrubs for lightly shaded areas.

6

CONSTRUCTING THE WALLS AND THE FLOOR

WHAT WORKS AS A SHRUB

ON DARK NIGHTS in early summer, the shrubbery in the backyard twinkles with tiny phosphorescent lights that grow stronger, then dimmer; that twirl upward, then stay still. These are the southern version of lightning bugs.

During the days of spring and summer, cardinals swoop in and out of the tangle of shrubs, the brunfelsias and bougainvillea, nesting and carrying on about it.

Fall and spring bring the migrating birds. Usually the tiniest warblers flit from branch to branch in the pines and the oaks, but redstarts and black-headed blue warblers will venture in, boldly, to hide in the aralias and palms, waiting for their turn in the birdbath.

Many little anoles inhabit the shrubs, coming out to sun on the big bromeliads beneath the front bedroom window. One of the dogs chases them, as do the cats.

Life teems in the shrubbery. The insect life alone would be impossible to keep track of, let alone the birds that use them for shelter, nesting, and food.

Berried shrubs—the elderberry, mulberry, wild coffee, beautyberry, bayberry—will guarantee birdlife in your garden. A diversity of shrubs planted so they offer various heights and thicknesses will provide perching, shelter, and nesting opportuni-

ties—particularly if you plant the perimeter of your garden with them, allowing some open spaces, water spots, and even a snag. See Chapter 11 for bird- and butterfly-attracting plants that can help you create a haven for wildlife.

And while temperate gardeners traditionally define a shrub as a low-growing, woody plant with many stems, subtropical and tropical gardeners are more generous. Shrubby vines, herbaceous perennials, large bromeliads, and gigantic aroids can all function as shrubs or mass plantings for our gardens. So think expansively when thinking shrubs, and look at many different kinds of plants.

Design considerations, too, will influence your choices. Among those considerations are unity, texture, and balance.

While a garden of all the same plants is restful to the point of boredom, a thousand different things in the yard can be unsettling or jarring. In a garden without any repetition, your eye will not have a natural resting area or line to follow easily.

Sometimes, though, a harmonious blend of different shrubs in a mixed border can work well, if you deal with half a dozen kinds and blend them skillfully.

Trying to achieve a compromise is where you begin to play with leaf color and texture, shape and form. You may find that round and scalloped leaves of *Alocasia odora* play nicely against the feathery, dark green leaves of a *Chamaedorea cataractarum* palm.

Or, the palmately compound leaves of *Schefflera arboricola* will contrast well with spiky leaves of walking iris.

For shrubs that provide background and reliability, the old faithfuls include orange jessamine (also called orange jasmine), Surinam cherry, ligustrum, podocarpus, pittosporum, and viburnum. They can be hedged, shaped, sheared, or allowed to grow into softly rounded forms. Some of these, such as the orange jessamine and the Surinam cherry, are on the Exotic Pest Plant Council's list of invasive plants as having rapidly expanding localized populations. They are not in Category 1, those plants widespread in Florida disrupting native plant communities.

Ficus benjamina hedges, which are grown into impenetrable and imperious walls of green in Palm Beach, are entirely too much work to consider. They want desperately to be trees of great size, and keeping them small is a full-time job.

When trying to decide, do a lot of looking; visit parks and gardens. Make notes when you see a landscaped yard you really like. Ask for help from your nursery, a landscape designer, or a landscape architect.

Because of the enormous variety of plants that can serve as shrubs, I have begun with native plants, grouped others according to use, and concluded with exotic shrubs.

Native Shrubs

Several native shrubs ought to be at the top of your list. Native shrubs benefit wildlife and birds, offering natural foods and hiding spots. Some are listed as small trees as well.

Silver buttonwood is a beautiful plant that can be shaped into a formal or informal hedge, while cocoplum has become such a stalwart of the landscape industry that it may be hard to find. These shrubs are durable and handsome, but they are not the only ones adapted to the local scene. Many others have just as much going for them and ought to be more widely used.

✓ **Sweet acacia,** *Acacia farnesiana*. Delicate compound leaves and round buttons of golden yellow flowers characterize this shrub or small tree of the Keys and the southern end of the Florida peninsula. It can grow to 20 feet or can be pruned to smaller size. Thorns along the twigs make it an effective barrier plant.

✓ **Saltbush,** *Baccharis halimifolia*. A seaside denizen that is recommended for wild gardens rather than domesticated havens.

✓ **Locustberry,** *Byrsonima lucida*. A low growing shrub (8 to 10 feet) with summer-ripening fruit. Springtime flowers have claw-like petals that open white and turn crimson. Summertime berries are attractive to wildlife. Simple, opposite leaves. The plant is drought tolerant, and can be found along the nature trail on Big Pine Key where summertime heat is ferocious.

✓ **Beautyberry,** *Callicarpa americana*. Adorned with grape-colored fruit in round clusters along the stems in late summer, fall, and winter, this plant grows 6 to 8 feet, with long, sprawling twigs. Cut back severely in late winter. Partial shade.

✓ **Spicewood,** *Calyptranthes pallens*. Grows tall enough to be a tree (15 to 20 feet) or can be used as a hedge, with pretty, pointy-tipped leaves. White flowers in late spring. Fruit is black when ripe. Sun or shade.

✓ **Bahama cassia** or **Bahama senna,** *Cassia bahamensis* 'Chapmanii.' 3 to 9 feet. A native to the pinelands and coastal strands and throughout the Florida Keys, this plant stays compact in sun, taller in shade. Compound leaves. Flowers are five-petaled, golden yellow, and attractive to sulfur butterflies. Drought tolerant.

✓ **Cocoplum,** *Chrysobalanus icaco*. Round, leathery leaves and soft red or green new growth. Short on the coast, to 20 feet or

Native shrubs grouped together create a mosaic of colors and textures and are attractive to many butterflies, such as this zebra longwing.

more inland in the Everglades. It can be injured in a freeze. One form has red new leaves; another has light green new leaves. The effect is quite ornamental. In the West Indies, the fruit is stewed.

✓ **Silver buttonwood,** *Conocarpus erectus* var. *sericeus.* The smaller and silver version of the buttonwood from the mangrove community; wonderful as hedge or small tree, although inland, it can get fungus if overly pampered.

✓ **Cordia globosa.** To 10 feet and as wide as it is tall. Tiny, sandpapery leaves with serrated edges on many twigs. Flowers appear year-round in round clusters, opening one or two at a time.

The drupes (single-seeded fleshy fruit) are red, and attract wildlife. Small butterflies and skippers are nearly always busy around this shrub.

✓ **Varnish leaf,** *Dodonaea viscosa.* A pineland resident that takes difficult conditions. Named for the tough resin-coated leaf surface that helps it survive dry conditions; leaves curl under on the edges. *D. viscosa* var. *viscosa* has big, soft leaves; *D. viscosa* var. *arborescens* is smaller and tougher; *D. viscosa* var. *linearis* has narrow leaves. Seed capsules are pinkish-green and shaped like little lanterns. They dry to brown and hang in clusters.

✓ **Golden dewdrop,** *Duranta repens.* Blue flowers and golden fruit are features butterflies and birds love. There is a white-flowered form. Julia Morton, economic botanist and director of the Morton Collectanea at the University of Miami, is among those who question whether this is a native; it also is found in the Bahamas, Central America, and northern South America. Though sprawling in habit, the plant can be pruned.

✓ **Coral bean,** *Erythrina herbacea.* Scarlet to red flowers in the spring will help locate this shrub or small tree (10 to 15 feet) on the edge of a hammock. A deciduous plant, it attracts hummingbirds with its flowers. Leaflets are shaped somewhat like an arrowhead. Paul Scurlock, in *Native Trees and Shrubs of the Florida Keys,* says the red seeds are poisonous.

✓ **Florida privet,** *Forestiera segregata.* Tolerates drought, salt, and alkaline soils and is a good hiding place for little birds. Has small leaves and twiggy branches. A pineland form has even smaller leaves. Male and female flowers on separate plants. Small, blue, olive-like fruit attracts birds.

✓ **Rough velvet seed,** *Guettarda scabra.* To 15 feet. Leaves are deeply veined, rough, and hairy. Small white flowers have a pink blush; velvety fruit turns red, then black. The pinelands/hammock plant takes drought.

✓ **Firebush,** *Hamelia patens.* Attracts hummingbirds and butterflies with slender, orange-red tubular flowers; grows quite large, to 20 feet or so. Sun or dappled shade. In more sun, leaves take on a reddish-bronze cast. Sensitive to cold.

✓ **Wax myrtle,** *Myrica cerifera.* A versatile large shrub/small tree that takes many conditions; root suckers may require pruning out. Use as a screening plant. Aromatic leaves smell of bay. Plants are either male or female. Fruit is waxy, bluish. Small birds use this shrub for shelter and eat its fruit.

✓ **Blackbead,** *Pithecellobium guadelupense.* A shrub or small tree from the very southern tip of Florida and the Keys. Leaves are leathery and round or notched at the ends; fragrant flowers are in little heads; black, bead-like seeds are suspended on pinkish red arils when the pods split open.

✓ **Wild coffee,** *Psychotria* species. Among the loveliest of shrubs with quilted leaves and bright red berries. *Psychotria nervosa* is the glossy-leaved variety that is most often used in landscapes; *P. ligustrifolia* from Key Largo has small leaves; *P. sulzneri* has dull green leaves and is sometimes called soft-leaved coffee.

✓ **White indigo berry,** *Randia aculeata.* Can be stunted in the wild but full in cultivation; seeds itself in mulch. White-skinned berries, which birds love, contain an indigo pulp. Once called blackberry jam fruit.

✓ **Maidenbush,** *Savia bahamensis.* This is used like a miniature version of cocoplum, but it will grow 8 to 10 feet. Small, leathery leaves are notched or blunt; red new growth. Drought and salt tolerant.

✓ **Inkberry,** *Scaevola plumieri.* A seaside, salt-tolerant plant with thick, succulent leaves at the ends of branches. 2 to 6 feet. Leaves are spatula shaped. Look for black fruit to indicate the native; white on the bigger, exotic (invasive) relative.

✓ **Necklace pod,** *Sophora tomentosa.* To 15 feet. The "tomentose" part is the hair on the leaves, giving the plant a gray cast. Yellow flowers on long, terminal spikes open from bottom up. Pods wrap tightly around seeds, hence the common name.

✓ **West Indian lilac,** *Tetrazygia bicolor.* With long three-ribbed leaves and panicles of white flowers with yellow stamens in spring and summer, fruit is purple-black. Can grow to 20 feet. Pinch tip ends to encourage fullness.

With natives, availability may be one factor in selecting plants. Choose from among those plants available for the ecosystem appropriate to your conditions.

If you live on the coast, you will need salt-tolerant plants. If you live inland, you will find temperatures in winter about 10 degrees colder than those along the coast, so you may want more cold-tolerant plants. Even within your small landscape, pockets of wind, sun, heat, and soil saturation may vary, creating microclimates.

Natural plant communities that once existed in your area will suggest suitable landscape plants, providing that drainage and soil have not been dramatically altered. Hammock plants are more easily adapted to varying conditions than pineland plants, and often are better suited for homeowners. Pineland plants require careful management, including controlled burning, as they evolved to withstand fire.

For help in selecting plants for natural habitats, see *A Guide to the Natural Communities of Florida,* published by the Florida Department of Natural Resources in Tallahassee.

The Atlas of United States Trees: Vol. 5, Florida, published by the United States Forest Service, is out of print but available at local libraries.

The Association of Florida Native Nurseries and the Florida Native Plant Society have produced a paperback book that outlines plants appropriate for various naturalistic plantings, "Xeric Landscaping with Florida Native Plants." Write the Florida Native Plant Society, P.O. Box 680008, Orlando, FL 32868.

Shrubs for Barriers

Some shrubs can be used defensively as deterrents to burglaries when strategically planted beneath windows or at vulnerable points of entry to the yard. Consider:

✓ **Agave,** *Agave* species. Various agaves are armed with needle-like tips. So dangerous are they that the tips must be removed if they are used in public areas. Remove tips within reach if you have children or pets that can fall into them.

✓ **Bougainvillea,** *Bougainvillea,* has not-so-subtle thorns. Winter is the showiest time for this flowering shrub. Keep it away from your sprinkler system, because it likes dry conditions. Prune ends in September for more branches on which flowers form.

✓ **Natal plum,** *Carissa macrocarpa.* Stellate flowers and plum-like fruit; has paired branching thorns on its branches.

✓ **Mediterranean fan palm,** *Chamaerops humilis.* The petioles are armed with sharp teeth, as are the leaf stems of washingtonia palms and Chinese fan palms. Pygmy date and other date palms have lower leaflets converted to long spines. Some palms are covered with needle-like spines along their trunks and even their leaves, such as tropical *Aiphanes* species.

✓ **Dioon,** *Dioon edule.* A rosette-shaped cycad with deep green, stiff leaves that are sharply tipped.

✓ **Crown-of-thorns,** *Euphorbia milii.* Grows so low that it won't present its thorns to any robber at windowsill level, but it will be painful to step in beneath the window.

✓ **Boxthorn,** *Severinia buxifolia.* A dwarf shrub with thorns along the branches. In the citrus family.

✓ **Limeberry,** *Triphasia trifolia.* This has sharp thorns hidden by its fine foliage.

Shrubs for Fragrance

Shrubs with fragrant flowers include brunfelsias, carissa, orange jessamine, gardenia, roses, and viburnum.

Lovely spicy fragrances—the clove aroma of the brunfelsia,

Chenille plant has long ropes of tiny red flowers.

particularly—are reason enough to plant these shrubs, in addition to the arresting flowers. (Roses are treated in a separate section; see Chapter 10.) Place them so you will be delighted with the fragrance near the entrance to your home, but think twice about mixing fragrances, particularly outside the bedroom window.

Gardenias take a little extra care. They should be grafted onto nematode-resistant *Gardenia thunbergia* stock to prevent the stunting and yellowing the microscopic worms can cause when invading roots. Additionally, since gardenias love acid soil, acid-forming fertilizer (12-6-8 or 12-6-10 containing ammonium nitrogen) along with compost and mulch are needed. Full sun and evenly moist soils prevent leaves from yellowing and dropping. Fluctuations in temperature, soil moisture, and thrip infestation can cause buds and leaves to drop. Gardenias are just that way.

Shrubs for Color

Shrubs for color are so abundant as to be overwhelming in number.

Begin with the colorful foliage of acalypha and run through the sanchezia. Calatheas and marantas—soft, herbaceous plants of the rainforest understory—offer luscious patterned leaves that are often large enough to serve as shrubs, but they're shade loving and cold-tender, and should be used beneath a protective canopy.

Crotons, perhaps the epitome of tropical foliage, are reappearing on the landscape after years of being shunned due to overuse in the 1950s. By planting them in masses rather than long, leggy hedges, the full effect of these beautifully colored plants can be appreciated. There are about 300 cultivars of crotons at Thomas Edison's home in Fort Myers, and nurseries are beginning to carry larger stocks.

Dieffenbachias and aglaonemas are succulent herbaceous plants often used in masses for a hedge or shrub effect. Both types of plants—and there are numerous cultivars available in both genera—are cold-tender and shade loving. Their striking leaves are patterned, striped, streaked, and marbled.

Ti plant, *Cordyline fruticosa,* is a red-leaved member of the dracaena family. The colors range from pink to maroon and deep red. Use with care for a vivid accent, not for a hedge.

Bromeliads add foliage color to the landscape. Large ones, in the Aechmea or Vriesea genus, are suitable as specimen plants or accents where a shrub might otherwise be used. The sun-loving bromeliads can be especially striking (see Chapter 8).

Shrubs for Seaside

If you have ever endured a windy day at the beach when the beach towels won't stay in place and sand menaces your eyes, you begin to appreciate the life of shore-front plants, or even plants behind the ocean-front dunes.

To endure in a seaside garden, plants have to take salt spray, salt-laden breezes, and generally windy conditions. Foremost in the ability to withstand such are sea oats. While you don't really classify grasses as shrubs, this wonderful, clumping grass with its tall seed heads is shrublike.

Sea oxeye daisy, *Borrichia frutescens,* a ground cover, is bush-like in appearance as it can grow to three feet, while inkberry, *Scaevola plumieri,* is another sprawly ground cover/shrub with succulent leaves at the ends of its slender branches.

Cocoplum, sea-grape, blackbead, cat's claw, coral bean, Spanish bayonet, necklace-pod, saltmarsh willow, buttonwood, giant leather fern, and golden leather fern all have good salt tolerance. Torchwood and joewood, two small trees from the coastal strands of the Florida Keys, are wonderfully tolerant of harsh, salty conditions. Florida privet, wax myrtle, maidenbush, white indigo berry, and bay cedar also can be added to the list.

Shrubs for Flowers

Ixora 'Norah Grant' has been developed to withstand alkaline soils and still produce big, bold clusters of deep pink flowers. It is a perfectly wonderful shrub, but it's planted much too often in a region where copy-cat landscape design is responsible for pedestrian plantings. 'Super King' is a bold red ixora that once ruled the roost, but it suffers magnesium deficiency when neglected. The dwarf ixoras, while cute, are a headache maintenance wise. So 'Norah Grant' prevails.

Thunbergia erecta is an African shrub in the Acanthaceae family that has deep purple flowers with yellow throats. The royal purple no doubt gives it the common name "King's-mantle."

Calliandra, or powder-puff, is one of those large shrubs or small trees that offers rosy-red winter flowers. And warm winters mean that some plants, such as allamanda and ixora, will never stop flowering but merely slow their profusion from a gush to a trickle.

Bauhinia is a genus with shrubby species, some quite tiny and others large. *Bauhinia punctata,* for instance, has pink flowers on its shrubby form. And there are small white flowering and yellow flowering bauhinias, too. Leaves on these orchid-trees-shrubs give the genus its name, commemorating John and Caspar Bauhin, sixteenth century Swiss herbal writers. The leaves appear to be deeply cleft but are fused compound leaves. The sterile bauhinia, Hong-Kong orchid tree, is the best for use by homeowners. It is grafted onto *B. variegata,* so ask to make sure you are getting a grafted tree.

Hibiscus has been hybridized until it's blue in the face, almost literally. And while the sunset colors are striking, I find the muddy

Congea tomentosa is a vining plant called "shower of orchids."

yellows and browns unattractive and overblown. Conversely, Anderson's Crape, the small pink-flowering hibiscus used as rootstock, is dependably pretty, and there's something quite beautiful about a pure yellow, red, or white hibiscus. Hibiscus bloom on new growth, so keeping them pruned is a sure way to forego their best trick. Hand-grenade scale and snow scale can be problems on hibiscus. Prune them off if you catch them in time. Never use Malathion; it will kill hibiscus. Orthene is a remedy.

Heliconias (see Chapter 8), like calatheas, are herbaceous plants that can clump or run in shrub-like formations, although they are not shrubs. These quintessential tropicals are outrageously dazzling with their compound inflorescences (flower stalks). One memory that always will stay with me is a tropical morning in Costa Rica spent wandering through dew-soaked stands of heliconias, listening to the catlike purrs of hummingbirds sipping nectar.

Exotic Shrubs

✓ **Chenille plant,** *Acalypha hispida*. May grow to 15 feet. The leaves are broad and toothed. The flowers are red on long ropes of blooms. Sun or shifting shade.

✓ **Copper leaf,** *Acalypha wilkesiana*. To 15 feet. Striking bronze or red leaves are large and toothed. Flower spikes are about eight inches long but flowers are inconspicuous. Use prudently. Water in the dry season.

✓ **Allamanda,** *Allamanda* species. A vining shrub that has yellow or purple trumpet-shaped flowers on new growth. Prune to shape in the late fall or early spring. Takes dry conditions.

✓ **Marlberry,** *Ardisia escallonioides*. To 20 feet. Leaves are glossy green. Terminal clusters of flowers and black fruit in late spring. Sun or shade.

✓ **Bamboo,** *Bambusa* species. Various other genera. Giant grasses that come primarily from Asia, but other countries as well. Use them as screens or background plants, but be sure to use clumping types rather than running types. The runners will be all over the neighborhood in no time. Bamboo needs plenty of water to become established, and then can be weaned to lesser amounts.

✓ **Annatto,** *Bixa orellana*. Lipstick plant. 10 to 12 feet. An accent plant, with heart-shaped leaves. Pink or white flowers in summer. Not often found, but can be a conversation piece when the spiny brown capsules split open in winter and reveal their orange-red seeds. The flesh on the seeds is used as dye, as food coloring, and even in lipstick. Grow in full sun.

✓ **Snow bush,** *Breynia disticha roseo-picta*. 10 feet. From the South Pacific. A beautiful shrub with delicate, thin leaves mottled in green, white, pink, and red. Sun or shade. Use in a mixed hedge.

✓ **Angel's trumpet,** *Brugmansia* species. 20 feet. Upside-down trumpet flowers with wonderful perfume come in shades of peach, salmon, and white. There are double forms, like trumpets nestled inside each other. Sun or light shade.

✓ **Lady of the night,** *Brunfelsia americana*. 10 to 20 feet. This Brazilian plant has glossy green leaves and cream-colored flowers that are moth-pollinated and quite fragrant. Does well in shade. *B. nitida*, from Cuba, grows to 6 feet; *B. undulata* from Jamaica, grows to 12 feet. *B. pauciflora*, yesterday-today-and-tomorrow, is a winter-bloomer so named because the flowers open purple, fade to lavender, then turn white. Its flowers smell of cloves.

✓ **Butterfly bush,** *Buddleja* species. 10 to 15 feet. Long, floppy branches ending in spikes of flowers. The leaves are woolly. Native to China. *B. variabilis* has lilac to purple flowers; *B. globosa* has yellow flowers; *B. volvilei* from the Himalayas has pink to maroon flowers. Sun.

✓ **Calathea,** *Calathea grandiflora*. 6 feet. Not a shrub, but a herbaceous plant that can be used as such. This calathea has large, smooth, plain green leaves, but other species have colorful variegations, stripes, or splotches. *C. insignis* is called the rattlesnake plant because the flower stalk looks like the upright tail of a rattler. *C. loesener*, *C. warscewiczii*, and others form large, attractive clusters of tropical foliage. Grow in shade with ample protection from wind and cold.

✓ **Powder-puff,** *Calliandra* species. 7 to 25 feet. A delicate and pretty shrub or small tree with bipinnate or twice-compound leaves and puff-like flowers, either red or pink, that occur in late fall and winter. Full sun.

✓ **Natal plum,** *Carissa macrocarpa*. 5 to 15 feet. A dwarf form grows 2 to 4 feet. Dark green, round leaves are leathery and there are two-pronged thorns on the stems. Slow growing. Flowers are star-shaped and fragrant; fruit is plumlike and edible.

✓ **Night-blooming jessamine,** *Cestrum nocturnum.* 8 to 12 feet. A fast-growing shrub with long leaves and greenish-white flowers that bloom in the full moon. Strong fragrance at night for moth pollinators. Sun or partial shade.

✓ **Snailseed,** *Cocculus laurifolius.* 15 feet. An attractive large shrub with elliptical leaves and prominent veins. Forms a good screen. Flowers in spring. Plant on five-foot centers, as the shrubs have long, lazy branches. Full sun, partial shade.

✓ **Croton,** *Codiaeum variegatum.* 10 to 15 feet; usually kept pruned shorter. Many cultivars. Use in masses of a prominent color; underplant with liriope or another ground cover.

✓ **Mexican heather,** *Cuphea hyssopifolia.* 1 to 2 feet. Neat, dense dwarf shrub with miniature white or purple flowers. It likes moisture to flourish. Full sun.

✓ **Surinam cherry,** *Eugenia uniflora.* 15 to 25 feet. Often pruned shorter. One of the most widely used hedging plants in South Florida, it nonetheless seeds readily. Birds love the fruit, which can be made into jelly or eaten fresh off the bush. New growth is a pretty maroon or pinkish red.

✓ *Euphorbia* species. 6 to 10 feet. Poinsettias and pascuita are two euphorbias prominent at Christmas, when the first develops red bracts and the latter has tiny white ones that cover the shrub like lace. Characteristic white sap can cause a rash. Can get scab. Fertilize regularly. Plant the poinsettia where there's no light at night; porch lights or street lights will delay bract and flower development.

✓ **Thryallis,** *Galphimia glauca.* Can grow to 8 feet or so, but usually shorter. Yellow flowers in the warm season and drought tolerance have catapulted this to popularity in recent years. Fine-textured, light green leaves. Sun or partial shade. Cut back hard to shape. Brittle.

✓ **Gardenia,** *Gardenia jasminoides.* Cape jessamine. 8 feet by 8 feet. Susceptible to nematode damage on its own roots. *G. thunbergia* is rootstock. Sun, fertile soil (use an acid-forming fertilizer or one marked for ixoras and gardenias), and moderate moisture are required. Flowers appear alone or in pairs in spring and summer.

✓ **Hibiscus,** *Hibiscus rosa-sinensis.* 25 feet. Long arching branches with terminal flowers in the warm season. Innumerable cultivars. Anderson's crape resists nematodes. Hand-grenade scale can be a problem. Don't use Malathion. If you catch it early, prune off infested twigs. Otherwise, Orthene is a systemic insecticide that will work. Allow ladybug beetles to control aphids. Occasional fertilizer and plenty of mulch will keep yellowing to a minimum.

✓ **Yaupon holly,** *Ilex vomitoria.* 25 feet. Narrow-leaved and fine-textured; excellent for shearing and formal appearance. Dwarf forms are *Ilex vomitoria* 'Nana' and 'Schillings Dwarf.'

✓ **Jatropha,** *Jatropha integerrima.* 10 to 15 feet. Can be pruned as a shrub. Red flowers most of the year appear in clusters; an open branching pattern. A good specimen or accent plant.

✓ **Shrimp plant,** *Justicia* species. Brazilian plume. To 6 feet. Copper or yellow bracts characterize shrimp plants. The yellow one is *J. brandegeana.* All are in the Acanthaceae family, which includes a large number of brightly flowering plants such as Ruellia, Crossandra or firecracker flower, Brazilian cloak, Jacobinia or flamingo plant, Eranthemum or tropical blue sage, and Thunbergia. They are cold-tender and can develop brown leaves when temperatures dip into the 40s.

✓ **Crape myrtle,** *Lagerstroemia indica.* To 30 feet or more. Clusters or panicles of flowers at the ends of the long stems range in color from white to lavender. These are warm-season bloomers; deciduous in winter. The roots are sensitive to transplanting and a large root ball is necessary, but the shrubs come back from hard pruning.

Sculptural and substantial, these Aechmea bromeliads have been used in this setting as accents or shrubs.
Chinese privet and a cycad (*Zamia furfuracea*) are mixed here as well.

✓ **West Indian holly,** *Leea coccinea.* To 8 feet. Wavy leaves on droopy stems give this shrub a distinctive, graceful look. The texture stands out when used in a mixed planting. Light shade.

✓ **Privet,** *Ligustrum japonicum.* Ligustrum. To 15 feet. Prune as a hedge or small tree. Forest green, stiff leaves are opposite, waxy. The new growth is light green. White, fragrant clusters of flowers in spring.

✓ **Chinese privet,** *Ligustrum sinense.* A variegated form has tiny leaves that are attractive as an accent.

✓ **Holly-leaf malpighia,** *Malpighia coccigera.* Dwarf shrub, 1 to 3 feet tall. Spiny leaves resemble holly. Flowers are pink with claw-like petals.

✓ **Medinilla,** *Medinilla magnifica.* A shrub in the melastome family, a widespread tropical plant family with characteristic veined leaves. The flowers appear in the warm seasons. The pink flowers have yellow stamens and purple anthers, and are followed by hot pink berries. Leaves are velvety. Remember its tropical nature, and provide cold protection by placing it on the south side of your house or surrounding it with cold-tolerant plants.

✓ **Orange jessamine,** *Murraya paniculata.* Large shrub in the citrus family with small, finely textured compound leaves with oblanceolate leaflets fatter toward the pointed tip than at the base. Small white flowers smell like orange blossoms. A carefree hedge with rounded natural shape.

✓ **Mussaenda,** *Mussaenda erythrophylla* and other Mussaenda species and cultivars in the Dona series. To 30 feet. Soft, pastel bracts surround small flowers. Cold-tender; may be burned back to the ground in cold winters. Full sun, well-draining soil.

✓ **Heavenly bamboo,** *Nandina domestica.* 3 to 8 feet. Feathery leaves on upright stems. The leaves turn red in the fall.

Sun or shade, but happiest when it's not too far into South Dade.

✓ **Oleander,** *Nerium oleander.* 15 to 20 feet. Drought tolerant, with many pink or white flowers in warm months. Can be defoliated by oleander caterpillars. All parts are poisonous; dwarf variety is best for home landscapes. Full sun. Salt and drought tolerant.

✓ **Plumbago,** *Plumbago auriculata.* 4 to 15 feet. Sky blue flowers on a low, frothy shrub. Requires little maintenance once established.

✓ **Aralia,** *Polyscias* species. To 25 feet. From the Pacific tropics, there are many forms of this shrub that easily root from cuttings and quickly form a hedge if you stick them in the ground rather close together and keep them moist until they take, then keep cut back. The leaves are toothed and may be solid green or green and cream. Related to umbrella or schefflera trees.

✓ **Crape jessamine,** *Tabernaemontana divaricata.* 10 feet. Fragrant night bloomer in the spring. White flowers in clusters. Fast grower. Sun or partial shade. *T. divaricata flore-pleno* is a double-flowered version.

✓ **Glory bush,** *Tibouchina urvilleana.* 15 feet. Purple flowers in the warm season. An undisciplined shrub that has soft, hairy leaves.

✓ **Limeberry,** *Triphasia trifolia.* 15 feet. Citrus relative with sharp spines and small lime-scented fruit that eventually turn red. The leaves are in threes, and flowers are fragrant. Sun or shade.

✓ **Viburnum,** *Viburnum* species. A number of species are available. *V. odoratissimum* is sweet viburnum. Use for formal hedge. Well-behaved, cold tolerant, and shade tolerant.

Planting shrubs is only slightly easier than planting trees. Using the shrub container as a guide, dig a hole a foot wider and as deep as the container is tall. Place the shrub in the hole so the top of the root ball is level with the soil surface. Use the soil from the hole to fill in around the rootball, watering in with a hose to eliminate air pockets.

Mulch two to three inches deep around the root zone, being careful not to stack mulch against the stems of the shrub.

Water every day for a week; every two days for the next four to six weeks; every three or four days for several more weeks until you reach week 12. Twice a week or less then may be sufficient.

Planting at the start of the rainy season, in late May or early June, will allow you to take advantage of Mother Nature. But don't be fooled by quick afternoon showers.

When you see sure signs of new growth—several shoots that are thriving—apply a light dose of fertilizer. Use a handful for shrubs under two or three feet.

Prune spring-flowering shrubs after flowering has finished. Prune plants that produce flowers on new growth (hibiscus, crape myrtle, and ixora) in late winter before the spring flush. Hibiscus also can undergo renewal pruning throughout the year for continuous blooming. Prune evergreen shrubs any time between March and October but not between November and the end of February, or you risk exposing new growth to damage from cold.

GROUND COVERS

Putting in an area of ground cover to replace grass is like giving yourself a gift: It saves labor, fertilizer, and mowing, and it adds interest to the landscape.

I use a variety of plants as ground covers, and my definition of the term is meant to be taken at face value. A ground cover simply covers the ground. It may or may not be meant for walking. Most of mine are not. Grass is, but grass is the ground cover I've been trying to reduce over the years.

I killed the grass in some areas using multiple layers of news-paper, watered down and covered with mulch. In other, larger areas, I used Roundup, a herbicide. Once the grass was dead, I scraped it away with a shovel and put down a several-inches-thick layer of mulch.

Then I bought various plants. I chose pilea for one area, bromeliads for another, ferns for a third. The beds continue to grow larger as the plants multiply. I find I have to add mulch every six months or so. Often I buy bagged eucalyptus mulch, but I also have called a tree service and had a dumptruck load of mulch delivered to the swale. Then I can spread it by the wheelbarrow.

Every time I work in these beds, I find big, squirmy earthworms in good rich soil. The artillery fern (*Pilea serpyllacea* 'Rotundifolia') has been in the ground four years now, and needs to be pulled out and replanted. The old stems have become woody and thick beneath the chartreuse, miniature leaves.

Bromeliad beds can stand a good thinning once a year to remove the old mother plants and space out the young pups that have formed at their bases. All I do to the fern beds is pull up runners as they escape their designated sites.

If you choose a plant that forms a thick cover, weeding will not be much of a problem. If you select bromeliads, crinum lilies, or another type of plant that allows light to penetrate to the soil, weeding will have to be done.

Ground covers may take several months to become established, during which time the soil should be kept moist. Planting, as with trees and shrubs, is best done at the beginning of the rainy season but may be done any time.

Among the native plants that serve as ground covers are these:

✓ **Sea oxeye daisy,** *Borrichia arborescens.* Silvery foliage and yellow flowers with yellow eyes; drought tolerant. Use in full sun. It thrives in damp places, such as low areas behind the dunes. It becomes almost shrub-like once established.

Pentas, bromeliads, colocasias, and sanchezias serve as shrubs at the entry of this home. Purple and yellow lantana and even caladiums are skillfully planted into this garden.

✓ **Swamp lily,** *Crinum americanum.* A swamp dweller that will do well as shrub or ground cover in a low spot prone to flooding. Large white flowers are fragrant. Grasshoppers love the succulent four-foot leaves. (*Crinum asiaticum* is the larger, non-native version.) I have watched them in the neighborhood survive on neglect.

✓ **Quailberry,** *Crossopetalum ilicifolium.* A sprawling little shrub with spiny leaves similar to American holly; comes complete with red berries. A shrub that's small enough to be used as a ground cover, like Mexican heather.

✓ **Golden creeper,** *Ernodia littoralis.* Succulent leaves serve as a water source in dire times. Tubular flowers can be pink, white, or red; "golden" in the name describes the berries. Do not be overly attentive. This will do well on rocky spots.

✓ **Blanket flower** or **gaillardia,** *Gaillardia pulchella.* Orange-yellow daisylike flowers. The flowers are produced many at a time, then they go to seed and disappear until the next batch of buds form and open. The foliage is gray-green, and prone to fungus if watered too much. These will spread.

✓ **Beach sunflower,** *Helianthus debilis.* Grows to one or two feet in height and produces yellow composite flowers. As its name suggests, this plant loves the sandy beach.

✓ **Spider lily,** *Hymenocallis floridana.* You will spot these occasionally in the sawgrass of the Everglades. The leaves are succulent and straplike, flowers white and fragrant. The flowers are tube-shaped, with long, fanciful ribbonlike extensions on the petals. Spider lilies like water. A Florida Keys relative, *H. latifolia*, also has fragrant summertime flowers. These will grow together over time when massed in beds. Either one takes salt spray. *H. palmeri*, from the pinelands, is listed by Alan Meerow in "Native Ground Covers for South Florida" (a pamphlet published by the University of Florida's Institute of Food and Agricultural Services) as "alligator lily." It grows to about a foot, or half to a third smaller than the other spider lilies with green flowers.

✓ **Beach morning glory,** *Ipomoea stolonifera*. Grows on sand and is used for stabilizing dunes. Funnel-shaped flowers are white.

✓ **Railroad vine,** *Ipomoea pes-caprae*. A relative of the beach morning glory, it has purple flowers. The two-lobed leaves suggested to taxonomists the imprint of a split hoof, so the botanical name *pes-caprae* means "goat's foot," according to Richard Workman in *Growing Native*.

✓ **Pineland lantana,** *Lantana depressa*. Compact with buttons of yellow flowers, this will develop fungus if overwatered. Blooms year round in full sun. Can get woody; cut back hard in the spring. Leaves have a refreshing herbal aroma.

✓ **Peperomia,** *Peperomia obtusifolia*. A familiar house plant, peperomia likes shady places. Related to commercial pepper, the minute flowers form on erect, slender stalks; leaves are round or somewhat pointed, with succulent stems that root easily. You'll find peperomia growing in the swamp on logs as well as in the hammocks.

✓ **Saw palmetto,** *Serenoa repens*. This palm is not a ground cover, but it is the predominant understory plant in pinelands and in some hammocks. The palm grows on a creeping stem, hugging the ground, and will serve as a ground cover after a long time. At Bok Tower Gardens in Lake Wales, the palmettos are kept on a regular irrigation schedule (watered twice a week) for the first year, then they're allowed to survive on their own.

✓ **Beach verbena,** *Verbena maritima*. Will spread over sand as well as rocky soils in full sun, lifting up bluish-purple flowers as it does.

✓ **Coontie,** *Zamia pumila*. The leaves of this plant suggest palms, but it is not a palm. It grows from a tuber in a hammock or pineland. Male and female plants form cones; female cones eventually open to expose red, fleshy seeds. They are slow growing. The atala butterfly's larvae (red and yellow caterpillars) feed on the leaves. The plants don't spread but will get larger. Watch for scale if you have too many planted too close; use soapy water to remove these insects.

Ferns are among the easiest of ground covers because they spread quickly, are kept in check by simply pulling them out, and hide a multitude of sins, from knuckly roots to falling leaves.

✓ **Leather fern,** *Acrosticum danaeaefolium*. From the low hammocks and swamps, leather fern makes an emphatic statement in a yard that can handle it. The fronds can grow up to 10 feet. Since it hails from low-lying areas it likes dampness, but is tough enough to take drying conditions.

✓ **Giant sword fern,** *Nephrolepis biserrata*. This has undulating fronds and grows in large mounds up to four feet tall.

✓ **Tuber sword fern,** *Nephrolepis cordifolia*. Less curly and shorter. It has a more controlled look, more regular pinnae.

✓ **Boston fern,** *Nephrolepis exaltata* var. *bostoniensis*. An excellent ground cover for areas beneath a black olive, mahogany, or oak. It spreads quickly on running roots.

Among the non-native plants appropriate for ground covers, consider bromeliads and certain aroids, such as philodendrons and aglaonemas (see Chapter 8). Others include:

✓ **Caladiums,** *Caladium* cultivars. In summer, these boldly colored foliage plants in the aroid family look pretty beneath the shade of an old oak tree. They die back gradually each winter, then return in early summer. You don't have to dig and save them from year to year.

✓ **Spider plant,** *Chlorophytum comosum.* Can have either solid green or variegated leaves and baby plants that develop on long stalks as offshoots.

✓ **Day lilies,** *Hemerocallis* species. These lilies like a light shade beneath oaks or other trees and are pleasantly fragrant. Golden, orange, yellow, rose, and other colors.

✓ **Lily turf,** *Liriope muscari* 'Green Giant.' Deep green leaf blades and tall spikes of purple flowers.

✓ **Mondo grass,** *Ophiopogon japonicus.* The best use of this miniature grass is beneath palms, such as licaula, seen at Fairchild Tropical Garden. It needs the least water in shade.

✓ **Pentas,** *Pentas lanceolata.* Plant these about 18 to 24 inches apart and let them develop into waves of year-round color. Even the dwarf varieties grow to two or three feet, with a true dwarf blue/lavender cultivar growing about a foot tall. The stems eventually become woody, and you may want to replace them after three or four years.

✓ **Aluminum plant,** *Pilea cadierei,* and **artillery plant,** *P. microphylla* 'Rotundifolia.' The aluminum plant has small, round leaves with a silvery cast and prefers some shade. It also likes more moisture than its relative. The artillery plant, so named for explosive shooting out of pollen from the small stems, is the color of a Granny Smith apple and makes a pretty contrast to St. Au-gustine or other ground covers. The stems of the artillery plant will dry up as new branches grow and spread over the top. Easily rejuvenated by clearing old stems and replacing with cuttings taken from the plant.

✓ ***Polypodium scolopendria*** *(Microsorium scolopendria).* One of the footed ferns, this has broad, flat fronds with deeply lobed edges. The fronds are held upright as the stems creep along the ground.

✓ **Purple queen,** *Setcreasea pallida.* A tropical purple stands out against any green. The plants are drought tolerant, but if not given care, they will grow in an open way that allows weeds to become established.

✓ **Walking iris,** *Trimezia martinicensis.* Small yellow (or white with yellow and blue markings) flowers on foot-long stalks; plantlets develop on stem ends and gradually bend over beneath their own weight to root again, hence the name. They like to grow in the shade of trees.

Ground covers not recommended: wedelia, because it spreads wantonly; oysterplants and wandering jew, both of which cause allergic skin reactions in some people.

VINES

Among the prominent features of the tropical rain forest are the lianas, or vines. Enormous, woody stems hang from the canopy, two hundred or more feet high. Lianas can link trees over several acres, making up much of the greenery (or total living weight called biomass) of what appears from the ground to be treetops.

In the subtropics, the vines are abundant but usually smaller than those in the tropics. Yet, after Hurricane Andrew, even the usually benign native vines became rampant, treacherous opportunists in the damaged forests. Vines usually begin in a sunny spot in the forest, such as a light gap left by a fallen tree or the edge of a clearing.

Ordinarily, vines thrive after hurricanes and are then shaded out of trees when the trees canopies recover. However, exotic vines have become so fierce that, even without a hurricane, they can take over hammocks, snuffing out understory plants and even trees. The Vizcaya Museum hammock has been plagued by vining pothos for years; sewer vine was thick in Matheson Hammock well before Hurricane Andrew; other natural areas throughout South Florida are filled with wood rose, air potato, jasmine, and others. A three-year program to eradicate the worst vines had to be undertaken in Dade County after Hurricane Andrew, costing millions of dollars.

Native vines that pop up around telephone poles or fences include Virginia creeper, wild grape, and the small passion flower, *Passiflora suberosa*. They produce fruit that provide for wildlife.

More spectacular vines for the garden are these:

✓ **Allamanda,** *Allamanda cathartica*. A vining shrub that will behave like a vine on a fence. Bright yellow funnel-shaped flowers throughout the warm season. Glossy green leaves. Occasional fertilizer, annual pruning if you wish to keep it more shrublike.

✓ **Pelican flower,** *Aristolochia grandiflora*. Also called Dutchman's pipe. A rubbery flower catches flies that slip into a deep pouch (which may be up to two feet long), pollinating the plant before escaping. Worth the conversation. Aristolochia is a favored larval food plant for swallowtail butterflies. The polydamas swallowtail, all black but for a row of yellow markings on the back wings, loves *Aristolochia ringens* as a larval food plant.

✓ **Bower plant,** *Pandorea jasminoides*. White funnel-shaped flower with pink throat.

✓ **Purple passion flower,** *Passiflora edulis*. Various cultivars are edible; 'Purple Possum' is self-pollinating and a good fruit producer, a rampant grower that can run fast and far in the rainy season.

✓ **Queen's wreath,** *Petrea volubilis*. Clusters of blue and violet flowers hang on this in early summer and are reminiscent of wisteria. The darker petals float away, leaving the lighter sepals. Prune in very early spring to stimulate growth and flowering.

✓ **Flame vine,** *Pyrostegia venusta*. In early spring, the brilliant orange flowers of the flame vine seem to drip from the back fences where this otherwise nondescript plant grows.

✓ **Chalice vine,** *Solandra guttata*. Spectacular chalices start out creamy, then turn golden. Purple stripes color the insides of the cups that hang from this poisonous vine with leathery leaves. Another name is cup-o-gold, and once you see the flower, you understand why.

✓ **Bridal bouquet,** *Stephanotis floribunda*. Fragrant, lovely white flowers all summer on this vine from Madagascar. If the plant does not thrive, suspect nematodes.

✓ **Jade vine,** *Strongylodon macrobotrys*. Glorious aquamarine flowers that hang in loose clusters called racemes; individuals are shaped like beaks and are velvety to the touch. From the Philippines.

✓ **Clock vine,** *Thunbergia grandiflora*. Flowers are big and blue with a white throat.

Pentas and periwinkles are two drought-tolerant plants that are useful for brightening shrub or flower beds without wasting water.

7

SAVING WATER

WATER-CONSERVING landscaping is based on a set of principles that are really common-sense ways of gardening.

In this first of several chapters that deal with special gardens and special plants, water-conserving gardening is of prime importance because we must make such a small natural supply of fresh water go so far—from city to farm field to Everglades National Park. In South Florida, tropical gardens are often created by using enormous amounts of water.

There are ways to create the effect of a tropical garden and still be water conscious. A grouping of tropical plants in and around a single tree, for instance, can be the centerpiece of a subtropical garden without making the entire landscape into a sponge. Plants grouped together according to water needs, plenty of mulch, less grass . . . all are principles of water-conserving landscaping that make sense and still allow us to make beautiful gardens.

Landscapes that conserve water are called xeriscapes. Like recycling newspapers or reusing a ceramic mug instead of a styrofoam cup for office coffee, water-saving gardening practices ought to become second nature to those of us who care for even a small part of nature. If we extend the metaphor, we see that because natural areas everywhere are managed, the Earth is a garden. Responsible stewardship of a part becomes responsible stewardship of the whole.

Conserving water in the garden is working with nature in many ways. An ideal xeriscape might be ringed with native trees and shrubs that don't require irrigation. A cold-tolerant landscape might well take the same form. Xeriscape gardens feature beds of plants and mulched areas, and so do gardens that work with nature instead of against it.

So in considering the principles of xeriscape gardening, think of them not as mandates from yet another government agency—in this case, the water management district—but as wise measures you can take to promote wise gardening.

Xeriscaping began in Denver in the early 1980s during a severe drought. It spread to California, Texas, Florida, and on to the rest of the country shortly thereafter. During the last years of that decade, drought in South Florida spurred the water managers to enforce strict water restrictions and promote model landscape codes for cities and counties that would mandate saving water and implement many of the xeriscape techniques.

As the South Florida Water Management District looked at water use during that critical time, it found that the region was using water at an embarrassing rate. Marco Island, for instance, consumed 695 gallons of water per person per day; Boca Raton lapped up 405, while the national average was 140. By 1991, water use in South Florida was reduced by restricting lawn irrigation between 9 A.M. and 5 P.M.

As water-saving gardening continues to be defined and refined, early admonitions have been softened to accommodate parts of the country where rainfall may be heavy but the need to conserve is chronic. Instead of calling for the elimination of grass, the National Xeriscape Council now recommends using it so irrigation systems can easily cover the area; rather than urging the planting of strictly native plants, the Council advocates appropriate plantings.

An excellent reference for xeriscape gardeners is a Council-endorsed book called *Xeriscape Gardening* by Connie Lockhart Ellefson, Thomas L. Stephens, and Doug Welsh, published by Macmillan in 1992.

The South and Southwest Florida Water Management Districts have books, landscape plans, and plant lists available free for homeowners who want a crash course in the techniques. Other courses are offered at community colleges and botanical gardens. The guidelines are easy to incorporate in your landscape planning, garden renovation, or day-to-day gardening:

✓ **Proper planning is the first principle.** It simply means that it's wiser to gather your thoughts about what you want your garden to do than to buy whatever catches your eye. Organize; strive for continuity and a sense of peacefulness, but also know that a diverse palette attracts various butterflies and birds and prevents widespread destruction of the entire garden by insects, disease, cold, or hurricane. Ask yourself how you will use your garden, and, if you eventually want a pool or patio, which plants should be put where in anticipation of that feature. Then plan a budget and time schedule so you can phase in your plantings. Trees first; shrubs and then the filigree.

✓ **A limited or manageable area of grass.** While grass pro-

Newly mulched beds have been created to replace grass in the first steps toward a water-conserving landscape.

vides a number of environmental "services," such as controlling erosion and filtering pollution, it consumes fully half the water for residential use. Design the grassy part of your yard to be easily irrigated so you won't waste water trying to hit the edges. If you have no need for grass—no children or pets—consider replacing it with ground covers and mulched beds.

✓ **Use an efficient irrigation system;** plug leaks; put it on zoned timers and use the latest and best heads as well as low volume emitters where possible. Water before sunup to avoid losing water to evaporation at midday. Home improvement stores are full of irrigation gadgets and systems, so you can upgrade your own system or have it done.

A year later, the ground covers are in place around palms and the big sculptural bromeliads, *Aechmea blanchetiana.*

Grass can be reduced by gradually enlarging planting beds around trees and palms as well as the foundation plantings. Here, I have used limbs lost from my trees in Hurricane Andrew to create borders on the beds.

✓ **Soil improvement is recommended** to help retain moisture, but in South Florida many experts question whether adding compost, manure, or peat to a planting hole is beneficial. It may, in fact, discourage roots from penetrating poor rocky or sandy soil beyond the planting hole. If you decide to amend soil, be sure amendments amount to no more than a third of the backfill. A better solution is to amend whole beds at once.

✓ **A still better solution is mulching** that gradually will add to the soil's organic content while mediating moisture and keeping down weeds. Mulching can reduce fertilizer use by half.

✓ **Drought-tolerant plants** are available for nearly every situation. Should you want a rain forest setting in part of your yard, that's possible, too, without consuming more than your share of water. Planning will help set up protected areas—using native canopy trees and shrubs as buffers against wind and sun—so you can cluster your water-demanding plants in one area. Select a single tree beneath which you cluster ferns, aroids, gingers, and other tender, water-loving plants (making sure the tree can withstand the water). Construct a high-rise sprinkler in the tree's canopy so rain can fall frequently on this miniature rain forest while the rest of your yard stays water thrifty.

✓ **Finally, maintenance**. How can maintenance save water?

A grouping of *Thrinax morrisii,* small native thatch palms, have been used effectively for sculptural value as well as water conservation by landscape architect Lester Pancoast. The rocks used for mulch emphasize the shape of the palms and saves water.

Start with keeping your grass mowed at three inches or higher. This will help the grass develop deeper roots that can reach deeper supplies of water, reducing the need to irrigate. If you allow the cuttings to remain on the lawn, the nitrogen in the leaves will be recycled back into the grass, reducing fertilizer needs. Keeping down weeds keeps out insect pests, and this reduces the need for pest control measures. It all adds up.

DROUGHT-TOLERANT PLANTS

After planting, no tree can endure without extra water; most re-

quire a lot of water to become established. So drought tolerance comes with age. More complete information on trees and shrubs is found in chapters 5 and 6, but here are brief descriptions of many suitable for water conserving gardens:

✓ **Sweet acacia,** *Acacia farnesiana.* A small tree to 12 feet with yellow, aromatic flowers in summer and fall.

✓ **Hong Kong orchid,** *Bauhinia* x *blakeana.* Blooms in winter with purple flowers; it is sterile and does not develop seed pods.

✓ **Black olive,** *Bucida buceras.* Fast-growing, big shade tree.

✓ **Spiny black olive,** *Bucida spinosa.* A dwarf (15 feet), thorny tree with ample character to deserve a place in a small yard or even a large pot.

✓ **Bulnesia,** *Bulnesia arborea.* Beautiful yellow-flowering tree with dark green, compound leaves.

✓ **Gumbo-limbo,** *Bursera simaruba.* The distinctive red-barked native hammock tree reaches 40 to 60 feet.

✓ **Jamaica caper,** *Capparis cynophallophora.* A small tree or large shrub; salt tolerant.

✓ **Floss-silk tree,** *Chorisia speciosa.* Floss-silk tree. Rapid grower to 50 feet, covered with thorns; pink fall flowers.

✓ **Buttonwood,** *Conocarpus erectus.* A salt-tolerant tree of the mangrove fringe that grows 30 to 50 feet.

✓ **White cordia,** *Cordia boissieri,* white cordia or Texas wild olive. 20 or 25 feet, with terminal clusters of white flowers all year.

✓ **Mexican calabash,** *Crescentia alata.* Small to medium tree with hard-shelled fruits that form on the slender trunks.

✓ **Royal poinciana,** *Delonix regia.* Sometimes wider than tall, spectacular scarlet blooms in summer.

✓ **Cockspur coral tree,** *Erythrina crista-galli.* Clusters of red flowers in the summer or fall; to 20 or 25 feet.

✓ **Stoppers,** *Eugenia* species. Small, understory hammock trees are good for small yards.

✓ **Lignum vitae,** *Guaiacum sanctum.* A beautiful small native tree; royal blue flowers with bright yellow stamens.

✓ **Blolly,** *Guapira discolor.* 35 to 50 feet. A native tree for various conditions with deep-pink fruit on the female.

✓ **Crabwood,** *Alteramnus lucida.* 15 to 30 feet. Native with notched or toothed leathery leaves.

✓ **Tulipwood,** *Harpullia arborea.* About 20 feet; once used on median of U.S. Highway 1 through Coconut Grove.

✓ **Jacaranda,** *Jacaranda mimosifolia.* 40 to 50 feet, with violet/blue flowers in spring and lacy, compound leaves.

✓ **Black ironwood,** *Krugiodendron ferreum.* 20 to 30 feet. Native and tough. Leaves are notched and wood is dense.

✓ **Queen's crape myrtle,** *Lagerstroemia speciosa.* 30 feet. Lilac-colored flowers in summer held above canopy.

✓ **Sapodilla,** *Manilkara zapota.* Medium height; leaves in clusters; rough brown-skinned, edible fruit. Wind tolerant.

✓ **Wax myrtle,** *Myrica cerifera.* Small, shrubby, multi-trunked. Takes wet to dry conditions. Bay aroma.

✓ **Jerusalem thorn,** *Parkinsonia aculeata.* 20 to 30 feet. Tiny leaves, yellow flowers; shallow roots.

✓ **Allspice,** *Pimenta dioica.* Small, upright shape. Big, simple leaves are aromatic.

✓ **Dade County pine,** *Pinus elliottii* var. *densa* and other pines are made for sand and rock; take seasonal flooding.

✓ **Jamaica dogwood,** *Piscidia piscipula.* 35 to 50 feet. A rapid growing pioneer tree from the Keys; cold-tender.

✓ **Frangipani,** *Plumeria rubra.* Small tree with open habit has perfumed flowers at branch ends in spring and summer.

✓ **Pongam,** *Pongamia pinnata.* Distinctive, compound leaf with wavy edges. Wind resistant; medium height.

✓ **Southern live oak,** *Quercus virginiana.* 50 to 60 feet. Native; wind resistant and excellent for shade, wildlife.

✓ **Paradise tree,** *Simaruba glauca.* 35 to 50 feet. A hammock tree; can drop limbs in wind; beautiful compound leaves.

✓ **Mahogany,** *Swietenia mahogani.* 60 feet. Shade tree with compound leaves, plum-like fruit, blackish bark.

✓ **Tabebuia,** *Tabebuia* species. Small and lovely flowering trees endure in difficult spots, but tenuously anchored. *Tabebuia caraiba* has been found growing in natural areas of South Dade County.

✓ **Wild lime,** *Zanthoxylum fagara.* 20 feet. Pretty, rounded compound leaflets with winged rachis; thorns.

DROUGHT-TOLERANT SHRUBS

Many shrubs can endure long dry spells, particularly if well mulched and weaned off heavy watering once established. Here are some excellent choices:

✓ **Bougainvillea,** *Bougainvillea* species. Can be kept as a shrub or allowed to climb a trellis. Flowers in the dry season.

✓ **Beautyberry,** *Callicarpa americana.* Will tumble and sprawl; bright purple fruits attract birds.

✓ **Rough velvet seed,** *Guettarda scabra.* A tough pinelands plant with sandpapery leaves and red berries.

✓ **Firebush,** *Hamelia patens.* Native to the hammock edges, a red-flowering shrub that can reach about 20 feet.

✓ **Texas sage,** *Leucophyllum frutescens.* About 8 feet, with dense silver leaves, purple flowers. Full sun.

✓ **White indigo berry,** *Randia aculeata.* A pinelands shrub that becomes full in cultivation; small leaves and pairs of thorns.

✓ **India-hawthorn,** *Rhaphiolepsis indica.* A dwarf shrub that has beautiful pinkish flowers.

✓ **Saw palmetto,** *Serenoa repens.* Low palm of the pinelands on prostrate stems. Fragrant spring flowers.

✓ **Necklace pod,** *Sophora tomentosa.* Native with silvery, fuzzy leaves and yellow flowers.

DROUGHT-TOLERANT GROUND COVERS

✓ **Golden creeper,** *Ernodea littoralis.* Vining beach shrub with yellowish leaves and tiny pink flowers.

✓ **Blanket flower,** *Gaillardia pulchella.* Salt tolerant. Spread from seed. Daisy-like flowers.

✓ **Beach sunflower,** *Helianthus debilis.* Pretty yellow flowers. The plant prefers the coast. Can grow to two feet.

✓ **African bush daisy,** *Gamolepis chrysanthemoides.* Small yellow flowers and delicate foliage.

✓ **Juniper,** *Juniperus conferta* 'compacta.' Prostrate form that likes full sun and grows like a carpet.

✓ **Kalanchoe,** *Kalanchoe* species. Succulent plant with red, yellow, or coral clusters of flowers. Use as a bedding plant.

✓ **Pineland lantana,** *Lantana depressa.* Clusters of yellow flowers on low-growing plant. Prune to keep from getting woody. *L. ovatifolia* variety *reclinata* is dwarf lantana. *Lantana montevidensis* is weeping lantana. Lilac-colored flowers in the sun.

✓ **Boston fern,** *Nephrolepis cordifolia.* It creeps on runners over shady mulch; pull it out where you don't want it.

✓ **Dwarf rhoeo or oysterplant,** *Rhoeo discolor.* Purple undersides on its rosette of spiky leaves.

✓ **Purple queen,** *Setcresaea pallida.* A beautiful jewel color of the tropics; light pink flowers.

✓ **Beach verbena,** *Verbena maritima.* Grows on coast or inland on poor soil. Has pretty blue/purple flowers.

A small, jewel-like tropical garden gracefully displays the patterns and textures of the exotic plants while keeping them organized in mulched beds.

8

TROPICAL PLANTS: THE FINISHING TOUCHES

SIMPLE OR COMPOUND, driptips dripping, leaves breathe oxygen into the thick tropical atmosphere of the rain forest where life so bountifully shows itself. These leaves play myriad roles. Folded heliconia blades become tents for miniature white fruit bats; rosettes form vases and provide nurseries and reservoirs for tadpoles and insects; red or iridescent blue pigments harvest photons of far-red light.

Arranged in spirals or opposite pairs, made with edges that undulate or stay entire, with surfaces that gleam or crinkle—tropical leaves are bold and impertinent by temperate norms, competing as they do for the life-giving light of the tropical forests by means of size or color or form. In deep shade on the forest floor, some shape their epidermal cells into lenses to catch and reflect what flecks of light they can. Some, like the juvenile aroid leaves, modify themselves into grasping tentacles to climb nubby bark until they reach the light, then they swell, lobe, and dangle on extended petioles to luxuriate in the tropical sun and rain. Others, once high up, coat themselves with hair to rebuff sun. Still others unfold from treble clefs called fiddleheads and spread their lacework wide.

Do the variegated ones want to appear already eaten, or are they merely warning against their own bad taste and toxic insides?

Because insects have proliferated in the tropics, leaves everywhere show signs of herbivory, their blades tattered and eaten and seldom whole. Plants survive, however, because they are filled with defensive chemicals, from quinine to calcium crystals, that shoo away the herbivores. These compounds, we have learned, are the sources of many medicines, including tranquilizers, steroids, and anti-cancer agents as well as local healing compounds, herbal teas, tinctures, and extracts. Perfumes, dyes, chewing gum, rubber, chocolate, vanilla, and cocaine all come from tropical plants, which are as complex internally as they are beautiful externally.

Flowers: fantastic flaunters to a fare-thee-well because in this great welter and wonder of plants, something has to attract a pollinator, be it color, form, smell, or sometimes all three. Scarlet, vermilion, fuchsia, violet, jade, lemon, magenta, chartreuse—they mean to stand out in the canopies of the great fluted trees, among the lianas, beside the palms.

In the tropical world, a whole galaxy of plants gives expression to evolution, each more beautiful and bizarre than the next. And they interact with animals and other plants in ways we just now are beginning to decipher. A certain euglossine bee collects scent packets from particular flowers, tucks them into his legs, and uses them to lure his mate. What or who is the instigator here? A hummingbird follows the same path through the rain forest every day, feeding on nectar in heliconia flowers that grow in the light gaps. Does the bird memorize this route or rediscover it daily as the flowers unfold and then die? An ant carries part of a leaf underground, then chews and regurgitates it onto a fungus garden where long, threadlike mycelia of the fungus consume it. The fungus no longer produces spores, but instead depends on the ant to carry and spread it from nest to nest. Where did it begin, this complexity and interdependence, and how will it end?

It begins with long, warm days, plentiful rain, the competition amidst plenty, and the urge toward survival. It expands and withdraws as the planet's icy poles shrink and enlarge. It is refuge and hothouse, it is serenity and violence, and more beautiful than you can imagine until you stand there, wet and sweaty and full of awe.

It may be ending with destruction by human use and need and overpopulation. It may be ending with the chainsaws that still have not stopped in spite of all we know.

As we struggle around the globe to deal with myriad issues of tropical deforestation, increasing appreciation and knowledge of these plants will help in the struggle to save them. Increasing destruction of them for the simple pleasures of using them in our gardens will not.

Ask, when buying tropical plants, how and where they were obtained. Do not buy plants collected in the wild unless you know they were properly permitted. Endangered is not an optional condition.

When you incorporate tropical plants into your subtropical garden, you must approximate conditions in which they grow naturally. For most tropicals, that means providing abundant moisture, humidity, and shade.

Yet not all of the tropics are in lowland, warm forests, nor are they all rainy year-round. Plants from high altitudes in the tropics evolved to take cool to often bitter cold temperatures and more or less constant mists and clouds. To grow these, you need specialized greenhouses with cooling pads and fans. Plants from tropical desert areas, on the other hand, need protection during the subtropical rainy season.

How can we grow tropical plants in our backyards without using too much water? How can we blend them into our own native flora? By creating a garden with a buffering perimeter of canopy trees and windbreaks of understory trees and shrubs. The canopy will shade, mitigate heat and cold, and help retain moisture, creating a protective microclimate.

If you don't have a natural canopy, then a shade house that is covered with 60 to 73 percent shade cloth will be your best bet.

Bromeliads are among the easiest plants to grow, since they practically grow themselves. Orchids require steadfastness. Most aroids need shade, although some adapt to sun and a few take cold. Tender ferns, such as maidenhairs, demand high humidity, but some can stand on their own and be allowed to wander about the garden at will, finding their own niches.

BROMELIADS

A rule of thumb for growing bromeliads is this: Bromeliads with soft, tender leaves, such as guzmanias, are shade lovers. Those with spiny, thick leaves coated with silver bands of hairs, such as aechmeas, can take some direct sun or very bright light. The hairs that look silver have evolved to reflect sunlight and retain moisture. Spanish moss has evolved to the point of having no roots or leaves, but merely tiny leaflike stems that take in water and food from rain.

Most bromeliads are epiphytes, or air plants. They attach themselves to trees or palms with clinging roots but they don't feed on the host like parasites. They have developed particular ways of obtaining nutrients from rainwater and decomposing organic matter in their cups. The leaves of bromeliads have special hairy cells called trichomes that, when wet, separate to allow water to collect on the leaf surface. When dry, the trichomes shut down over these miniature reservoirs. Rainwater contains a scant amount of nitrogen and can provide some nutrients to the plants, while the organic matter around their roots and dissolving in their cups also provides vase-shaped bromeliads with minerals.

In the dry season, the bromeliad cups are natural water sources for many insects, amphibians, and reptiles. In the tropics, certain small tree frogs carry their eggs to hatch in the water-filled urns.

An easy way to grow bromeliads is to attach them to trees. You can staple them through the base, attach them with plastic wire (the slender colored wires inside telephone line are ideal), or use twine that will disintegrate. As they produce offshoots, they'll gradually colonize their site.

If you pot them, use a soilless potting mix that drains quickly or, and I like this best, an orchid mix with perlite and small wood chips. You can sink the pots into beds of mulch and move them forward in the bed for better show as the plants come into flower. Prop them in limestone or cap rock crevices. Grow them on driftwood. You can even grow them in empty terra cotta pots if you splash them often with water.

Mosquitoes will breed in the water collected in bromeliad cups. If you have bromeliads in the ground, an every-other-day spritz with the hose to wash out the cups will help reduce the mosquito population, but without using chemicals, mosquitoes come with the territory.

Snails love to hide in the tight rosettes of leaves or even in the centers. Diatomaceous earth around the bromeliad bed discourages them from crawling there (see Chapter 4). If crowded in beds with little air circulation, bromeliads develop scale. The small black dots are the hard-shelled insects; yellow spots on the opposite sides of the dots tell you that sucking insects are at work. You can rub them off with your fingers. Or clean out your beds, separate the plants, and give them more air, allowing the scale gradually to disappear. (Cygon is a chemical used by commercial bromeliad growers to control these pests.)

A water-soluble fertilizer such as 20-20-20 can be used occasionally, mixed at half-strength. At Fairchild Tropical Garden, the bromeliads on display are given one-quarter-strength soluble fertilizer once a week to keep them in showy and robust condition. Neoregelias, which develop intense red, purple, or scarlet centers before blooming, can turn green and lose their color with too much fertilizer, and patterns in leaves can fade.

Generally, *Neoregelia*, *Aechmea*, and *Bromelia* species develop colorful leaves and can take more sun than the softer, spineless *Vriesia* and *Guzmania* species. Some tillandsias and guzmanias are native to South Florida. Spanish moss is a *Tillandsia* that occurs throughout much of the South. Florida's prehistoric Indians used the curly gray Spanish moss in making pottery.

When your bromeliads are in need of watering, their leaves will roll inward; when overwatered, they'll flop out. After Hurricane Andrew, bromeliads all over South Florida sent up flower stalks and bloomed.

Among those massed beneath palms in my yard, clambering over mango limbs, attached to palms or growing in pots: *Aechmea chantinii*, *A. coelestis* 'albomarginata,' *A. fasciata*, *A. blanchetiana*, *Bilbergia zebrina*, *Guzmania lingulata*, *Neoregelia spectabilis*, *Tillandsia cyanea*, and *Vriesea gigantea*.

Tillandsia cyanea has feather-shaped pink inflorescences that spurt purple-blue flowers that smell like cloves. *Neoregelia spectabilis*, the fingernail bromeliad, was situated beneath an avocado nearly a decade ago and has produced a hillock of plants, many of which I have merely cut off, repotted, and moved to other locations.

P.S. The branched flower spike of *Aechmea blanchetiana* is yellow and red and lasts for months. After a while, I get tired of looking at them, so I cut them, put them in a big vase on the floor, and use them as a flower arrangement.

AROIDS

A philodendron flower stalk, the spadix, is surrounded by a protective leaf called a spathe. It is a construction that characterizes the entire aroid family of plants, a family that includes aglaonemas, anthuriums, spathiphyllums, pothos, and even water lettuce (*Pistia stratiotes*).

If you look at a philodendron spathe and spadix closely, you'll notice the center part of the white, fleshy spathe is pinched in the middle, and it opens and closes. It opens when the female flowers are ready for pollination. It closes when insects arrive for the task. It opens again, after the fact and when the male flowers along the top of the stalk have shed pollen. That way, the insects carry off pollen to the next open female flowers.

Dan Nicolson, taxonomist and aroid specialist at the Smithsonian Institution for more than a quarter of a century, classified philodendrons as advanced in aroid evolution, whereas anthuriums, which stick out naughty-looking spadices and advertise them with brightly colored spathes, are the most primitive.

In between are many of the tropics' most resplendent plants. Among them are some that adapt well to landscape uses. The bird's-nest anthuriums are good specimens for planting beneath trees. The leaves are tall and leathery, arranged in a rosette. They're quite long, broadening near the ends, though some types stay narrow. They grow on mounds of white roots that increase in height as the plants age. Try this type in a tree; transplant by cutting the root clump at ground level.

Philodendron selloum. Commonly planted, it is tough and pretty with deeply lobed leaves that have undulating margins. It

Epitomizing tropical flowers and leaves are this ginger relative, *Hedychium gardnerianum*, and aroid hybrid, *Philodendron giganteum* x *P. eichieri*.

forms a clump. *P. bipinnatifidum* is similar but more deeply lobed so it looks frillier.

Philodendron x *evansii*, a hybrid that's a cross between *P. selloum* and *P. speciosum*, is a giant elephant ear type. *P.* x. *evansii* is a tree climber. The leaf surface is glossy, slightly lobed, and undulating. Big leaves can reach a couple of feet across and three to four feet long.

Philodendron hastatum has arrow-shaped leaves when young that develop a hastate base—little wings grow on either side of the petiole.

Anthurium clarinervium has dark green and velvetlike leaves etched with light colored veins. Two other less cold-tolerant anthuriums that have the velvet texture are *A. magnificum* and *A. crystallinum.* The epidermal cells on the leaf's surface are hemispherical, reflecting light at many angles and creating the velvet effect. Ordinarily, epidermal cells are flat.

Monstera deliciosa, Mexican breadfruit, has deep lobes and holes in its leaves (they form well before the leaf unfurls, probably so the wind won't shred the leaf), which are roundish and striking. The fruit tastes of a blend of pineapple and banana, hence the species name, meaning delicious, but they must be eaten only when completely ripe or they are poisonous. Wait until the sections begin splitting apart to know when to eat them. When monsteras get too large for their spot, cut off a portion of the corky stem and lay it in a layer of mulch, water for a few days, and watch it grow.

Many philodendrons have been hybridized and even patented, such as 'Red Princess' and 'Red Emerald.' The leaves are deeply colored, usually red, wine, or wine with pink splotches. Some leaves are silvery, others are variegated or marbled. The decorative value of these plants can be lost by over-use, but when one or two are grown they bring a tropical feel to the garden, and they are particularly useful for patio or house.

Caladiums also are members of the aroid family, the Araceae, as are alocasias and colocasias. The latter genera, from which come the elephant ears, look as if they belong; the caladiums are so brightly colored, they look like prodigal sons. Dieffenbachias, aglaonemas, and homalomenas, as well as lesser known genera such as *Colletogyne, Asterostigma, Carlephyton* and *Gonatopus, Calla,* and *Dracunculus* round out the huge group. A particularly bizarre one is Amorphophallus, which looks much like what its name implies and smells of carrion, attracting flies that pollinate it. Annually, it grows on a green and gray blotched and bumpy slender stem, produces an enormous inflorescence, then dies back.

Caladiums are bulbs that thrive in our summers if given some shade. Like philodendrons, they have been hybridized repeatedly. They are spotted, pink-veined, white-veined, green-veined on pink, multicolored . . . endlessly varied. Once planted in well-draining organic soil, they appear on their own in the spring and disappear in the winter when the days shorten. Like all bulbs, they will rot if they sit in water. But unlike northern bulbs, they do not have to be dug up each winter. You can simply ignore their spot in the ground, withholding water except for rain. When they appear, resume watering and fertilizing.

Dieffenbachias are produced by the millions in Florida for use as interior plants. They have big, showy, beautifully marked leaves, and they grow upright on a thick, succulent stalk. If your garden has shade and protection from the wind, try a few of these in the understory. If not, use them inside.

Aglaonemas fare better outside than dieffenbachias because their leaves are smaller and will not tear as easily in the wind, as they grow lower to the ground. Their markings are just as pretty, and they can be used in shady places as ground covers or singly as specimen plants.

Alocasia cuprea, quite a rare plant only a few years ago, has gained in popularity because of its leaves, which seem to be made of quilted patent-leather: silver-green on top, maroon on the underside. It can take morning sun, but not afternoon sun. They'll shrink back and try to grow away from too much light. *Alocasia sanderiana* has an arrow-shaped leaf, a polished finish, and bluish veins against a deep blue-green background.

Some lovely gardens in South Florida have been created with aroids, but many of these are work-intensive. Collectors often spray to prevent fungus and bacteria that spread so easily in moist, humid areas where plants are close together. You can grow some of these plants without devoting every free minute to them if you choose carefully, provide good drainage, water regularly every two or three days (daily if you grow them in lava rock), and allow for good air circulation.

Growing mixes can range from rock to a complicated recipe used by the Marie Selby Botanical Garden in Sarasota. The rich Selby mix holds moisture. It is one part Canadian peat moss, one part fir bark, and one-half part limestone gravel for weight, with the inclusion of the fungicide Banrot, minor elements, dolomite, and slow-release fertilizer. A prepackaged soilless potting mix, amplified by either perlite or a medium orchid bark or fir bark, will suffice.

Use a soluble fertilizer with micronutrients (consider a 30-10-10 because these plants need higher nitrogen for foliage production) or a micronutrient foliage spray when needed to supplement slow-release fertilizer. Mulch, compost, and a regular granular fertilizer with micronutrients work well.

FERNS

About 400 million years ago, the ferns became. And comely they still are.

Tied to a watery heritage (following the liverworts and mosses ashore but developing more sophisticated internal circulation and support systems as well as true roots), ferns have two separate plants in one life cycle: the sporophyte, or familiar fern stage, produces spores, and the gametophyte, a heart-shaped plant (prothallus), produces male and female sex organs and gametes. The spores are developed in cases that dry and pop open. They are carried by wind, and when they land in watery spots, they germinate to become the heart-shaped prothalli. On the underside of the prothallus, male and female organs develop. When these tiny organs are mature, sperm are released to swim to the eggs. The offspring then grow and develop fertile fronds on which the spore cases form to complete the cycle.

This whole system developed 200 million years before flowering plants (coal is the ancient ferns' legacy) and still works wonderfully well.

Ferns love cool, moist mountainsides in the tropics, but will grow in various habitats. They grow diversely, from those called filmy ferns, just a single cell thick, to those that become tree ferns. Water ferns are host to blue-green algae that grow in chambers inside their bodies.

Maidenhair ferns native to South Florida grow in moist, humid niches of limestone solution holes. String and hand ferns pop up in the boots of sabal palms. *Blechnum serrulatum* is a sword fern often called a dwarf tree fern. It, too, grows in solution holes. An unfortunate change is occurring in the Florida wilds, however: as drainage and a lower water table have dried out solution holes, the delicate maidenhairs and other high-humidity ferns have begun to dwindle, and more robust (often exotic) ones are taking their place. Life does not stand still even for descendants of the land colonizers.

Bird's-nest ferns, like bird's-nest anthuriums, have long, straplike leaves that grow in a rosette around a central stem. Debris and moisture collect in the bowl of leaves and allow this fern to grow

Maidenhair fern, accented by deep pink impatiens, is tender and lovely in tropical corners of the garden.

on rock. Bird's-nest ferns are a brighter green than anthuriums and have a more delicate look to them.

Asplenium serratum, a bird's-nest fern from the Everglades, has serrated margins and fronds that are about two feet long.

Rare shoestring fern (it looks like its name and grows in the old boots of sabal palms) and strapleaf ferns are native to Florida, the latter growing on logs, collecting debris around it, and taking nutrients from the debris. This is a good way to grow yours.

Footed ferns—davallias, polypodiums, and aglaomorphas—grow on rhizomes or hairy, creeping stems. In the spring, when new leaves come out, new roots form at the same time.

Once a frond produces spores—and every fern has its own spore pattern—it declines and gradually dies.

Polypodium polypodioides is the native Florida resurrection fern. It is brown and curled when dry, and after a good rain it is green and healthy-looking again. *Polypodium scolopendrium* is the hand-shaped, running fern that makes a ground cover before you know it.

Staghorn ferns are in the genus Platycerium. These big, showy ferns have two types of fronds: fertile, forward fronds that are divided at the tip like horns, and shield fronds, those flat, round fronds that cover the roots. Tropical and epiphytic, staghorns have gone through waves of popularity among Florida gardeners, but you'll find them hanging in trees in every neighborhood.

If grown on a tree limb, staghorns soon are happily attached all around the trunk. In nature, they like the upper canopies of trees; in cultivation, we put them closer to earth, although longer ladders make for loftier staghorns.

When mature, the fertile fronds will develop suedelike patches on their undersides. These are masses of spore cases. They start out light green and turn brown.

I have one that has been growing for years in the crotch of a mango tree. Having once read that banana peels were good for staghorns, supplying potassium in abundant amounts, I flipped a peel into the top of the shield fronds. The staghorn remained virtually unchanged, as far as I could tell, except that it drew fruit flies.

Because this big bowl collects leaves and debris, once a staghorn is established on a tree, it needs little fertilizer. When it requires water, the fertile fronds will shrivel. If you poke the shield fronds with a finger and water drips out, it's too wet.

Elkhorn ferns have apple-green, entire, upright fronds with a dark vein down the center of each. The top of the blade is ruffled to different degrees. Mine was started years ago, and came close to dying because I assumed it would thrive on its own. When I added potting soil, fertilizer, mulch, and began watering regularly, it suddenly became vigorous, deepened its color, and took off. Not all ferns take equally well to benign neglect.

Boston ferns are really Florida natives, called Boston because that's where they gained their popularity in the nineteenth century (see ground covers in Chapter 6).

Tree ferns from Australia and Hawaii are lovely additions to our gardens. They grow on upright masses of roots that resemble trunks. New fronds, called croziers, emerge from the center of the crown, tightly curled and covered with hair either dark or light tan, and, in the case of the Australian tree fern, they are a skin irritant. The plants take a fair amount of light, high humidity, and moisture.

Use 20-20-20 on potted ferns. Don't fertilize deciduous ferns in winter. In the growing season (April 1 to mid-October), alternate with 30-10-10 or occasionally with fish emulsion. A teaspoon of soluble fertilizer per gallon of water is ample. Ferns used in beds beneath trees, scrambling over mulch, do fine on their own.

HELICONIAS

Ornate as temple paintings of the Maya, heliconias bespeak ceremonial rites and rituals. Their bizarre flower stalks must have been as highly regarded by the ancient peoples of the New World jungles as the lotus was in Egypt.

Scientists have known for years that the flowers produced within the colorful bracts are pollinated by birds in many cases, by small mammals in others, but only recently did the Smithsonian Institution's John Kress discover that a Madagascar member of this family, the traveler's palm, is pollinated by lemurs.

Related to bananas, heliconias flourish on the edges of the rain forest or in the light gaps of the canopy. With leaves that are banana-like and paddle-shaped, these giant herbs produce their inflorescences from a central stem. The flowering stalks may be held upright or allowed to dangle upside down. Individual boat-shaped bracts are arranged on the stalks in a spiral or opposite each other. Tubular flowers are found inside the bracts.

I remember many years ago seeing an arrangement of heliconias and cycad leaves at a sugar plantation in Colombia, outside Cali in the Cauca River valley. This combination, in a large ceramic pot, was stark and lovely at once. And while there were orchids hanging from the trees at this rich finca, and peacocks strutting the grounds, it was the pot of heliconias on bare wood planks, set against a white-washed stucco wall, that spoke of a particular way of life in South America that was under siege and passing, and to be lamented for its disappearing elegance.

I've seen heliconias growing in the red soils of Amazonas, the volcanic earth of Central America, on mountainsides in Puerto Rico. They never fail to dazzle. Their relatives include gingers, costuses, marantas, cannas, and birds-of-paradise, all of which are exotic in some way. In recent years, the great, bold stalks have become more common, even showing up in giant floral arrangements in office building lobbies, yet that does nothing to take away from their mystique.

When grown outside the subtropics, heliconias slow their growth in cool weather, and can suffer damage in cold. They grow on underground stems, so they will quickly resprout after freezes if the stems have survived. Waterlogging is worse than cold, since it will rot the rhizomes. They are what gardeners call heavy feeders, particularly the *Heliconia psittacorum* types and, more particularly, when the psittacorum types are grown on limestone or alkaline soils.

Joseph Fondeur, a nursery owner in Broward County who wrote growing instructions for the Smithsonian's valuable handbook *Heliconia: An Identification Guide,* advises fertilization with balanced, soluble fertilizer at least once a month.

The small psittacorums in my garden will darken their color quickly after being fertilized, but just as quickly, it seems, they fade again. They like to have their beds fluffed annually—that is, they like being dug up in spring, having their roots trimmed to be replanted in new peat moss, cow manure, and compost. And they respond to a semi-annual drench of chelated iron by turning green once more.

Other types of heliconias are better suited to subtropical conditions. The huge clump of *H. caribaea* x *H. bihai* var. Jacquinii that grows near my psittacorums shows no signs of phlegmatic temperament. *Heliconia stricta* cv. 'Bucky' has fabulous scarlet bracts on four-foot leafy stems, a nice size for a home garden.

Heliconai caribaea, H. stricta, H. wagneriana, and *H. rostrata* are old favorites with such beautiful coloration and form that any gardener wanting a tropical corner ought to try them—providing the area is roomy, sunny, and well-drained. The plants will die when inundated with salt water, but will grow near the ocean if protected from salt spray.

Their need for frequent watering means you should be selective and judicious about including them in your garden. A protected and sunny spot on the south side would be suitable. In the wild, they may be found by streams or on river banks. This suggests that you experiment with putting them near lakefronts or canal banks.

The Heliconia Society International was begun in 1985. It has helped popularize these plants while expanding knowledge of their types and habitats. Its annual sales are sources of unusual heliconias, often plants new to cultivation. Flamingo Gardens and Arboretum in Davie, Florida, is one of the society's repositories. Others include Andromeda Gardens in Barbados; Jurong BirdPark, Singapore; Lyon Arboretum, Honolulu; National Tropical Botanical Garden, Kauai; Jardin Botanicao Robert y Catherine Wilson, Costa Rica.

Contemporary plant scientists and explorers are busily trekking through the rain forests of Ecuador, Peru, and Central America for new heliconias, not unlike the eighteenth century explorers collecting for botanic gardens in England and Europe. That age of discovery brought to the Royal Botanic Gardens, Kew, probably the most famous flowering member of the family, the bird-of-paradise.

Birds-of-paradise, which were discovered by Sir Joseph Banks at the Cape of Good Hope in 1773, were named for King George III's German-born wife, Queen Charlotte Sophia, Duchess of Mecklenburg-Strelitz. Queen Charlotte was a patron of botany, and the

Orchids are thought of as tropical, but they grow around the globe. This is *LC* Irene Finney 'Chicago,' one of the first I bought.

botanic name for this plant is *Strelitzia reginae, reginae* meaning queen.

Bold orange bracts with blue and white flowers looking like bird plumes, these highly regarded plants take about eight years to flower. The white bird of paradise, by the way, *Strelitzia nicolai,* is named for Czar Nicholas I, and was discovered between 1772-1775. The birds, for some years, were included in the genus Heliconia. In our subtropical climate, the stems on birds become zigzagged when warm and cold weather alternates in winter, speeding up and slowing down growth. If the winter is warm, the birds grow all year.

ORCHIDS

Obsession begins with a cattleya.

Seldom can anyone grow one orchid without growing two, or two without three. The first one is most often a cattleya, frequently given as a birthday or Mother's Day present, perhaps bought on a whim. A capricious notion, and then comes the shade house. It happens that way.

Of all the flowers there are to grow, the orchids are the most alluring. The largest families of flowering plants, with perhaps 30,000 species, orchids also have a large repertoire of abilities: they can flower underground or in treetops, they may look like stars, swans, moths, lady bees' bottoms, or creepy spiders' tops. They seem to be made of glass, eggshells, silk, crepe de chine, wax with warts and whiskers.

They are evolution's playthings, undergoing speciation from tree to tree in biologically rich niches of Ecuador. They are growers' trinkets, filling endless pages of *Sander's List of Orchid Hybrids,* begun in 1906 and now on compact disk.

Romantic as cathedral glass, little red cattleyas and violet vandas, cinnamon ascocendas and spotted paphiopedilums, pure white

phalaenopsis fascinate us all. The glorious claret and golden lips of *Cattleya aurea* surrounded by the lemon yellow petals are unsurpassingly beautiful, but just as wonderful are the tiny pink and rose cascades of *Aerides feildingii.*

A whole mythology encases them. The story might seem to be apocryphal: Charles Darwin, upon seeing the foot-long spur on *Angraecum sesquipedale,* hypothesized that a moth with an equally long but coiled proboscis pollinated it. Darwin reasoned that the moth uncurled its tongue to drink nectar from the bottom of the spur. Many years later, after Darwin's death, the moth was discovered.

Vanilla comes from an orchid, and at one time, all our vanilla flavoring came from *Vanilla planifolia* or *V. pompona* and *V. tahitensis.* Because these orchids had to be hand pollinated for ample production, the cost gradually nudged the market toward synthetic flavoring. *V. planifolia* grows in Mexico, Central and South America, the West Indies, and even the Everglades, where it vines up trees and puts out one-day flowers in April.

When a collector named Swainson shipped mosses and lichens from Brazil to William Cattley in England in 1818, he used what he believed were "trash" plants as packing. The trash bloomed, and that lavender flower with its purple lip is called *Cattleya labiata.*

In the Everglades, the orchids are more modest than Mr. Cattley's namesakes, but they are just as worthy. The clamshell orchid, *Encyclia cochleata,* has an upside-down, hooded flower that looks like a seashell with streamers; the ghost orchid, *Polyrrhiza lindenii,* is leafless until producing its white, spidery flowers; cow's horn or cigar orchid, *Cyrtopodium punctatum,* has giant pseudobulbs and sprays of greenish-yellow spotted flowers. Often, the little night-flowering epidendrums and shy terrestrials of the Everglades are unnoticed. They proliferate in certain open prairies and hammocks. Tourists on Anhinga Trail, the most popular in Everglades National

Park, rarely remark on the tiny orchids in the pond apple trees alongside the boardwalk.

There's an interloper orchid appearing throughout the state in hammocks and woodlands. It's an African and South American terrestrial orchid, *Oeceoclades maculata,* that looks like a sansevieria when not blooming. Listed on the Exotic Pest Plant Council's list of most invasive, it nonetheless has defenders among orchidophiles who maintain it wouldn't harm a fleabane.

One of the delights of orchids I find most appealing is their scent. They smell of licorice, lemon, chocolate, vanilla, carnations, and medicine. When browsing through an orchid house, I'm likely to stick my nose into each flower and take a whiff. *Rhyncostylis gigantea,* with its rose-purple pendant stalk of small, waxy flowers, has a spicy smell I'm mad about but other people hate. And *Encyclia cordigera* (once called *Epidendrum atropurpureum*) has worked its way into my shade house solely by virtue of its chocolate aroma.

Flower scent is purely practical. It attracts insects for pollination, including moths, flies, bees, and butterflies (these orchids have vivid colors, too). Calaway Dodson and L. van der Pijl elaborated on the phenomenon in *Orchid Flowers: Their Pollination and Evolution* in 1966. Botanists at the University of Florida received a National Science Foundation grant in the late 1980s to study fragrance-producing cells in orchids, called osmophores, and the differences among them. In a more immediately practical vein, breeders at Stewart Orchids in California market their "fragrant plant of the month" to connoisseurs.

Orchid genera with fragrance include: *Angraecum, Aerides, Catasetum, Cattleya, Cynoches, Dendrobium, Epidendrum, Oncidium,* and *Rhynchostylis.* And occasionally a warm-growing *Cymbidium* from the ensifolium complex.

Select warm-growing orchids from low altitudes and tropical climates for hot subtropical summers. Generally, the orchids that hobby growers find easy to grow include cattleyas, vandas, oncidiums, phalaenopsis, and dendrobiums.

There are few basic conditions to meet, and growing orchids can be relatively easy. While they will survive without your complete attention, they will look their best and healthiest with regular care. For instance, water vandas daily and feed monthly in winter, biweekly or weekly in summer if you grow them as captives.

All manner of ideal temperature ranges are given for various genera in orchid culture books, but if you grow them in a shade house or on trees as a hobby, you take what God gives you. (Otherwise, you'll end up with glass houses, cooling pads, fans, and other incidentals.) If you become a serious grower, there are plenty of the equally devoted among the members of the many orchid societies in Florida and around the world to whom you may turn for advice. Orchid fanciers are among the most active of all plant society members.

If you want to grow orchids and other plants in a more casual way, then a few good trees or a shade house will be ample. You'll want to buy a watering wand that attaches to the end of your hose to spray water on the plants. To apply fertilizer, I use a siphon attachment that screws onto the outside spigot; a rubber siphon tube drops into a bucket of extra-strong fertilizer (15 times the normal strength because it's diluted when watering); the hose screws onto this, and fertilizer is mixed and sprayed as I water.

Cattleyas like bright light. About 50 percent shade is the all-purpose recommendation in Florida—about the shade an oak tree provides. If the leaves on your cattleyas are dark green and the plants won't flower, the most likely cause is too much shade, so gradually move them to more light. Yellow-green leaves are good with these plants. I grow them on trees or in a pre-packaged mix

Licuala grandis, a beautiful palm, is surrounded by a collection of tropical aroids, including anthuriums and philodendrons.

Anthurium clarinervum is a deceptively tough velvet-textured aroid that enlivens a garden with its beautiful veination.

of tree fern, bark, charcoal, and perlite in terra cotta orchid (or azalea) pots that are shallow with extra drainage holes.

Cattleyas grow on creeping stems or rhizomes. They produce a new shoot with each new flush, while maintaining the old for some time after flowering. This is called sympodial growth. Each new leaf is on top of a water-storing organ called a pseudobulb. Because they store up water, cattleyas like to dry their roots somewhat between waterings, so you can count on watering them every two, three, or four days, depending on the weather (too much water and they won't produce roots, says a commercial grower). Windy, mild days will dry a clay pot in a hurry, whereas overcast, sunless days will not. Always water early in the morning so plant leaves can dry before sundown—a rule of thumb for all plants, including orchids.

Vandas and their hybrids and relatives, the ascocentrums and ascocendas so popular in Florida, are without the water-storing capabilities possessed by cattleyas, so these orchids need watering daily unless it's overcast.

Vandas are monopodial, or one-footed, growing on an upright stem, producing leaves first to one side, then the other, one at a time. They come in three forms: terete, with leaves rounded like pencils; semi-terete, with leaves forming a V; and strap-leaf, with flat leaves. Most take a lot of sunlight, but the flatter the leaf, the greater the danger of sunburn.

Phalaenopsis orchids are favorites for late-winter, early-spring flowers. They are monopodial, and have flat, succulent leaves. They like shady conditions—55 to 73 percent shade. Put them in the back of the shade house. And their big, fleshy roots like to be kept moist in sphagnum moss (without being soaking wet). Phals in my shade house thrive, planted in plastic pots to help retain moisture, in New Zealand sphagnum moss, with either volcanic rock or styrofoam peanuts on the bottom for drainage. A mix of sphagnum moss, coarse perlite, tree fern, and a few redwood chips is a growing mix developed by Miami grower-teacher Ethyle Knapp.

When flower stalks form, keep the plant facing the same direction all the time, or the stalks will twist and the flowers will open every which way. Commercial growers sometimes recommend a single drench of one tablespoon of Epsom salts per gallon of water when flower spikes first form to strengthen them; others apply the drench weekly until spikes are six inches long. Epsom salts are the kitchen cupboard version of magnesium sulfate.

Evergreen **dendrobiums,** *Dendrobium phalaenopsis* types, are grown in the same bright conditions and potting mixes as cattleyas, in either plastic or clay. They flower on new canes and grow year-round. The deciduous dendrobiums, *Dendrobium nobile* types, require more shade for their thin leaves, and only occasional water when they're leafless. They bloom in early spring.

Oncidiums with pseudobulbs are treated like cattleyas, and can take 50 to 70 percent shade. Water every two or three days in the summer, a couple of times a week in winter. Equitant oncidiums, the miniatures, must dry between waterings. Because I'm a waterer, I often lose these little ones, even though I grow them in clay for fast drainage.

These orchids generally like more water when they are actively growing and less water when they begin to harden leaves and set buds. When orchids are actively growing, soluble 20-20-20 fertilizer used at quarter-strength weekly or half-strength every two weeks is ideal. The more light, the more fertilizer and water will be required. Place plants on benches or hanging in your shade house so new growth faces south or southeast for the sun. And if you put orchids in trees, attach them on the south side to protect them from winter's northwest winds.

Eventually, you will find the difficult growers or conditions that make them so. For instance, many red cattleya hybrids may have as one parent the cool-growing *Sophronitis coccinea.* This, like other red cattleyas, is a little trickier to bring through summer than others. Don't be discouraged if you fail. Simply try another, easier orchid.

Vanda coerulea, the blue vanda, won't flower in summers that are too hot. *Vanda tessellata,* a species from India and Malaya, is a tough plant that flowers almost continuously in the summer. It thrives in full sun, except during midday. *Cymbidium pascelis* 'Autumn Leaves' is a warm-growing cymbidium that flowers faithfully in spring, with tiny flowers on long sprays. The flowers are white with stripes the color of red-hots. Other cymbidiums won't do well in South Florida.

Paphiopedilum concolor is a beginner's lady slipper. It has mottled leaves and small yellow flowers with red dots and delightful little pouches. The paphiopedilums with mottled leaves are warm growers, best suited for subtropical conditions. *LC* Erin 'Bill Teel,' a green orchid with a rose-violet lip, bloomed many years for me in the fall, while *Cattleya* 'Wendy Patterson,' a wonderfully fragrant white with light lemon throat, has bloomed in the spring for years.

LC Irene Finney 'Chicago' was an oldtime hybrid I bought as a bare root cutting without a pot. There were three bulbs on her in 1979, and she cost $5. It took until 1984 for her to produce her first purple flowers. This orchid, with its lavender sepals and petals and yellow and purple lip, is a consistent, tough, and wonderful plant that still surprises and delights, and has been joined recently by Irene Finney 'York.'

How do I remember all these things? I keep records (less well now than early on) with photographs attached. Try this; it also helps identify plants if the tags have been lost.

Of utmost importance also with orchids is the matter of using sterile tools when repotting and manicuring. A virus is spread easily, and many of my vandaceous orchids have been infected by sloppy disregard for cleaning between every cut. The black streaks that appear on the leaves are symptomatic of the disease and reduce vigor in the plant and number of flowers. Flowers may become deformed or have color breaks, with two tones appearing where there should be one. Dip your cutting tools in trisodium phosphate for two to five minutes between cuts. Or use an alcohol dip or 1:10 Clorox mixture.

Years ago, I covered my shade house with rolls of clear plastic in winter, rolling up the sides in warm weather, dropping them in cold snaps. I find that's too much work nowadays, and I prefer to carry the orchids into the Florida room before a cold front hits, and carry them back out when the weather warms up. If you want to cover your shade house, remember to attach the plastic over the top and down the sides so the sides won't blow up and out in the wind of a cold front. Raise the plastic for ventilation during sunny days during the cold spell.

Cold can damage plants and create an opening for fungus. Before and after cold, some commercial growers spray with fungicide as a preventive measure. It is better to protect plants than use chemicals.

When the days shorten and the light is less intense in winter, move vandas into sun, and give the cattleyas and dendrobiums more light. I roll back the cloth on my shade house in November, allowing sun to stream in. This has to be done gradually to avoid burning plant leaves. Big, brown circular spots that turn black are the results of sunburn. Then, in late February or March, I re-cover the house again.

In very hot summer months, sprinkle orchid leaves with a quick spritz of water in the early afternoon to cool them. Don't let water remain in the crowns of phalaenopsis, as they are prone to rot; prop pots up on one side so water drains out of the crowns. Once they get some size on them, these orchids tend to bend over, as they do on tree limbs, to avoid crown rot disease.

Thrips sometimes attack orchid buds as well as leaves. They can cause the bud to drop or distort the flower. Malathion can be used against thrips on leaves, but will cause flower distortion if used on buds. Cygon is another product that can be used.

Aphids and the other sucking pests sometimes infest orchids; snails and slugs can work their way into the pots, and even roaches will hide in pots. Use Malathion for the sucking pests; slug bait and roach bait for the others.

Black rot is a fungus disease of new growth and leaves, causing black, soft areas. Don't overwater, be sure there's good air circulation in your shade house or patio, and use Tersan or Kocide. Remember that bacterial rots are slimy or watery and spread much faster than fungal diseases. Manzate can be used.

Repotting Orchids

When the new shoots of the cattleyas begin creeping over the pot's edge, and the phalaenopsis medium begins to break down and the vanda is too big for its basket, it's repotting time. Take a day to do it right, and assemble your materials first: hand shears, sterilization mix or Bunsen burner to flame-clean tools, new pots, and new media (use the appropriate medium for each genus).

Soak cattleyas in a bucket of clean water to soften and loosen the roots from the sides of their pot. This may take a while, so repot vandas or other orchids while you wait.

When the roots slip loose, carefully remove the plant from the pot. With a chopstick or similar tool, clean potting material from the old roots. If roots are brown and shriveled, cut them off; if they're healthy and fleshy, covered with the special white cells that absorb water and nutrients, handle them carefully.

To successfully divide cattleyas, look at the plant and determine where a natural division can be made so there are at least three to five new bulbs on the young plant. Eliminate brown and shriveled old bulbs at this time. Cut the plant's rhizome and carefully untangle the roots.

Place in a terra cotta orchid pot with the oldest bulbs against the side so new growth goes toward the center of the pot. Hold the plant with one hand, add mix with the other, and pack it tightly. Use a bulb clip to secure the new plant in place, but don't let it stay on for more than a few weeks or it will distort the growth.

Water the plant well, and put it in a darker area of your shade house. Then, keep the new plant drier than normal for a few weeks until new growth begins. Gradually return to the old location and resume normal watering patterns.

Divide vandas by cutting off the top of a large, old plant with three or more roots. Simply place the new top in a wooden basket with horticultural charcoal, tying the stem carefully in place so the wind won't blow it around. Keep the old stem, and a keiki or two will sprout at the top. A keiki is a new plantlet, or baby, if you will.

If the old vanda is in a basket that's too small, soak the roots until they're pliable, then carefully wrap them and the old basket into the nest of a new and bigger basket. You can place new charcoal around the coiled roots. Again, keep the top and bottoms shadier and drier than normal until you see new growth.

Phalaenopsis keikis sometimes develop on long stalks after the flowers. Wait until there are a few roots to support the plant, then cut the umbilical stalk and carefully pot the keiki in sphagnum moss. At other times, new plants will develop at the base of the phalaenopsis, and can be removed when there are sufficient roots to keep them alive on their own. You might wait until a keiki is two or three inches across before removing it.

Dendrobium keikis develop naturally at the ends of old canes, and can be removed when they have a few good roots. When you overwater these orchids, new plantlets sometimes form instead of flowers.

Paphiopedilums, or lady slippers from Asia, flower with each new growth. The best time to repot them is when a new plantlet is just beginning to form at the base of the old.

There are many wonderful guides to orchids. Once hooked, you'll begin buying your share. Rebecca Tyson Northern's *Home Orchid Growing* is a classic, and a good place to begin. Many orchid books are written by the British, who have had centuries of experience, but their conditions and terminology are quite different and you may find them daunting. A good new paperback that is beautifully photographed is *Orchids Simplified*, by Henry Jaworski. Local growers throughout Florida, the Caribbean, and Latin America are expert on local conditions.

Lady palms surround the base of a royal palm at The Retreat, home of the late palm collectors Arthur and Margaret Langlois in Nassau. The home now belongs to the Bahamian National Trust and the palms are cared for by the International Palm Society.

9

PALMS AND CYCADS

AS MUCH AS ANYTHING, it is the palms that imbue our gardens with a feel of the tropics and the subtropics. The feathery fronds of the pinnate palms, the coconut, queen, and chamaedorea; the sturdy, assured shape of the palmate fronds, the Bismarck, Bailey, and thatch. Fluttering on a southeasterly, posing, idling, fretting out a storm, flashing undersides of silver, revealing crown shafts of ivory, red, orange, and blue, the palms sway.

They are sly in their ability to charm, lacking showy floral displays and mouth-watering fruit. Instead, they offer a growing enchantment.

As you begin to notice the cabada's handsome ringed trunk, the coccothrinax fibers woven as if on a loom, the borassus's ebony polish, the areca's slender grace, you discover that you have been seduced into growing them.

And what at first seemed merely green turn out to be gray, blue, olive, or seafoam unfolding as mahogany, pink, rose, or copper fronds on trunks that are as solemn as columns, ringed with thorns, fat in the middle, or smooth as glass.

After you have noticed all those qualities, you notice you have found crannies for squeezing just a few more into the corner of the garden where last year you said nothing else would fit.

There are quite wonderful palms for our landscapes, and there are collector's palms that require cold protection and coddling on a grand scale, such as the exquisite sealing wax palm (*Cyrtostachys renda*) that is difficult to a fault to bring through any weather cooler than 50 degrees. Remember when planting them that they look wonderful in groups; they are visually pleasing in odd-numbered clusters of staggered heights. However, giants or particularly interesting palms can be strategically placed by themselves to show their form or special character. Palmate palms as background can be used to show off pinnate, smaller palms in a foreground bed. The native ones are where you should begin. Get to know them, use some of them, have them hold up and endure. Then fiddle with the rest.

NATIVE PALMS

✓ **Paurotis palm,** *Acoelorrhaphe wrightii.* A clumping, palmate palm from the Everglades that has shaggy fibers on slender and sometimes curving trunks that are 15 to 20 feet tall. The round palmate fronds are drawn with a light hand. Needs ample water.

✓ **Silver palm,** *Coccothrinax argentata.* Quite silvery on their underside, the palmate leaves are held on slender stalks or petioles. Individual segments of the fronds arch, resembling falling water.

Coccothrinax leaves are called palmate, because their leaves are like fingers coming off a hand.

✓ **Buccaneer** or **Sargent cherry palm,** *Pseudophoenix sargentii.* On a staunch blue-gray trunk, the young buccaneer palm has a resolute demeanor. Its fronds are pinnate and grow on a single plane when very young, before gradually positioning themselves around the axis. An attractive and worthy palm, endangered in the wild.

✓ **Needle palm,** *Rhapidophyllum hystrix.* Central and north Florida native, with a short trunk covered with sharp needlelike spines. The fronds are palmate but divided like fingers. Cold tolerant.

✓ **Royal palm,** *Roystonea* species. Enormous columnar trunk with huge, graceful fronds, awesome and splendid. From wetland areas, they like their roots in the water table, and will taper their trunks to a point if denied proper care. Royal palm bugs sometimes shred emerging fronds.

✓ **Cabbage** or **sabal palm,** *Sabal palmetto.* The state tree. Fronds are costapalmate; that is, they are rounded like palmate fronds but have an arching extension of the stem down the middle and fold to either side. The trunks are often left with old leaf stems clinging to them (these are called boots), and in the wild ferns germinate and grow in these tight spaces. A champion survivor of hurricanes, it is a drought-tolerant palm of medium stature, rugged, round headed, and square shouldered.

✓ ***Sabal miamienses.*** A species identified only within the last decade, this sabal is indigenous to a restricted area from Martin County south. Fairchild Tropical Garden is cultivating and propagating it.

✓ ***Sabal minor*** and ***Sabal etonia*** are trunkless species or rarely taller than a few feet if the stems arch up. *Sabal minor* is called the dwarf palmetto; *Sabal etonia* is the corkscrew or scrub palmetto.

✓ **Saw palmetto,** *Serenoa repens.* As much a part of Florida as the beach and mosquitoes. A prostrate, hairy stem allows it to grow along the ground and survive the periodic fires of the pine ecosystem. In shade, the stem will head up as if looking around. In Palm Beach and Martin counties, palmate fronds have a bluish cast.

✓ **Key thatch,** *Thrinax morrisii.* Also called brittle thatch. Circular fronds are somewhat silvery underneath. A small but sturdy palm, good for entrance gardens.

✓ **Florida thatch palm,** *Thrinax radiata.* A good grower, with palmate leaves and a nubby hastula, that point at which the blade emerges from the stem, in this case shaped like an "outie" belly-button. The fronds are large, bending at the ends, and the trunk slender. Fruits ripen white.

COMMON LANDSCAPE PALMS

There are so many palms from which to choose that a complete list would be impractical. In addition to the natives listed previously, these are some of my favorites that I grow or know to be available. The spring and fall palm sales held by the South Florida chapter of the International Palm Society, as well as Ramble, the annual two-day fund-raiser at Fairchild Tropical Garden, are two good sources for new and unusual palms.

✓ **Aiphanes,** *Aiphanes* species. Rainforest palms that are studded with sharp spines on the trunks as well as undersides of the leaves. *Aiphanes erosa* has pinnate fronds that look as if they were scissored bluntly on the ends. *A. caryotifolia* has wedge-shaped leaflets on its arching fronds that also are spiny on the stalks. Both of these are extremely attractive but difficult to work with because of the hypodermic-like spines.

✓ **Bismarck palm,** *Bismarckia nobilis.* Enormous fronds are blue-green to light gray. An impressive palm that deserves a place of honor in the garden. From Madagascar, the palm does well in South Florida. Dioecious. Leaf stems are covered with woolly wax that may help the big leaves slip up and out of the growing point.

✓ *Chamaedorea* species. In the understory of Central American rain forests, tiny palms thrive in the low light. These chamaedoreas sometimes have splayed fronds—that is, they are pinnate but don't separate into leaflets, such as *Chamaedorea ernesti-augusti* or *C. metallica.* They often have bright orange flower and fruit stalks with black berries for an ornamental touch in the shadowy subcanopy. *Chamaedorea elegans* 'Bella' is the reliable parlor palm that's been in cultivation for a hundred years, and it's still hard to beat for a potted plant in a corner. The newer species that have recently been discovered, named, and accounted for are described by California specialist Don Hodel in *Chamaedorea Palms: The Species and Their Cultivation.*

✓ **Cabada palm,** *Chrysalidocarpus cabadae.* Related to the areca palm, this is a taller palm with pinnate fronds that are coarser and tend to twist at the ends so the tips parallel the trunks. The trunks are marked like bamboo, green with white rings. Clumping and fast-growing.

✓ **Areca palm,** *Chrysalidocarpus lutescens.* A full sun, multi-trunked palm that has lovely arching fronds with a yellowish tint. The palms are so overused as to be a cliché in South Florida, but they are fast growing, which explains their demand. Used as a screen, the palms often are planted within a couple of feet of each other—far too close. With age, the clumps can be large and tall.

✓ **Old man palm,** *Coccothrinax crinita.* West Indian in origin, the old man has thick, light brown thatch on its trunk, as if the trunk were bearded. Responds well to regular fertilizer, water, and mulch. The round, stiff fronds are retained for many years.

✓ **Coconut palm,** *Cocos nucifera.* A nineteenth century shipwreck supposedly dumped thousands of coconuts on the beaches of Palm Beach, where they took root. This most useful of palms has been transported, either by man or by floating nuts, across the tropical oceans and around the world. In Florida, the lethal yellowing disease destroyed most of the graceful Jamaican tall varieties in the 1970s, although a handful escaped destruction. Nowadays, Maypan coconuts that are resistant to the disease are being used instead. The lethal yellowing disease still is present in South Florida, however, and coconuts as well as many other palms occasionally can be seen with characteristic flagging, yellow fronds.

Cocos means "monkey" in Portuguese and refers to the monkeylike face on the nut. The palm probably originated in the Pacific or Indian Ocean islands. Quite tall, coconuts are heavy-headed with long fronds. They take up more space than you think, so allow room.

Severe cold damages the fronds, and even if they do not fall off immediately after a freeze, they will drop several weeks later because of weakened crowns.

New varieties take more care than Jamaican talls, and often have a yellow, hungry look to them. Golden Malayan, particularly, can quickly become undernourished. Do not use a string trimmer around the base of this or any other palm, as the plastic line eats into the trunk and cuts off newly developing roots, making the palms prone to toppling over and creating entry opportunities for disease.

✓ **Bailey palm,** *Copernicia baileyana.* Slow-growing, massive palm with a thick gray trunk and big, stiff, round leaves in a full crown. The backs of the leaf stalks are colored in yellow and green stripes, and the edges are armed with wicked, skin-ripping spines. Regal in all aspects, this is a stunning palm.

✓ **Hurricane** or **princess palm,** *Dictyosperma album.* New leaves are pinkish, and leaflets of the pinnate fronds are often held together by long reins of tissue on the edges. The fronds arch up quite high while older fronds droop and twist, so the overall effect is like water sprayed from a fountain. Beneath each leaflet's midrib, there's a thin but broken line of woolly fuzz. When flowers form, the crown shafts swell considerably.

✓ **Kentia palm,** *Howea fosterana.* Deep woodsy green pinnate fronds that arch perfectly in planters are a characteristic that has made this a premier interior palm. It can grow well outside in shade. It takes cold well.

✓ **Bottle palm,** *Hyophorbe lagenicaulis.* A swollen, Coke-bottle shape gives this distinctive palm its common name. Thick, pinnate fronds are held in a rainbow arc, and the long-necked crowns are smooth green over a gray base. Prone to potassium deficiency that causes older fronds to become flecked with orange. May require special care, including spring and fall applications of potassium sulfate and magnesium as well as use of special palm fertilizer.

✓ **Spindle palm,** *Hyophorbe verschaffeltii.* Some orange is in this palm on the leaf stem, called the rachis. Individual leaflets tend to come out in different planes. A swollen section in the trunk accounts for the name.

✓ **Red latan palm,** *Latania lontaroides,* **Blue latan palm,** *L. loddigesii,* and **yellow latan palm,** *L. verscheffeltii.* The red latan palm has juvenile leaves and leaf stems edged in red. The blue latan has leaf edges and leaf stems edged in blue; the yellow has these same areas colored yellow. When young, they may be confused with bismarck palms; when older, the trunks are taller and more slender and leaves less stout. Wonderful palms for a dignified, solitary landscape statement.

✓ **Chinese fan palm,** *Livistona chinensis.* Easy-care palms that are attractive and grow relatively fast. The stalks are edged in thorns, so working with them can be tricky. Handsome, palmate fronds have splits in the tips and ends that droop.

✓ **Triangle palm,** *Neodypsis decaryi.* When the fronds emerge from the central growing point, they are magically moved to one of three points, forming a triangle around the axis of the trunk. They emerge with fuzzy wool on them, and the crown is nicely colored in chartreuse, yellow, gray, and tan. They like fertilizer and water; they may struggle in limestone.

✓ **Canary Island date palm,** *Phoenix canariensis.* Huge, solid trunked and genuinely splendid, but susceptible to lethal yellowing and ganoderma butt rot. While many of the wonderful old specimens were lost in the 1970s and 1980s, these are once again being planted. Care must be taken with this and other arid-growing palms not to overwater or reduce air flow around the trunk.

Phoenix dactylifera, the fruiting date palm of the desert, will grow well in South Florida but won't produce edible fruit because of the humid and rainy conditions. Dactylifera and other date palms will hybridize, and these can be difficult to tell apart.

Chinese fan palms, *Livistona chinensis*, at Fairchild Tropical Garden.

✓ **Pygmy date palm,** *Phoenix roebelenii.* Slight of stature but substantial, this palm withstood much buffeting in Hurricane Andrew and held onto its turf and fronds with determination. Like all phoenix palms, the feathery fronds taper toward the base into sharp spines. The trunk is knobby from old leaf stems, and quite often curved. A good palm for restricted spaces, it's drought tolerant, too.

✓ **Solitaire palm,** *Ptychosperma elegans.* For sun or shade, with proportions that make it useful in small yards. The trunk is straight and green (turning gray with age) with regular leaf scars, and the fronds are nicely proportioned with neatly trimmed ends. Fast growing. Fruits are small and red; they germinate freely.

✓ **Lady palm,** *Rhapis excelsa.* From southern China, the fronds are more like fingers than palms, since the segments are fat and deeply veined. Trunks are slender, with black fibers. An attractive palm for screens or even as a tall hedge, the lady palms (there are many species, including dwarf and variegated ones) are often used for indoor potted plants since they hold up well in low light. They sucker to form clumps.

✓ **Queen palm,** *Syagrus romanoffzianum.* Vastly over-used in the South Florida landscape, where it is ill-suited to the high pH soil, the queen palm nonetheless can be a glorious specimen if treated right. Its pliable leaflets come out from the central rachis at about 45 degrees, so from a distance the resulting full crown appears to be in soft focus. Untended, the fronds shrink in size and vigor. Without regular applications of fertilizer and supplemental manganese, they often become distorted, developing what's called "frizzle top" and eventually starve to death. Other Syagrus relatives include the *S. coronata*, a beautifully crowned palm, and *S. amara* from the West Indies.

✓ **Veitchia** species. Veitchias are slender, quite tall palms that are extremely fast growing. They are hard to tell apart; Alan Meerow, author of *Betrock's Palms for the Landscape*, does so by the way the fronds are held at angle above or below the horizon line. So does George Stevenson in *Palms of South Florida*. Here is the key: *Veitchia winnin*, lower leaves below horizontal; *V. montgomeryana*, lower leaves at horizontal; *V. joannis*, below horizontal and fruits three times, the size of *V. winnin*; *V. mcdanielsii*, above horizontal. All are susceptible to lethal yellowing disease. The Christmas palm, *Veitchia merrillii*, is the shortest and most suited of the Veitchias to the small or average landscape, but it is the most susceptible to disease. However, there are some Christmas palms in the landscape that have escaped lethal yellowing disease.

✓ **Foxtail,** *Wodyetia bifurcata*. An Australian palm with fronds that fluff out around the rachis, this is a fast-growing and cold-tolerant palm. The trunks are gray and ringed. The crown looks like a starburst of green from a distance.

Many other palms are suitable to outdoor use, and are becoming more available through the annual sales of the South Florida Palm Society.

PALM CARE

Research into the care and feeding of palms done at the University of Florida's Agriculture Research and Education Center in Fort Lauderdale has increased wide appreciation of palm needs in a subtropical setting. A significant recent finding is the effect of potassium deficiency on many palms, a deficiency that is widespread on sandy and rocky soils. Orange and yellow flecking and discoloration of older leaves were once thought to be simply senescence, but now are known to be symptoms of a lack of potassium.

These research efforts are supported by the International Palm Society, which was founded in South Florida.

Discoloration of leaves reveals micronutrient deficiencies ranging from manganese to iron shortages, just as it does in trees and shrubs. But because palms are slower growers, it often takes longer to correct these inadequacies. Fertilizers have been—and continue to be—developed for South Florida's conditions. The latest University of Florida recommendation is to use a 12-4-12-4 fertilizer with micronutrients several times a year. The nitrogen and potassium (the 12s) are in balance because it has been found that they both leach from porous soils at about the same rates. In addition, they are supplied in slow-release form in this "palm special" (formulated especially for palm needs). An extra heft of magnesium is added, along with vital minerals needed in lesser amounts. A fertilizer with a 10-5-10 balance of macronutrients also may be used.

Fertilize three to four times a year: in February/March, June, September, and November. If you fertilize only twice, do so in the spring and fall. The fall application is important to bring palms through possible cold. Palm metabolism slows considerably during cool winter months, and some of the fall application of fertilizer may still be around and unused, ready for uptake in early spring; the spring application will supply minerals for the nudging out of new foliage.

The amount recommended is three pounds for a small palm, such as a thrinax or coccothrinax, broadcast around the palm under the canopy; five pounds for a medium to large palm, such as a grown queen palm; and eight pounds per palm for large palms, such as coconuts, royals, and Bismarcks.

Palms in the ground longer than two years are fertilized twice a year at Fairchild Tropical Garden, Miami's botanical garden that specializes in palms and cycads.

Lethal yellowing, the disease of palms that killed most of South Florida's lovely Jamaica tall coconuts as well as many other popular palms, still is present in the region. There is no known cure, and even treating with antibiotics only delays death.

Palms highly susceptible to LY include: *Cocos nucifera*, except for resistant varieties now being released, such as the Maypan; *Arenga engleri*, *Corypha elata*, *Pritchardia* (this Pacific palm is

Cycas revoluta, ancient plants from the age of the dinosaurs, are included in this palm garden.

being widely planted once more in Key West, where LY seems to be in remission), and *Veitchia merrillii*.

Other susceptible palms include *Borassus flabellifer*, *Caryota mitis*, *Caryota rumphiana*, *Caryota urena*, *Chrisalidocarpus cabadae*, *Dictyosperma album*, *Hyophorbe verschaffeltii*, *Latania* species, *Livistona chinensis* and *L. rotundifolia*, *Nannorrhops ritchiana*, *Phoenix canariensis*, *Phoenix dactylifera* and *Phoenix reclinata*, *Syagrus schizophylla*, *Trachycarpus fortunei*, and *Veitchia montgomeryana*.

A palm considered susceptible to LY may not get the disease.

The same is true of palms susceptible to other palm diseases, such as leaf-spotting diseases and bud rot. Copper-based fungicides and mancozeb are often used against fungal diseases.

There is no known cure for *Ganoderma zonatum*, or butt rot. This fungus occurs in mature palms, often from arid climates. The incidences of the disease have begun to increase in South Florida. The presence of bracket mushrooms, or conchs, at the base of the trunk indicates the organism at work in an advanced stage, as the conch is the fruiting body. Wilting and browning fronds occur as the disease advances.

Keep shrubbery, annuals, and heavy mulch away from the bases of palms susceptible to the disease.

Palms at Fairchild Tropical Garden that have been observed to be susceptible to Ganoderma include:

Acoelorrhaphe wrightii, *Acrocromia aculeata*, *Arenga tremula*, *Attalca* species, *Bactris major*, *Brahea brandegeei*, *Brahea dulcis*, *Chamaerops humilis*, *Chrysalidocarpus cabadae*, *Chrysalidocarpus lutescens*, *Copernicia curtisii*, *Gastrococos crispa*, *Livistona chinensis*, *Nannorrhops ritchiana*, *Phoenix canariensis*, *Phoenix reclinata*, *Phoenix roebelenii*, *Ptychosperma macarthurii*, *Roystonea altissima*, *Roystonea oleraccae*, *Roystonea regia*, *Sabal causiarum*, *Sabal palmetto*, *Scheelea* species, *Serenoa repens*, *Syagrus oleracea*, *Syagrus romanoffzianum*, *Syagrus schizophylla*, and *Washingtonia robusta*.

CYCADS

If birds are descendants of dinosaurs and lizards in their current diminutive forms, the cycads are their evolutionary plant equivalents, having appeared about 250 million years ago. Although flowering plants began nudging cycads into corners in the Cretaceous period, about 100 million years ago, they nonetheless prevailed for a good 150 million years. In virtually every dinosaur exhibit, you'll find a cycad lurking in the fore- or background (you ride through them in EPCOT's dinosaur display) just as surely as you'll see *Archaeopteryx* hung somewhere in the sky.

These ancient plants, in the family Cycadaceae, usually are called living fossils, but in fact, they are evolving like the rest of us. At this time, there are about 150 species in 10 or 11 genera. Thanks to Knut Norstog when he was at Fairchild Tropical Garden's research center, we've caught on to one of their secrets—they are pollinated by weevils and beetles rather than wind. But we also know that they are fast disappearing from the wild as their niches are being destroyed, despite their ancient lineage.

Looking somewhat palmlike, cycads are used as hardy accent plants that require little care. Many have leaves that are extraordinarily tough, without the first hint of being real working parts. When new and unfolding, they are quite supple, even soft, as the leaves are not yet covered with their protective waxy coating.

Cycads have been thrust into the postmodern age with prehistoric survival skills that include cones as bearers of their sexual parts, but the sperm in the pollen actually swims, so they bridge the gap between conifers and primitive ferns. A beetle carries the pollen to the female cone, and the sperm then swims to the egg.

Cycads have two kinds of roots: a tap root and coralloid roots. The latter are shaped like coral, as the name suggests, and grow up instead of down. Inside these "coral heads" are blue-green, nitrogen-fixing algae.

The fronds, or leaves, of cycads grow in a rosette, and are pinnately compound and sometimes armed with menacing spines. *Encephalartos horridus* is aptly named for its gray-green leaves and horrid spines. Fronds are preceded by scale-leaves, or cataphylls, protectively sharp and needlelike. When you notice the central stem of a cycad bulging upward and cataphylls appearing, you know it won't be long before the fronds will flush.

Cones develop annually after the plants mature, and these can be colorful or soft and fuzzy. When female cones develop seeds, they swell and gradually open, often exposing and dropping brilliantly colored seeds—one type of which is dispersed by elephants, which conjures up images of dinosaurs doing the same thing millions of years ago.

For subtropical gardens, cycads of the Caribbean, Florida, and Mexico are best, including species of *Ceratozamia, Dioon, Microcycas,* and *Zamia. Zamia pumila* is native to Florida, and played a large role in pioneer lives. A starch called arrowroot was extracted and processed from the underground stems by early settlers. Arva Parks's *Miami: The Magic City* features a 1915 photo of Mr. and Mrs. A.B. Hurst in the midwinter parade of that year riding a float advertising their starch "for pies, pudding, pastry" made in Little River. The float is decorated with cycad leaves, of course.

The starch industry nearly eliminated the little zamia, and development pushed it onto the endangered species list, but it now is widely grown in nurseries and is even used in mass plantings as a type of ground cover. It is the favored larval food of the threatened Atala butterfly, and can be chewed to bits by the red and yellow caterpillars that then pupate beneath the skeletonized fronds. At Fairchild, which has one of the world's finest collections of cycads, Chuck Hubbuch, the curator of palms and cycads, was faced with a delicate decision when the threatened species threatened to endanger the endangered one. Which to save? He compromised and devised a program of hand-picking some caterpillars, allowing others to feed.

Bailey palms, *Copernica baileyana*, are truly majestic, as seen in this grove at Fairchild Tropical Garden.

Well-drained soil is a requirement for these plants with underground stems. Even for upright-growing cycads, such as the King Sago (*Cycas revoluta*), this is a must. Those in pots should be repotted annually to eliminate compacted soil that results in poor root aeration.

Palm fertilizer with slow-release nitrogen and slow-release potassium is good for cycads, too. If you wish to use it, apply in early March before new leaves appear in spring and summer, and again in October to harden plants for winter because leaf tissue develops over winter.

When you see yellowing new leaves, you're looking at iron deficiency. When you see brown spots on new leaves, it's manganese deficiency. Treat with drenches of iron or manganese sulfate when new leaves are flushing. Liquid Green is one of the commercial products that contains all the minerals needed.

When older leaves begin to yellow, the plant is probably suffering from magnesium deficiency; scatter Epsom salts around the base of the plant and water in as a remedy. A half cup ought to do nicely; a quarter cup if the plant is small.

Plant or transplant in spring, before the new leaves flush (which can be from April to July). Don't wait until the new leaves have appeared; if you damage them, you're stuck with them for a full year. And if you plant from seed (*Zamia furfuracea* is a prolific seed-bearing plant), you may wait from one to nine months for seeds to germinate. These are slow, deliberate plants that have had time on their side.

A variegated agave, *Agave augustifolia* 'marginata,' is among the plants armed with sharp leaf points. It is surrounded by a fragrant *Brunfelsia americana*, whose flowers open purple and fade to white, and yellow flowering kalanchoes.

10

TOUCH, TASTE, AND SMELL IN THE GARDEN

EXPERIENCE THE GARDEN in every way.

If you relish only one reward with but one of your senses, you're missing myriad pleasures and possibilities. As early as the twelfth and thirteenth centuries, non-utilitarian pleasure gardens were being cultivated in England and Europe. These many centuries later, we sometimes forget what the Middle Ages knew, that such gardens are "trewly close to paradys."

Of course, any garden can be a pleasure garden. To appreciate it as such, you simply allow your curiosity to get the better of you: wonder how things touch, taste, and smell; then touch, taste, and smell.

Begin by feeling the breeze play on your cheeks and tousle your hair, telling you the planet is traveling through unforeseen time—and you don't want to miss a minute.

Listen to the natural sounds that fill the air: the insistent high-pitched chirping of crickets, the buzzing and humming of wings, the mournful cooing of doves.

Hear the soft *sushing* of leaves; the ticking pinnae of coconut palms; brittle pods scraping and popping, their brittle seeds pinging on landing. Hear bamboo culms clacking.

Touch the garden, the parts and prickles—the sandpaper leaves of *Guettarda, Cordia*; the satiny surface of *Musa* and her large-leaved large clan. Feel on your cheek or your lips the velvety leaves of costus, ginger, satinleaf trees. Run your hand over the hemplike textures of thrinax palm thatching.

Smell the mustiness and fustiness as well as the perfume. Sniff the musk of the stoppers, the licorice of liverworts, the spiciness of lemon grass, allspice, garlic vine, bay. Wake up one midwinter morning and know, just by the overripe air, that the mangoes are flowering. Learn to recognize summer by the too-sweet albizias, the night-blooming jasmine, hedychium, crinum, redolent roses, and (some think reeking) gardenias.

Taste whatever it is that pleases your palate because subtropical gardens are ready producers of mangoes, citrus, mamey, and more.

Perhaps short-changed in its array of dazzling flowers, the native flora nonetheless holds some remarkable surprises.

Sea-grapes make a jelly that once was the all-purpose souvenir of Florida, sweet bottled amber captured in apple-sized jars. The fruit of wax myrtle makes bayberry candles. Soapberry makes lather.

White indigo berry of the pinelands and hammocks once was called blackberry jam fruit. Guess why. The fruit of the fiddlewood may remind you of raisins. The terpene-rich myrtles enliven the hammocks with fragrance of skunk and menthol. The foreign aromas of melaleuca, guava, eucalyptus, and bay rum are from the same family.

The pines give us rich-smelling resins distilled into rosin and turpentine. The rest of the pinelands residents—the rough velvet-seed, pinelands lantana, and varnish leaf—bear rough-textured leaves meant for survival. They call out to be touched.

More things are edible than eatable in our woods, such as the pond apple and cocoplum fruit. In the Fakahatchee Strand, that wonderful deep trough in the Big Cypress Swamp, naturalized citrus are reminders that humans once lived here and prized their grapefruit even among the mosquitoes and the cottonmouth snakes.

When planning a garden with touchable, smellable, tastable parts, remember to select from among the plants best suited to your soil, elevation, and exposure, and to place these within reach—along a pathway or edging the patio.

Fruit trees may drop their bounty at whim, so plant them where the harvest, no matter how succulent, won't make a mess. Herbs give off great clouds of fragrance when you sprinkle them with a hose; put them in a rich, well-draining bed in a lightly shaded spot near the kitchen for convenience and olfactory pleasure.

Roses in the subtropics need particular care. Plant them in full sun, in the richest of soils in raised beds around which air circulates freely.

FRAGRANT PLANTS

Brugmansia species. Once called *Datura*, the angels' trumpets hang their flowers upside down and let the fragrance spill out. Sun or light shade; poisonous.

Brunfelsia species. The winter bloomers range in color from creamy yellow to purple turning white, with the aroma of cloves. Partial shade. In summer, *B. nitida* will provide episodic flushes of fragrant flowers.

Buddleja species. Butterfly bush. Various colors of flowers on the ends of long, unruly growth. Full sun.

Carissa macrocarpa, natal plum. Spicy fragrance in the star-shaped flowers. Sun.

Cestrum nocturnum. Night-blooming jessamine. Said to bloom during the full moon; this sprawling West Indian plant gives off a heavy perfume. Sun, light shade.

Citrus species. Sweet-smelling white flowers on the various types, from oranges to grapefruit. Full sun, good drainage.

Crinum americanum, C. asiaticum. The swamp lily and tree crinum lily. Moist conditions for the first; dry for the latter.

Gardenia jasminoides. Sweet and perfumy. Full sun; mulch for even soil moisture.

Hedychium coronarium. Butterfly ginger with heavy scent in the white flowers. Good soil moisture.

Hemerocallis species. Day lily. Spring and summer bloomers with a soft lemon scent. Light shade.

Jasminum officinale. White flowers used in perfume.

Lantana species. Herbal fragrance to the leaves when rubbed. Full sun to pine tree shade; will get fungus if too wet.

Lysiloma latisiliqua. Wild tamarind's white staminate flowers are small but fragrant. Full sun, good drainage.

Magnolia virginiana. Sweet bay magnolia has a wonderful spicy fragrance, even if the flowers aren't as showy as the southern magnolia. Moist soil for this swamp plant.

Myrica cerifera. Wax myrtle leaves smell like bay. Takes many conditions.

Nicotiana. Sweet scent in the night-blooming flowers. Use in full sun.

Orchids. From chocolate encyclicas to vanilla-scented cattleyas. See Chapter 8.

Passiflora species. One-day flowers that are fragrant throughout summer. Full sun with trellis or fence for vining.

Pimenta dioica. Allspice. The leathery leaves of this small to medium tree are spicy-smelling, as are as the fruit used for flavoring. Full sun.

Prunus myrtifolia. West Indian cherry. Small tree with leaves that smell of hazelnuts or prussic acid when crushed. Sun.

Stephanotis floribunda. Madagascar jasmine is a common name for this sweet-smelling creamy flower. Sun.

Viburnum odoratissimum. Sweet viburnum is the common name because of sweet-smelling flowers. Sun.

ROSES

No other flower has a more romantic history or more romance associated with it.

Roses evolved in four areas: Europe, America, Asia, and the Middle East. Roses captivated Cleopatra, Marie Antoinette, and even Thomas Jefferson, who ordered his from William Prince's Long Island nursery. The history of the rose increases in complexity, beginning about 150 years ago when the China tea-scented roses were taken to Europe and crossed with once-a-year bloomers to beget hybrid teas.

American roses probably included the swamp rose; the *Rosa nitida*, a deep pink; the prairie rose, also pink; a thornless pink, and some others. They had rich autumn foliage.

In Florida, hybrid roses are widely but laboriously grown. The heat of the southern end of the peninsula quickly depletes the resources of roses, and they tend to be shorter-lived than in the north.

Most roses require a lot of care, but this old-timer, Charlemagne, is content to lounge among the shrubs.

Nematodes, too, take their toll, and so grafted roses are the best survivors. Rootstocks are *Rosa fortuniana* (also called Double White Cherokee or Evergreen Cherokee) for South Florida; *Rosa multiflora* for central and northern Florida; 'Dr. Huey' is a second choice. 'Queen Elizabeth,' 'Big Ben,' and 'Swarthmore' grow well on their own roots here.

Roses, like vegetables, need at least six hours of full sun daily. Morning exposure helps dry dew and avoids fungus, although fungal disease black spot is outrageously prevalent in the southeastern United States. Old roses are disease resistant.

The best location is an open area in the center of the yard that has been built up into a raised bed full of organic matter, composted manure, peat moss, calcinated clay (such as a cat litter without perfumed additives), compost, and coarse sand. Mulching is necessary to help retain soil moisture for water-loving roses and to keep down nematode populations.

Rose experts in South Florida say to plant in September. Give roses three inches of water a week. Organic fertilizer is often recommended, such as a 100 percent organic 6-6-6, although 7-3-7 with extra magnesium works, too. Fertilize every two weeks from October to May, and use a slow-release fertilizer over the summer. Fertilize frequently at half strength to keep plants vigorous. Prune so the center of the plant is open to air circulation to minimize fungus, and when cutting roses for indoors, cut very long stems.

Beetles love white roses, but are present only four to six weeks a year. Rose growers may have to apply fungicides every seven to 10 days in the summer to prevent black spot on hybrid teas. Spider mites may bronze the foliage in dry weather.

The work involved, plus the frequent use of pesticides, eliminates these plants from my garden. The same is true of tomatoes. While I love roses and tomatoes, there are places better suited to growing most of them than our climate.

FRUIT TREES

Citrus, mangoes, avocados, and bananas are foods of the subtropical garden that are not essential crops but purely delicious pluses.

Citrus, *Citrus* species. Grafted citrus (buy 'Cleopatra' rootstock for rocky, alkaline soils; sour orange for sandy soils) give you fruit within three to five years. Ten to 15 years is the wait for seedlings to bear fruit, and the trees are especially thorny. Citrus need full sun and excellent drainage. Plant at the beginning of the rainy season.

Plant a citrus no closer than 15 feet from the house and no closer than 20 feet to another tree. This will allow these small trees ample room to grow. Plant them so the root ball is at the same level in the ground as it was in the pot. Too deep, and you're asking for root or foot rot disease; too high, and the root ball will dry out.

Keep the base of the tree free of weeds and grass; if you want to mulch for aesthetic reasons, do so lightly. There is danger of fungus diseases with citrus. Palm Beach County extension agent Gene Joyner grows citrus with several feet of mulch added yearly, but the mulch is kept away from the trunks so the trees appear to be rising from the centers of bowls.

Water daily for the first week or two after planting, giving your young tree at least five to 10 gallons at each watering. Water every other day for two to four more weeks. Gradually reduce watering to once a week. During the dry season of the young tree's life, water weekly, but once the trees have reached maturity, natural rainfall may be sufficient (except in drought).

Fertilize with a balanced 6-6-6 for the first year, applying a small amount often. Increase the amount of fertilizer but reduce the number of applications as the trees age. In the third year,

Sugar apple is both a delicious tropical fruit and a touchable one.

switch to a citrus fertilizer, 8-2-10-3. The 3 percent is extra magnesium required by citrus and other fruit trees.

Prune out deadwood or shape slightly, but never cut back hard or hatrack.

Sometimes, when citrus are young and growing vigorously, they will produce dry, pulpy fruit. This could be from the vegetative vigor. If your citrus produces fruit the first or second year after planting, you may want to remove the fruit. That way, the tree isn't stressed and can put on more substantial growth, hence more carrying capacity.

Cold snaps can contribute to dry fruit. Rough lemon rootstock also produces dry fruit, as can lack of nutrients. Cool weather, on the other hand, converts carbohydrates to sugars and sweetens citrus. It also will put color in the peel.

The problem of fruit splitting comes from giving the tree too much water (an especially rainy season may do it naturally). Because of the tendency for root rot, you should plant trees where they don't get water from lawn irrigation—this will reduce the splitting fruit problems, too.

Key limes are highly prized fruit in South Florida and the Florida Keys. (Limes and lemons are not as cold tolerant as oranges and grapefruit.) Limes can produce all year, though summer is the peak season. Key limes are so loaded with flavor that a handful will do for a pie. Key limes flourish on much less fertilizer and water than other citrus. Use a half-strength application once or twice a year, and water only in the dry season once the tree is established.

Oranges and grapefruit are associated with the image of Florida. The winter fruit once so prized they were given in Christmas stockings are available by the bushels from trees in the backyard. Tangerines, limes, lemons, grapefruit, calamondins, kumquats . . . you even can find trees with several varieties grafted onto one. Floridians know that oranges do not have to be orange to be mature; they are gassed for the benefit of out-of-staters. Pick them when they taste good, providing you have a good idea of the cultivar you grow and its season of maturity.

Whiteflies and sooty mold are problems on citrus. Whiteflies are sucking insects that feed on plant juices. The honeydew they excrete falls to the leaves below. Gradually, a black mold will grow on the secretions, covering the leaves. By using an insecticidal soap

Haden mango, a luscious fruit of the tropics.
Courtesy of Larry Schokman, The Kampong

on the insects (in their larval or crawler stage) you also can help eliminate the mold.

The orange-dog caterpillar may show up on your citrus. It looks like a large bird dropping that, when threatened or touched, sends up two red horns meant to scare the daylights out of you. Commercial growers hate this creature because of the leaves it consumes. However, it is the larval stage of the giant swallowtail butterfly. Be generous.

Mango, *Mangifera indica.* Tropical to the nth degree, the mango is a succulent, beautiful fruit. The mango tree, which can grow to 50 feet, also is a lovely ornamental with a symmetrical canopy of long, leathery leaves that start out pink, as delicate looking as batwings. Some trees are more upright than others, but generally, they're wider than they are tall. A mature tree will need a fair amount of space, away from paths, because fruit that drops can turn to mush if allowed to remain on the ground or after the squirrels and birds get to them.

For highly alkaline soils, the Turpentine and No. 11 rootstocks are used. After planting, you can mulch around the trees, making sure the mulch is kept a foot or so away from the trunk.

Grafted mangoes will bear in three to five years. Once a tree reaches a good size, the harvest will be more than enough for a family; you'll find yourself carting fruit to work, offering them to neighbors, making pies, chutney, salsa, and ice cream. Eat them as real Floridians do, leaning over the kitchen sink.

As with citrus, the non-bearing trees benefit from a balanced fertilizer (6-6-6 or 10-10-10), while mature, bearing trees do best with 8-3-9-3 or a similar fruit tree fertilizer. In alkaline soils, foliar sprays of micronutrients may be needed, while in acid soils, the micronutrients can be applied as a drench to the ground.

Apply a small amount of fertilizer (beginning with a quarter pound) every couple of months during the first year, increasing to a pound. By the time a tree is a large, mature specimen, between 20 to 35 pounds may be applied annually, split into two, three, or four applications. Make those in February-to-March, June-to-July, and October. My mango produces dependably, though I may fertilize it only every other year. I mulch beneath it instead.

Mango trees flower in the winter to early spring and produce fruit over the summer and into fall, depending on the variety. Commercial fruit varieties are designed to be picked green for shipping; those grown by homeowners usually fall or are picked when the color says ripe, although you can pick them green (when the shoulders have rounded out) and let them ripen in the windowsill. Later in the year, avocados will keep the sills full.

Anthracnose and powdery mildew are both fungus diseases of concern when growing mangoes. The first, which occurs in periods of rain and high humidity, can cause a loss of flowers, twigs, and fruit. However, if the trees have plenty of room, air circulates well through them, and if you plant resistant varieties, you won't have to undertake a spray program. Powdery mildew occurs in the dry season, and sulfur is used against it.

My mango tree is prone to anthracnose, but I don't spray. The tree is large, and reaching all its parts would cover me with chemicals. (The labor-intensive program involves neutral copper alternated with a fungicide applied every three weeks from flowering to the time when fruits are nearly ready to pick.) Furthermore, while the fungus mars the appearance of the fruit, it doesn't do a thing to the quality and flavor unless the fruit sits out too long. Most often, I just have fruit with teardrop-shaped black stains running down the sides until I peel and eat them. After Hurricane Andrew, the crop was almost free of the fungus.

My tree is an Irwin, a variety quite susceptible to the disease. The tree came with the house. Other susceptible varieties are Smith, Haden, Ruby, Fascell, Lippens, Julie, Zill, Sensation, and Palmer. Resistant varieties include Earlygold, Saigon and Carrie, Tommy Atkins, Van Dyke, Glenn, and Keitt. My favorite fruit is the Edward, also moderately resistant but not widely grown.

For a number of years, commercial mango growers in Dade County watched their trees suffer a decline in vigor and bearing. Eventually, they found the cause to be nutritional deficiencies in manganese and iron. As with other organisms, stressed, undernourished trees are prone to secondary infections. Keeping your trees in good health is a way to help them fend off attacks from diseases and insects.

Mangoes are related to poison ivy, poisonwood, cashews, and pistachios—all of which can cause skin irritations, rashes, and itching. Sometimes a rash from handling mango fruit can be avoided by wearing rubber gloves to skin the fruit. Sometimes it takes a number of years to develop a reaction to the oil in the skin of the fruit.

For an excellent reference, see *Mangos: A Guide to Mangos in Florida*, Richard Campbell, coordinating editor, published by Fairchild Tropical Garden.

Avocado, *Persea americana*. Avocado trees range from medium to large (40 to 60 feet) with brittle limbs that can be broken in storms. The fruit on those grown in Florida, the Guatemalan and West Indian types and their hybrids, are large with bright green and bumpy skins, and once were called alligator pears. The flesh is light yellow, with smooth pulp. A third race from Mexico is small and black-skinned, with a much higher oil content. These avocados are grown and marketed chiefly in California.

Avocados generally are said to bear large crops every other year, but that really depends on the variety. You can allow fruit to stay on the trees for a long time—convenient storage if ever there was any.

Avocados flower and put out new leaves at the same time. Flowers do a tricky thing: they open first as female, close, and then open as male flowers. The stigmas may or may not be receptive when the second opening occurs. And there are two types: A, which has flowers that open in the morning of the first day, stigma receptive, closes and opens in the afternoon the second day, when pollen is shed and the stigma may or may not be receptive; B opens in the afternoon of the first day, with stigma receptive, closes, then opens again the morning of the next day, when pollen is shed and the stigmas may or may not be receptive. So for cross-pollination, A and B types are recommended. However, self-pollination from wind and neighborhood trees ordinarily means that homeowners don't have to worry about planting A and B.

A University of Florida fact sheet, "The Avocado," lists 31 varieties and their flower types. Among the more commonly grown varieties, A types include Donnie, Dupuis, Simmonds, Nadir, Russell, Waldin, Choquette, Lula, and Brooks-late. The B types include Hardee, Pollock, Booth-8, Booth-7, and Hall.

Avocados will come down with root rot in flooding or badly drained soils, so locate your tree carefully. Once the trees are established, watering in the dry season helps growth and fruit set. Thrips and mites often attack avocados, with leaves becoming discolored. This usually occurs in winter before the leaves are shed prior to development of flowers and new growth, so it's best not to do any spraying. A variety of fungal diseases can affect the trees and fruit in summer, but are usually not serious for the home grower. In alkaline soils, these trees may benefit from an annual drench of iron.

Keeping the tree pruned properly is of more concern. In Hurricane Andrew, overgrown, long-limbed avocados were badly torn apart.

Avocados, by the way, are related to the South Florida native called red bay, *Persea borbonia*, which has small, black-skinned, one-seeded fruit in the late summer. It grows in the wetter hammocks of the Everglades.

Banana, *Musa* species. Bananas are not trees, but large herbaceous plants that grow on underground stems. What you call the trunk is really a tightly packed whorl of leaves.

Marie Neal, author of *In Gardens of Hawaii*, tells the story that once all bananas held their fruit erect until the mountain bananas defeated the lowland bananas in battle. Ever since, the lowland bananas have hung their heads in shame.

Probably the oldest domesticated fruit, the banana we eat today may have come from Southeast Asia. Parentage may include the related *Musa acuminata* from lowland Malaysia and *Musa balbisana* from higher latitudes, although DNA testing is under way to pin the parents down. The plant was carried into Indochina, Burma, and Thailand. *Musa paradisiaca* from Thailand was mentioned by Mohammed in the Koran, and, according to Charles Pickering's *Chronological History of Plants* (1879), they were seen growing in Alexandria in 1520. From Egypt, they were taken to the Canary Islands; Europeans took them to the West Indies, then to Central and South America.

Bananas were first imported to our country in 1804. By 1857, William Bliss began a banana importing business, bringing bananas to Boston from Baracoa, Cuba.

The fruit we prefer are sterile. Those tiny black dots in the centers are reminders that seeds once lived there. The edible bananas are propagated vegetatively from their underground stems. Most often, at fruit tree sales, bananas are sold as leafless corms the size of baseball bats. New green leaves will emerge from the center. Once planted and thriving, new plants sucker from the base.

Bananas take full sun, plenty of fertilizer and water, and protection against wind and cold. A southern exposure is ideal. Bananas frozen to the ground will come back from underground corms.

Bananas are giant herbs, not trees. They need a lot of fertilizer and water to thrive, so should be kept in just a single area of a garden.

Bill Lessard, a banana expert in South Florida who grows 50 kinds of bananas, recommends the Grannain (a type of dwarf Cavendish), Mysore, and Rajapuri as well-suited for home yards and for resistance to nematodes, insects, and diseases except sigatoka. While mulching heavily can help reduce some nematode populations, one type won't be deterred by mulch. Nematodes attack roots and interfere with the uptake of water and nutrients, so bananas go into decline. There are chemical treatments, but most require applicators to be licensed.

Panama disease is devastating to bananas, and the small-fruited apple banana, so popular in South Florida for many years, was all but eliminated by this fungus. Lessard, in *The Complete Book of Bananas* (1992), describes the symptoms as occurring first as a blackened area on the stem near the ground. The disease spreads upward and the whole plant yellows and dies.

Bananas require a lot of fertilizer or composted manure. The flagging and scantiness of leaves can often be traced to a lack of nutrients. Young plants need a balanced fertilizer the first few months. Then, because the fruit contain so much potassium, that element is needed in the greatest amount by the plant. A 3-1-6 ratio is a long-recommended analysis. Lessard likes a 3-1-9 ratio, but even a fruit tree fertilizer will work.

Begin with a pound of fertilizer every two months, working up to five or six pounds when the plant begins to flower and fruit 10 to 15 months later. A one-pound coffee can holds two pounds of granular fertilizer.

Once a year, spray your bananas with a foliar spray containing the micronutrients manganese and zinc. If bananas are not sufficiently fertilized, their large leaves can flag, discolor, yellow, and die. Copper can be included in the mix to prevent fungus. Copper is helpful against airborne sigatoka disease that causes yellowing and dead areas on the leaves. And while at least one fungicide is effective against sigatoka, it is too powerful for homeowner use.

A bunch of bananas is the whole stem of fruit; a hand is an individual cluster; an individual fruit is a finger. Bananas are ready to harvest when the edges on the fingers begin to round out.

After harvest, remove the main stalk of the banana and limit the number of suckers coming up around it to three or four. Be careful when working with bananas, as the sap stains clothing and stains cannot be removed.

In Thailand, where banana leaves are used as food wrappers and the flowers are eaten raw or as a cooked vegetable, there is a superstition against planting the type called Banana with a Hundred Hands, says Pimsai Amranand in *Gardening in Bangkok*, because this especially prolific plant has a spirit living in it.

Assorted tropical fruit that may be found in increasing numbers in the subtropics include annonas, carambolas, mamey sapote, lychees, jaboticaba, and passion fruit. Treat them much like other fruit trees, making sure they are placed to get full sun and good drainage, apply balanced fertilized when they're young, and a fruit tree fertilizer (8-2-10-3) when they begin to bear. Here's a quick sketch of these fruits.

Sugar apple, custard apple, and **atemoya**; *Annona* species. Small trees from the West Indies and Central America. To about 20 feet. These are aggregate fruits, rather wonderfully ferocious looking with raised warty bumps on the atemoya that smooth out somewhat in the sugar apple. The flesh is custard-like, with flavors varying in different types. Soursop is the most cold sensitive of the annonas. Sugar apple is sweetest and used for ice cream, milkshakes, and mousse. Atemoya keeps longer on the tree and is resistant to the chalcid fly that lays eggs in annona fruits. After the larvae disappear, a disease can enter the holes and mummify the fruit. The chalcid fly is the main pest and worry with these tropical fruits. Keep the fallen fruit off the ground and dispose of them before they can attract disease. Ambrosia beetles bore into young stems; prune off deadwood.

Carambola or **star fruit**; *Averrhoa carambola*. Now commercially grown in South Florida, the carambola is another Malayan or Southeast Asian fruit, called *kurmurunga* in Sanskrit. There are tart and sweet varieties, as well as one called the Arkin that blends both. The sweet include MaHa, Fwang Tung, and Thai Knight (for Robert Knight, Jr., the Miami scientist who collected it in Southeast Asia). Tart cultivars are Star King, Golden Star, Newcomb, Thayer, and Younghans.

Called star fruit because slices are star-shaped, carambolas can be used to float on punch, decorate salads, make into wine, and for a variety of sauces.

The trees bear when quite young and over a long period, from June through January. Branches are weeping, with compound leaves and small leaflets. The waxy fruit are borne on the inside of the canopy. Thin the canopy somewhat to allow light in and encourage ripening. Provide cold protection. Some varieties need cross-pollination: Arkin and Star King are best grown together for that reason.

Jaboticaba, *Myrciaria jaboticaba*. Native to southern Brazil, the jaboticaba stays a small tree in South Florida (but not in Brazil) and produces grapelike fruit on the branches and multiple trunks. Jaboticaba is a pretty tree, notorious for a long period of juvenility. Fruit growers have found it takes anywhere from 10 to 20 or more years before the trees bear.

Wine and jelly makers use the fruit like grapes. The trees are small and make pretty patio specimens. Regular irrigation and mulch are important. Water faithfully during the dry season and when the tree is young, and use an annual iron drench on rocky soil.

Lychee, *Litchi chinensis*. A beautifully symmetrical tree with long, shiny, and compound leaves, the lychee originated in southern China. It grows to about 40 feet, with fruit that are a staple of Chinese cooking. The fruit has become popular in the last few years in the United States. Fruit is contained in bumpy, red-skinned shells that hang in clusters like jewels, ripening from May to early July, or when they deign to appear.

Trees like cool months prior to flowering (February and March) and hot, humid weather thereafter for abundant fruit production. Warm winters often upset the lychee cart, resulting in scant supply.

University of Florida fruit experts say the trees like an abundance of water; they do best in acidic sands, but will grow on rocky soils if minor nutrients are supplied. In sandy soils, they require a couple of applications of fertilizer every year; in rocky soils, up to four applications. When, in 1974, Wilson Popenoe wrote the introduction to the reprint of his famous book, *Manual of Tropical and Subtropical Fruits,* he noted that Hawaiians believed lychees "had best be considered a beautiful ornamental tree for the dooryard, which every once in a while produces a fine crop of beautiful and delicious fruit."

Mamey sapote, *Calocarpum sapote.* With a pink to reddish flesh inside a rough, brown skin, mamey sapotes are a delight to cut open. The leaves cluster distinctively at the ends of the twigs; the fruits hang like small footballs, taking up to 18 months to mature, so two crops occur on the trees at once. When in need of water, the leaves droop. Cuban May beetles feed on the leaves; red spider mites can occur in dry weather.

Passion fruit, *Passiflora edulis.* A premier butterfly larval food plant, the passion vine is fed on by a variety of caterpillars, including those of the julia, zebra, and Gulf fritillary. 'Possum Purple' is the best cultivar for nematode resistance and edible fruit; as a rootstock, *P. laurifolia* resists nematodes. You may need two for cross-pollination, planted six to 10 feet apart on a trellis or chain-link fence. Use balanced fertilizer on small plants, and high-potassium (8-4-12) on fruiting plants. Watch for fungus that quickly kills, so don't let the plants become matted.

Passion fruit sorbet is heavenly.

Weather influences when fruit appears, of course, but here are some general guidelines to fruiting. Fruit listed for June generally continue all summer. Avocados appear in July and run through October or November, depending on the variety. Mangoes start maturing in May and continue through July.

June: Pineapple, mamey sapote, Key and Persian lime; calamondin, lychee, Barbados cherry, sapodilla, banana, passion fruit, tamarind.

July: Avocados begin; soursop, longan, figs.

August: Sugar apple, *Monstera deliciosa* (fruit of the aroid), guava.

September: Sea-grape, carambola.

October: Atemoya, kumquat, macadamia.

November-December: Citrus.

January: Papaya, black sapote, governor's plum, mysore raspberry.

February: Custard and star apple, carambola (second big crop of season), loquat.

March: Wax jambu (pink fruit with crisp flesh, mild flavor).

April: Jaboticaba.

May: Mango.

Golden orb weaver, a common spider of the Everglades, is beautiful and perfectly harmless.

11

CREATURE FEATURES

SEEING NATURE at work, says Annie Dillard in *Pilgrim at Tinker Creek*, is a matter of keeping your eyes open. "I'm always on the lookout for antlion traps in sandy soil, monarch pupae near milkweed, skipper larvae in locust leaves. These things are utterly common, and I've not seen one."

Sometimes, I think, it is also a matter of lagging behind, crouching down, and searching out. Sometimes it's blind luck. But mostly, these days, it is a gift.

In nearly a quarter of a century of living in South Florida, I have seen a long list of wild creatures, from cottonmouths and pygmy rattlesnakes to river otters, black bear, panther, deer, and crocodiles, but not often and not many. A single otter, bear, and panther have made my list. At last count, Florida has some 48 endangered species, more than any state east of the Mississippi, and more than 270 endangered plants, according to the Center for Plant Conservation. More exotic amphibians and reptiles inhabit the state than native ones slithering through the shrubs. Exotic parrots, parakeets, starlings, and mynahs compete with the cardinals and doves and the other homebodies. Exotic fish called tilapia compete with bass in the Everglades; Norwegian rats compete with native and benign wood rats in the Keys.

Yet the greatest threat is from expanding urbanization that has imperiled the existence of such lowly creatures as frogs and turtles, lizards and skinks.

When little ringneck snakes emerge from shrub planters and Everglades racers drape themselves over the ligustrum twigs, I feel privileged to have their company. Before the ferns grew thick and the palms grew up, I purposely left stacks of dead branches piled here and there around the edges of the yard so snakes could find shelter.

Not that we don't have urban fauna. We do. As neighborhood pines die back, pileated woodpeckers occasionally travel through, stopping to pound out grubs and bugs from the old branches. At dusk or dawn, you can catch glimpses of screech owls as they glide noiselessly from pine to pine or from pine to poinciana. Mourning doves like these tall roosts, too, as do the parrots, blue jays, and mynahs.

Cardinals are first to announce the dawn, and mockingbirds spend long summer days on high perches singing incredibly lovely songs. In the spring and fall, the redstarts and black-throated blue warblers and the other migratory and tiny birds flit through the trees and squeak around the birdbath.

While the foxes have managed to cling to a marginal existence in cities and suburbs, they seem only to do so by accident and a hole in the fence, yet opossums and raccoons somehow flourish in the urban chaos.

So it is heartening to watch the increasing popularity of gardens purposely planted with food and shelter for birds, butterflies, snakes, and the like.

Butterfly gardens and native plants will not save the panther, the bobcat, the Everglades mink, or any of the other large creatures of the wild places. Only deliberate conservation efforts aimed at saving big expanses of habitat along with connecting corridors will accomplish that.

What butterfly and native gardens will accomplish is to allow a handful of birds and insects into our world and perhaps get us to open our hearts to those struggling on the margin. They will teach our children how birds, animals, and insects depend on plants, how one creature transforms into another, how beauty emerges from lowly and sometimes undesirable things. They may foster a sense of nurturing and kindness.

BUTTERFLY GARDENS

Native plants, from oaks to Spanish needle, are natural nectar and larval food plants for about 100 different butterflies and skippers in the subtropics. It can come as a surprise when we see the oaks and the coontie, the wild tamarind or the passifloras being eaten by caterpillars. Too often, we forget that these things are cyclical—that the first half of a butterfly's life is spent in caterpillar form, eating everything in sight. To successfully attract butterflies and have them stay in the garden, both nectar flowers and larval food plants are needed, along with a high tolerance for ragged edges.

Because the food web is a complex set of balances and not necessarily a tale of happy endings, birds are likely to find butter-

Zebra longwing butterflies are South Florida's most visible butterflies. They roost from dusk to dawn in protected spots of the garden.

fly gardens attractive, too, as caterpillars can make a fine meal; wasps may parasitize caterpillars and use them for their own larval food; ants can destroy the pupating creatures wrapped in their chrysalises.

In South Florida, trees and shrubs play nearly as big a role as flowers in attracting moths and butterflies. *Guettarda scabra*, velvet seed, is pollinated by a sphinx moth and so attracts this huge insect at night. Firebush and necklace pod, Bahama cassia, cordia and saw palmetto, wild coffee and oaks are butterfly plants, attracting these insects during the day when they fly, warmed by the sun. (Notice that on cold and cloudy days, few butterflies take to the wing; they simply can't fly on days when they aren't sun-charged.)

Biologists are beginning to unravel some of the other plant/insect and plant/animal interactions in the subtropics, just as they are working in tropical rain forests. In Everglades National Park, botanists have found 89 plants, from cocoplums to wild tamarinds, that have little glands called extra-floral nectaries on their leaves or leaf stems. Ants are attracted to these sources of sugar and repel other insects that might eat the leaves or damage their food supply.

Planting a native corner, perimeter, or whole native yard is a good way to watch not only birds, butterflies, and moths, but the complex and fascinating smaller world of insects, snakes, anoles, and frogs.

A PINELAND PLANTING FOR BUTTERFLIES

One approach to butterfly gardening is native gardening. South Miamians Henry and Kathy Block planted a native pineland habitat that has turned out to be a magnet for butterflies, though it was not planted solely for that reason but rather to try and reestablish a small piece of natural Florida.

Exotic trees on the high rock ridge in the front yard were taken out and the stumps ground to the soil level. Then, about 50 small pines and 45 nursery-grown saw palmettos were planted. The young pines were spaced about 10 feet apart to allow the fallen needles to provide a natural mulch.

In addition to the pines, the miniature woods were planted with myrsine, coontie, Bahama cassia, prickly pear, lantana, twinflowers, verbena, and bracken. Also planted were American beautyberry, a shrub that attracts birds as well as butterflies; blue porterweed, a wildflower; silver and sabal palms; white indigo berry, and wax myrtle. Around the edge of the planting that bordered the street, landscape architect Peter Strelkow designed alternating groupings of white indigo berry and wax myrtle. In the wild, white indigo berry is often scraggly and small; in cultivation, it's a handsome shrub. Wax myrtle, which travels across many soils and moisture gradients in Florida, can be full and rangy or pruned and shaped.

Reestablishing a pineland community such as Block's is not duplicating or re-creating an authentic native system. Not enough is known yet to do that, and the pinelands system is a particularly difficult one to mimic on a small urban scale because it is maintained by fire. To keep a pinelands healthy and free of hardwoods, fire or some equivalent such as mowing must periodically sweep through. By clearing and pruning palmettos and shrubs (the necklace pod, for instance, takes a hard pruning in the spring in order to keep it shrubby; lantana needs pruning to keep from getting woody and leggy) the re-created pinelands can look like a native system without being the real McCoy.

In the pinelands, even ersatz urban ones, the opportunity exists to attract myriad butterflies and birds. Sulphurs love nectar from necklace pods, and they use cassias from pinelands for larval food plants. Liatris, porterweed, lantana, and other flowers of the pinelands are used by zebras, sulphurs, Gulf fritillaries, julias, and skippers. Monarchs fly to the orange and yellow milkweeds.

Several years after planting, Block's pineland is struggling to survive. Many of the young pines did well at first, but have begun to yellow and die, while the white indigo berry is seeding itself rampantly. Block believes the pines are having trouble because roots were left in the ground and are decomposing, creating a soil too rich for pines while allowing the indigo berry to do too well.

In a different part of his yard, a group of pines and saw palmettos planted on rocky ground is doing extremely well.

Nonetheless, on a bright afternoon the plantings are brimming with butterflies. Block often takes a caterpillar into the house along with some of the plant on which it is feeding to let his daughters watch the metamorphosis. He has had a malachite swallowtail float through on one occasion and five daggerwings on another, as well as clouded and orange-banded sulphurs. The milkweed and native passiflora have prospered in the unmown areas of the yard. The green shrimp plant, *Blechum brownei*, has gone undisturbed because it is larval food for malachites.

Begun when the understanding of pineland restoration was more primitive than it is today, the first pine planting at Henry Block's house may eventually have half a dozen remaining and healthy pines and a healthy understory. Block has tried burning it, and believes this can be a successful technique in even as small an area as his when conditions are right.

If you do not want to re-create a pinelands, a sunny spot devoted to pentas, firebush, passiflora, parsley, and a citrus tree, surrounded by a hedge, will serve as a small-scale butterfly garden.

Blue and pink porterweed and pentas are fast growing and drought tolerant, and form mounds and drifts of color. Butterflies are attracted to areas of color. Small butterflies generally go to small flowers, and large butterflies to larger ones, but that's not a hard and fast rule.

Find a sunny spot where your butterfly garden can thrive—remember, butterflies need sunshine to fly and feed. You might consider surrounding flowers with larval plants for the butterflies you'd like to attract. Plant them so the flowers will be protected from wind but not shaded out. Locate trees—citrus for swallowtails, strangler fig or short-leaf fig for daggerwing caterpillars, live oak for hairstreaks—on the north with taller shrubs such as hamelia (this can take some shade). Plant shorter plants on the south, so you don't shade out the flowers. Dwarf pentas can provide a middle zone, as they grow two to three feet tall.

Many butterfly plants are weedy, and care is minimal. Spanish needle, green shrimp plant, native passion vine, and porterweed are drought tolerant. Pentas like a little more water than the others, but don't put them near the sprinklers.

Beach sunflowers will not tolerate overwatering or overfertilizing, nor will lantanas or gaillardias. They get fungus from too much water.

Nonetheless, water is important for any kind of wildlife in your garden, even butterflies. Filling a terra cotta saucer with sand and keeping the sand moist is one way to give butterflies a drinking station near the flowers.

Butterfly gardening books are available from paperback to coffee-table types. A particularly handy one has been published by the Florida Native Plant Society called *Butterfly Gardening with Florida's Native Plants*, by Craig Huegel. Cooperative Extension offices carry lists of butterfly plants and butterflies, and Butterfly World in Coconut Creek (see the Gardens to Visit list in the back of this book) is an extraordinary example of what can be done, complete with museum, passion flower pergola, feeding stations, and viewing areas for watching butterflies emerge from their chrysalises. Butterfly gardening classes are offered regularly at Butterfly World.

Wildflowers

Wildflowers are attractive to butterflies. For wet areas, try these subtropical wildflowers and watch to see what shows up.

✓ **Sea oxeye daisy**, *Borrichia frutescens*. Low-lying damp areas behind the dunes are home. Yellow petals and yellow discs with gray-green leaves. Robust once started; to three feet tall.

✓ **Coreopsis**, *Coreopsis leavenworthii*. Sometimes called tickseed. Yellow petals with dark red to brown eye.

✓ **Fleabane**, *Erigeron quercifolius*. Small pink asters found on damp roadsides.

✓ **Blue flag iris**, *Iris virginica*. Naturally occurring at the edge of a prairie and pineland, iris like low-lying areas that stay damp. Not a butterfly flower, but a lovely native.

✓ **Pickerelweed**, *Pontederia cordata*. Purple-blue flowers on long spikes. Found in ponds, ditches, wet areas. Pickerel weed needs to be damp, but not necessarily in the water.

✓ **Arrowhead**, *Sagittaria lancifolia*. White flowers with yellow eyes on long stalks; arrow-shaped leaves. Plant in or at the edge of a pond.

For moist to damp areas, use these wildflowers:

✓ **Brown-eyed susan**, *Rudbeckia hirta*. Golden petals and brown eyes. Roadsides and damp swales.

✓ **Blue-eyed grass**, *Sisyrinchium miamiense*. In the lily family, a perennial that grows in the open, damp prairie.

✓ **Spiderwort**, *Tradescantia ohiensis*. Purple flowers with prominent yellow stamens. Open in the morning.

✓ **Ironweed**, *Vernonia blodgettii*. Same conditions as fleabane. Tiny flowers have beige petals and maroon centers.

For dry areas, here are some wildflowers:

✓ **Dwarf twinflower**, *Dyschoriste oblongifolia* var. *angusta*. Tiny white flowers pop out sequentially up a little stalk.

✓ **Gaillardia**, *Gaillardia pulchella*. Orange petals and a dark eye or yellow petals and a yellow eye. A drought-tolerant sun-lover.

✓ **Man-in-the-ground**, *Ipomoea microdactyla*. Delicate, reddish-pink flowers on this morning glory. On the threatened species list and rarely seen in the woods. It likes to run or climb from an underground tuber.

✓ **Pineland moss rose**, *Portulaca pilosa*. Shrubby, succulent leaves and colorful little flowers that open in the morning.

✓ **Wild petunia**, *Ruellia caroliniensis*. Purple, funnel-shaped flowers. Two forms: a creeping form and an upright one. Upright is a hammock plant that prefers more moisture than the pineland creeper.

✓ **Skullcap**, *Scutellaria havanensis*. Skinny upright plants with tiny purple flowers. A plant of the dry pineland scrub.

✓ **Goldenrod**, *Solidago sempervirens*. Seaside goldenrod. A beachfront plant that grows to about five feet tall.

✓ **Goldenrod**, *Solidago stricta*. From moist pinelands. This species likes some moisture.

✓ **Beach verbena**, *Verbena maritima*. Bluish-purple flowers in clusters on the tips of long branches. It can take beachlike conditions or pineland settings.

These wildflowers take variable conditions:

✓ **Yellowtop**, *Flaveria linearis*. Long, linear leaves and flat heads of bright yellow flowers for dry, sunny areas.

✓ **Blue porterweed**, *Stachytarpheta jamaicensis*. Said to be brought from Jamaica for its medicinal values, this is a pinelands resident. Smaller than the robust exotic sold for butterfly gardens.

For a free poster-brochure, Wildflowers of Florida, write: Division of Plant Industry, P.O. Box 147100, Gainesville, FL 32614-7100, Attn: Wildflower Brochure.

Nectar Plants

Plants that attract butterflies by offering nectar include:
Milkweed, *Asclepias currassavica, A. tuberosa*
Spanish needle, *Bidens alba*
Butterfly bush, *Buddleja officinalis*
Powder-puff, *Calliandra haematocephala*
Cordia, *Cordia globosa*
Golden dewdrop, *Duranta repens*

Gaillardia, *Gaillardia pulchella*
Firebush, *Hamelia* patens
Sunflower, *Helianthus* species
Lantana, *Lantana*
Blazing star, *Liatris* species
Pentas, *Pentas lanceolata*
Brown-eyed susan, *Rudbeckia hirta*
Wild petunia, *Ruellia caroliniensis*
Salvia, *Salvia coccinea*
Goldenrod, *Solidago* species
Necklace pod, *Sophora tomentosa*
Blue porterweed, *Stachytarpheta jamaicensis*
Beach verbena, *Verbena* species
Ironweed, *Vernonia* species

Larval Plants

Larval food plants for butterflies include:
Torchwood, *Amyris elemifera*
Butterfly milkweed, *Asclepias tuberosa*
Climbing aster, *Aster caroliniensis*
Crabwood, *Ateramnus lucidus*
Tarflower, *Befaria racemosa*
Green shrimp plant, *Blechum brownei*
Jamaica caper, *Capparis cynophallophora*
Bahama cassia, *Cassia chapmanii*
Citrus, *Citrus* species
Butterfly pea, *Clitoria mariana*
Cordia, *Cordia globosa*
Rabbit bells, *Crotalaria pumila* and *C. rotundifolia*
Pineland croton, *Croton linearis*
Beggar's tick, *Desmodium* species
Strangler fig, *Ficus aurea*

Short-leaf fig, *Ficus citrifolia*
Pop ash, *Fraxinum caroliniana*
Green ash, *Fraxinum pennsylvanica*
Milk pea, *Galactia* species
Dune sunflower, *Helianthus debilis*
Scarlet hibiscus, *Hibiscus coccineus*
Dwarf lantana, *Lantana ovatifolia*
Pepper grass, *Lepidium* species
Sweet bay magnolia, *Magnolia virginiana*
Wax myrtle, *Myrica cerifera*
Passion vine, *Passiflora* species
Red bay, *Persea borbonia*
Swamp bay, *Persea palustris*
Laurel oak, *Quercus laurifolia*
Southern live oak, *Quercus virginiana*
Blackbead, *Pithecellobium guadalupense*
Cat's claw, *Pithecellobium unguis-cati*
Willow, *Salix caroliniana*
Wire weed, *Sida acuta*
Goldenrod, *Solidago* species
Beach verbena, *Verbena maritima*
Spanish bayonet, *Yucca aloifolia*
Yucca, *Yucca filamentosa*
Coontie, *Zamia pumila* and other zamias
Hercules club, *Zanthoxylum clava-herculis*
Wild lime, *Zanthoxylum fagara*

For an excellent book on butterfly gardens, see *Gardening for Butterflies and Children in South Florida* by Anne Kilmer, printed by *The Palm Beach Post*. Contact the Palm Beach County Cooperative Extension Service or Mounts Botanical Garden, 531 N. Military Trail, West Palm Beach, for information on obtaining a copy.

A NATIVE GARDEN FOR BUTTERFLIES AND BIRDS

A diversity of plantings will draw a diversity of wildlife, especially when designed around the perimeter of your yard.

A Coral Springs garden planted by naturalist Judy Sulser draws blue jays, mourning doves, grackles, cardinals, mockingbirds, red-wing blackbirds, oven birds, brown thrashers, warblers, blue-gray gnatcatchers, downy and red-bellied woodpeckers, and occasionally a red-tailed hawk and kestrels.

Gardener Sulser says the long list of birds tells her she has been successful, even in a suburban setting, and allows her to follow the rhythms of nature despite the impact of man.

There are two bird feeders among the plantings for the seedeaters such as cardinals. But the birds, especially warblers, love the wild tamarind for finding insects (which are attracted to the blossoms), the berries of the wild coffee and *Cordia globosa*, elderberry (a special hit with the mockingbirds), Florida privet, and blue porterweed.

For butterflies, three red bay trees serve as larval food of the palamedes swallowtail (cardinals love this tree, too); citrus and wild lime feed caterpillars of swallowtails; cassias host sulphur butterflies; milkweeds draw the monarchs; parsley feeds caterpillars of black swallowtails; limber caper is for the Florida white butterflies; necklace pod hosts sulphurs; and golden dewdrop attracts a wide variety of butterflies.

Hummingbirds occasionally come to the red/orange tubular flowers of the firebush, *Hamelia patens*, while lizards find cover in the Fakahatchee grass.

Sulser has combined native passion vine, *Passiflora suberosa*, with a coral honeysuckle vine on a mailbox trellis by the front drive. The honeysuckle hides the tattered passiflora after caterpillars have eaten it back to nothing more than a few stringy stems.

A female anhinga, lacking oil in her feathers, dries her wings after diving for a fish. The female has buff neck and head; the male has black neck and head.

All the berries and the shrubs also help feed opossums and raccoons that make a living in the urban environment.

One summer, Dade County naturalist Roger Hammer erected a purple martin house in his South Dade yard and was surprised to have a community of insect-eating bats move in. South Florida doesn't have many naturally occurring bats—only the stray and endangered mastiff bat and a few mosquito-eaters that happen by. So each evening that summer, just at dusk, Hammer's friends gathered in lawn chairs and watched the bats fly out for their night's feed.

Snags, downed logs, and brush piles are other homes for wildlife, but cats and dogs are a deterrent. Frogs and lizards that eat the insects will be dinner for the snakes, owls, and hawks.

FOOD FOR BIRDS

To attract birds to your garden, you can buy wild bird mixes or put out nuts, dried raisins, or even fruit slices. You also can plant a variety of shrubs and trees that have bright or plentiful berries or, like oaks and wild tamarinds, host an abundance of insects that attract birds.

- **Hummingbirds:** nectar in bright, tubular flowers, such as firebush or even some clerodendrums, bottle brush, powder-puff, and floss-silk tree
- **Red-headed woodpeckers:** acorns, berries, insects
- **Yellow-bellied sapsuckers:** running sap, especially from black olive trees
- **Purple martins:** dragonflies, beetles, and other insects
- **Blue jays:** insects, lizards, and rodents
- **Mockingbirds:** berries from dahoon holly, elderberry, cabbage palm
- **Brown thrashers:** insects and fruit
- **Cedar waxwings:** fruit from short-leaf fig, hollies, mulberries
- **Warblers:** insects, small seeds, wax myrtle fruits, lancewood and spicewood fruits
- **Cardinals:** fruits and sunflowers at feeders
- **Indigo** and **painted buntings:** insects, berries, primarily seeds
- **Grackles:** grains
- **Spot-breasted orioles:** tropical fruits, insects

Plants that will bring birds to your yard, compiled by the Broward County Parks and Recreation Department, include:

Trees

- *Bauhinia* x *blakeana*, Hong Kong orchid: hummingbirds
- *Bursera simaruba*, gumbo-limbo: parrots, parakeets, and other fruit-eating birds
- *Chrysophyllum oliviforme*, satin leaf: warblers, cardinals, gnat-catchers
- *Coccoloba diversifolia*, pigeon plum: mockingbirds, catbirds, robins, woodpeckers
- *Cordia sebestina*, Geiger tree: hummingbirds
- *Ficus aurea* and *Ficus citrifolia*, strangler fig and short-leaf fig: mockingbirds, cardinals, blue jays, catbirds, cedar waxwings, and woodpeckers
- *Guapira discolor*, blolly (female): fruit-eating birds
- *Ilex cassine*, dahoon holly (female): cardinals, mockingbirds, cedar waxwings
- *Lysiloma latisiliqua*, wild tamarind: warblers, gnatcatchers, and flycatchers
- *Morus rubra*, mulberry: fruit-eating birds
- *Myrica cerifera*, wax myrtle: fruit-eating birds
- *Nectandra coriaceae*, lancewood: fruit-eating birds, especially veeries and thrushes; good nesting for mockingbirds
- *Pinus elliottii* var. *densa*, slash pine: doves, blue jays, warblers, owls.
- *Quercus virginiana*, live oak: Southern; woodpeckers, vireos, warblers, blue jay, grackles, owls
- *Simaruba glauca*, paradise tree: fruit-eating birds
- *Swietenia mahagoni*, mahogany: nesting for birds

Shrubs

- *Ardisia paniculata*, marlberry: mockingbirds, catbirds, cardinals
- *Byrsonima lucida*, locustberry: mockingbirds
- *Calliandra haemetocephala*, powder-puff: hummingbirds
- *Callicarpa americana*, beautyberry: mockingbirds, cardinals, bulbuls, brown thrasher, catbirds

Marsh rabbits are shy during the day but are easily seen as they eat tender shoots at dawn and dusk.

- *Calyptranthes pallens*, spicewood: fruit-eating birds; good shelter for smaller birds such as warblers, wrens
- *Chrysobalanus icaco*, cocoplum: fruit-eating birds
- *Hamelia patens*, firebush: hummingbirds
- *Hibiscus rosa-sinensis*, hibiscus: spot-breasted and Baltimore orioles, hummingbirds, painted buntings
- *Malpighia glabra*, Barbados cherry: fruit-eating birds

- *Malvaviscus arboreus*, turk's cap: hummingbirds, painted buntings
- *Murraya paniculata*, orange jessamine: mockingbirds, catbirds, cardinals
- *Myrcianthes fragrans*, Simpson stopper: mockingbirds, catbirds, cardinals
- *Psychotria* species, wild coffee: cardinals, bluejays, catbirds
- *Rhus copallina*, southern sumac: catbirds, mockingbirds, cardinals, sparrows
- *Sambucus canadensis*, elderberry: fruit-eating birds
- *Sophora tomentosa*, necklace pod: hummingbirds, warblers
- *Stachytarpheta fruiticosa*, blue porterweed: cardinals, sparrows
- *Tetrazygia bicolor*, tetrazygia or West Indian lilac: mockingbirds, blue jays, and cardinals

Vines

- *Parthenocissus quinquefolia*, Virginia creeper: catbirds, flickers, great-crested flycatchers, mockingbirds, robins, brown thrashers, warblers
- *Pyracantha coccinea*, firethorn: mockingbirds, cardinals, blue jays, catbirds, cedar waxwings, woodpeckers
- *Vitis species,* wild grape: fruit-eating birds

One of the best books available for Florida birdlovers is *Florida's Birds, A Handbook and Reference,* by Herbert W. Kale II and David S. Maehr, illustrated by Karl Karalus. Pineapple Press, 1990, $19.95.

More than a year after planting, a little hammock planted near the protective canopy of a wild tamarind tree has taken hold and grown considerably. It contains firebush, crabwood, satin leaf, gumbo-limbo, blolly, and is edged with wildflowers.

12

RESTORING THE SOUL

THE 10,000-year-old subtropical Everglades ecosystem is just out of the egg in evolutionary terms. The central Florida ridge, on an old dune system once surrounded by prehistoric seas, rises 200 feet down the middle of the peninsula and may be 25 million years old. By comparison, tropical rain forests may have developed 150 million years ago. Even the relatively recent emergence of the Isthmus of Panama connecting the northern and southern continents in the Western Hemisphere occurred two and a half million years ago.

Only in the last 200 years, barely a blink of time's eye, have we altered the planet so dramatically that much of the biological complexity is threatened. The Everglades teeters on survival's precipice; panthers vanish along with wading birds, turtle grass, and the entire complex food web in between.

Remnant habitats are being threatened by exotic plants moving with man around the world, transforming unique landscapes into vistas of sameness.

More than 400 plants are invading Florida, some disturbing whole ecosystems, others just getting a toehold in the ditches. Botanists say that up to 27 percent of what grows in Florida's wild areas comes from foreign shores. The climate in the subtropics is agreeable to many plants out of their home environments, without natural checks of insects or disease. Some biologists fear that a simplified, global system may be developing that will reduce biological diversity to only the strongest weeds—be they animal or plant.

Florida is not unique in experiencing drastic change from human impact. The Midwestern prairie, arid California, and the ancient forests of the Northwest have been changed in this country while around the world deserts grow, rain forests shrink, and even the poles now are compromised. Disappearing with these changes are vast libraries of evolutionary data and whole catalogs of species we haven't named, classified, or screened for medicinal or food use, much less encountered or watched with wonder.

And yet, like a bud beginning to swell, there's a growing concern that we must redress these wrongs. We must choose plants selectively so they don't escape into natural areas. But we must go one step further. We must try to restore the land.

Some of this work has begun. Early stages of the Kissimmee River restoration, for example, have shown that it is possible. River restorations seem generally to be easier than other types, but in the Midwest, prairie restoration is working well. Restoration biology is venturing into sea grass beds, deserts, tropical dry forests, tropical wet forests and, tentatively, into the backyard.

From beyond the garden's limestone wall, the baby hammock seems as insubstantial as the dwarf pentas in front.

It is true that saving parts won't save the whole. Only when we begin to think, plan, and work regionally will we make any difference in saving whole functioning systems. But on our home grounds, we can grow threatened plants of various habitats, ensuring, at least, the survival of some vital genetic information. We may combine it in ways different from those found in nature, but nature is change itself—evolution made flesh and bone, stick and stone, dominant and recessive. We should give it a shot.

How to begin?

Outline what you want to accomplish with your natural garden, just as you would with any landscape project: do you want a visual buffer? Shade? Energy conservation? Butterflies and birds? What kind of soil and hydrology exist in your yard?

Look around the neighborhood for telltale remnants of historical plant communities. Are there old pines left? Ancient oaks? Cypresses?

If you have high or low spots, you will want to measure the drainage in these areas. If you have areas where water stands for days, you can plant wetland plants such as cypress, dahoon holly, and red maple. If you are high and dry, hammock or pineland plants are your best bet.

In re-creating habitat, the hammock community is easiest for

A young hammock planting replaced tropical birds of paradise, pagoda plants, and ferns in this poolside garden near Kendall.

most home gardeners, since pinelands are fire dependent. Many hammock plants tolerate a wide range of soil types. So make a general list, then whittle it down to the plants that can work for your specific needs, such as screening. George Gann-Matzen, habitat restoration specialist in South Florida, says you should consider different growing patterns when you get to this point of planning: a lancewood tree, for instance, tends to keep limbs and leaves quite far down on the trunk, and would make a better screening plant than a paradise tree that has long, lanky limbs with leaves clustered at the ends.

Also, check with local nurseries to find out what plants are available. There are about 50 native plant nurseries throughout Florida (see Chapter 6 for how to write for a directory), and many nurseries carry commonly grown trees and shrubs such as cocoplum, live oak, and mahogany. But some plants may be hard to find, like the infrequently used velvet-leaved coffee *Psychotria sulzneri* or some of the more unusual tropical trees, shrubs, and wildflowers.

Pineland plants are tough survivors when they become established. Dade County pine, *Pinus elliottii* var. *densa*, is slightly different from southern slash pines in that it has a denser bark and a protective cluster of long needles around the growing point. Saw palmetto has an underground or prostrate stem and may lose its

A small house and yard in Homestead appear to blend in perfectly with the non-native neighborhood. . . .

fronds to fire, but quickly resprouts. Coontie, the native cycad, *Zamia pumila*, also has an underground stem and resprouts after fire.

Many pineland shrubs have especially tough leaves to withstand drought: velvet seed, varnish leaf, wax myrtle, pineland lantana.

Hardwood hammocks, on the other hand, are more moisture loving. Hardwoods can invade a pineland and convert it to a hammock within 25 to 50 years. All they need is a moist solution hole. Pioneer plants, such as lysiloma, oak, and poisonwood, which thrive in less humidity than other hardwoods, sprout first. These in turn create microclimates of shade and humidity as they grow, allowing other species to join them.

Pioneer plants, then, are good candidates for starting your hammock. (For a more complete description of these trees, see Chapter 5.)

Lysiloma latisiliqua, the wild tamarind, is a quick grower. Not exceptionally long-lived, it eventually may be shaded out by other, bigger hammock trees, but it serves well initially and lives for many years.

. . . but the backyard has been converted to a native planting with trees from the Keys and mulched paths. Fakahatchee grass in the left foreground covers the septic tank drain field.

Judy Sulser's native garden surrounds her pool in Coral Springs, a development in Western Broward County. Sulser keeps a record of the birds and butterflies attracted to her garden.

Quercus virginiana, the Southern live oak, is a longer-lived pioneer. A grand old oak at the Charles Deering Estate in Dade County is estimated to be 150 to 200 years old and marks an old Indian burial ground.

Bursera simaruba, gumbo-limbo, casts a light shade, is a fast grower, and will quickly build your hammock canopy.

Stoppers are especially useful small trees for subtropical gardens that have limited space. Crabwood, satin leaf, paradise tree, pigeon plum, and wild tamarind are among my favorite trees. They make a beautiful domesticated woods.

Before selecting native trees—or any plants—for your garden, visit natural areas, parks, preserves, and experience the feel of a real Florida setting. Take along a plant identification book, a notebook and a pencil, and make notes on what you like, what you don't like, and what grows where.

BUILDING A HAMMOCK

I have worked with a friend to build a hammock in Coconut Grove. Our planning and planting processes have proceeded in stages; the first phase was selecting and planting the trees (both canopy and understory) and some hedges for privacy the first year. The second year, we added wildflowers—they will eventually be shaded out but we enjoy them in the meantime. In time, we'll add the ferns and subshrubs.

First, we drove to several parks and natural areas in South Florida to look at the kinds of plants my friend wanted to include. We made lists. We noted where things grew in these hammocks: what grew in the interior and what was on the edge, how big or small they grew in a natural setting.

We spent a day measuring the distance between trees at the Vizcaya hammock, near my friend's home. The trees there are slender-trunked and quite close together, growing in the same rocky conditions we faced.

Next, we looked at nurseries to compare these plants in cultivation. Wild coffee grows in the interior of the hammock; in those shady conditions, is a slender plant. It also likes the edges, where it's fuller and more robust looking. We wanted to plant a coffee hedge, and we knew it would do best with light shade instead of sun. We transplanted some scraggly coffees beneath the wild tamarind and added some nursery-bought plants. Within a year, the hedge looked like a hedge. One recalcitrant shrub eventually took after Hurricane Andrew shook it.

Next, we examined our list, and determined whether certain trees were cold or wind sensitive. The paradise tree, which we wanted to use, can be damaged in wind, so we decided to put it in the center of our miniature forest. The crabwood and blolly are of small stature but serviceable and nice, so we located them in a spot where they would serve rather than show off. The satin leaf, on the other hand, has such beautiful foliage we wanted it to be seen. So it grows on the edge of the hammock.

A Jamaica caper has found a spot all to itself to be shown off as a specimen because of its beautiful shape, flowers, and the silvery undersides of the leaves. A blackbead, a small tree or shrub that is from the southernmost mainland and Florida Keys as well as the Bahamas, has been included in the understory for conversation's sake: the seed pods on this legume crack open and black, bead-like seeds dangle from long, coiled, pink-to-reddish arils.

The entire yard is not given over to natives; other areas beneath several large oaks are being planted with palms, tree ferns, aroids, heliconias, calatheas, coleus, and other tropicals. An herb garden gets filtered oak-tree light just outside the kitchen, where it is handy for cooking. The oak's protection has allowed some herbs to survive the hot and humid summers.

Two years after we put many of the trees in the ground, they tripled in size. After the trees grow substantially enough to prune the bottom limbs, the hammock will be ready for understory plants and shrubs. Not so long a time to wait for your very own forest.

A KEYS HAMMOCK

Thelma Thomas's small garden in Homestead, designed by Peter Strelkow, illustrates the wonderful naturalistic effect that can be achieved within a restricted space using West Indian trees of smaller stature from the southern mainland and Florida Keys.

The garden was not an attempt to re-create a hammock, but instead to evoke a woodsy feeling in a suburban setting.

Measuring only 75 by 130 feet, the back half of the Thomas lot was designed to utilize mostly native plants while retaining bromeliads and pentas to attract butterflies. The Strelkow design was an appealing one, with mulched pathways running through paradise, black ironwood, West Indian cherry, and satin leaf trees. Wild coffee, West Indian lilac, and white and Spanish stoppers served as hedges or walls for the forest room, buffering a streetside fence and wrapping the little woodland inside.

A governor's plum tree was allowed to remain; beneath it Mrs. Thomas's bromeliad collection grew in filtered light. That tree was toppled by Hurricane Andrew, but the small trees were not badly injured, even though Homestead took the brunt of the storm.

A simulated hammock, citified, if you will, is appropriate for an urban/suburban setting because it is controlled and can be made to blend in with the neighborhood. Nonetheless, it makes berries and flowers available for wildlife, reduces care to a minimum, and, most important, provides a sense of place.

A PINELAND AND A HAMMOCK

Linda and Roger Blackburn, living in a suburban area of Miami on half an acre, were fighting a losing battle to keep alive their Dade County pines, even using nutrient injections. George Gann-Matzen, ecological restoration specialist, suggested they work with their yard as a system rather than piecemeal, and here's what they did.

They cleared birds-of-paradise, exotic ferns, and other tropicals from their front yard, exposing the long-neglected saw palmettos and pines. They planted a few pine saplings and waited to see what would reestablish itself.

Ground cherry, pineland croton, coontie, gopher apple, and three-seeded mercury, all pineland natives, appeared. But the initial spurt ceased once the remaining fertilizer in the soil was used up, so Gann-Matzen added additional pineland denizens to increase diversity.

Around the backyard swimming pool, a narrow strip of land was planted with hammock trees and shrubs to quickly buffer a two-story house. Gumbo-limbo, satinleaf, pigeon plum, myrsine, and other hammock plants were used.

All of the mature pines were killed by Hurricane Andrew, but the hammock has prospered. Half a dozen pine saplings remain in the front yard, where oak seedlings have become plentiful. As the plants sort themselves out, they will compete to gain light, space, and a rightful position in the yard. This is the process of succession. This is nature at work.

WATER FOR WILDLIFE

Water in the landscape is one way to draw birds and wildlife, whether you have a yard like that of Bill and Jean Harms, measuring 50 by 140 feet, or an acre of land.

Besides being intensely planted with more than 70 different kinds of native plants, the Harms yard contains a small wading-pool sized water feature, only 18 inches deep, rigged up with a recirculating pump. In another area, three terra cotta saucers have been stacked on a wire stand so a trickle of water overflows from top to bottom over the three-tiered birdbath. And while the habitats are in miniature, the lure of water, food, and shelter has brought in red-bellied woodpeckers, kingbirds, shrikes, buntings, hummingbirds, hawks, swallows, flycatchers . . . in all, 54 species of birds and 34 species of butterflies, six different snakes, a toad, and a green tree frog.

Many homes are built around retention lakes in South Florida. These shores can become wetlands. Cypresses, a maple, a clump of paurotis palms, leather ferns and beach lilies, pop ash and pond apple will all do well in such a setting—and attract squirrels, raccoons, opossums, snakes, ospreys, anhingas, buntings, and redwing blackbirds.

When building a freshwater wetland, remember that a pond or lake shore that is irregular offers more hiding and nesting sites than a smooth-edged one. The shore should gradually slope into the water. Cordgrass, blue flag iris, soft rush, and maidencane can be planted in the shallow water. A mid-zone that slopes from six inches to three feet deep may be planted with sagittaria and pickerelweed, while the deep part of the slope, from three to five feet in depth, can hold spatterdock, water lilies, and bulrushes.

For information on Florida nurseries that carry aquatic native plants, write to: The Bureau of Aquatic Plant Management, Technical Services Section, 3917 Commonwealth Blvd., Tallahassee, FL 32399.

In South Florida, Tree Tops Park has a manmade marsh that is a textbook example of how to create a freshwater wetlands (an 11-acre marsh and four-acre lake) with lessons for even small projects.

When the Everglades were drained around the turn of the century, the marsh in this part of Broward County was turned to pasture and upland areas were planted in citrus. Gradually, urbanization eliminated most of the cattle and groves. At Tree Tops, a wax myrtle thicket developed over what had been marsh. In the early 1990s, the county built a landfill, destroying some natural areas; as a mitigation project, it restored the marsh. Over two years, the myrtle was removed, the mucky soil excavated, and a lake dug. Then, two feet of soil covered over with the original muck was put back, and 200,000 marsh plants went in. A transition zone of red bay, dahoon holly, wax myrtle, willows, and spartina linked the wetland to the hammock.

When canoeing there on a winter's afternoon not long ago, I watched blue-wing teal and woodstorks, little green and blue herons, gallinules, and white ibis around the marsh. It seemed like a little poiedce of the everglades.

When canoeing there on a winter's afternoon not long ago, I watched blue-wing teal and woodstorks, little green and blue herons, gallinules, and white ibis around the marsh. It seemed like a little piece of the Everglades

APPENDIX

INVASIVE PLANTS

ABOUT 27 percent of the plants growing in Florida's natural areas are exotics that have arrived since Europeans appeared in the 1500s.

Why be concerned?

Out of their native habitats, plants often multiply too rapidly because they have no natural predators or they find the climate so agreeable they can grow into every available space. They may so completely fill those niches that the natives no longer can thrive.

That has happened at an alarming rate in this century, particularly when plant exploration brought pretty and useful new plants to American shores for decent and honorable purposes.

We are wiser today, with thousands of acres of wetlands being devoured by Australian melaleuca trees, hardwood hammocks being overrun with jasmine and air potato vines, and pinelands being suffocated in Burma reed.

The loss of biological diversity is high when these exotics so vigorously impose themselves on the landscape. A dense melaleuca stand, for instance, has fewer than five species per acre as compared with a natural wetlands diversity of greater than 20 species an acre.

The Exotic Pest Plant Council is a nonprofit group of federal, state, county, and university biologists, environmental resource managers, and botanists in Florida. The group has a committee on invasive species that keeps track of plant scoundrels overrunning the land. Some of the most invasive plants are well known—melaleuca, Brazilian pepper, Chinese tallow tree, Burma reed. Others less known and less invasive are poised to make the jump from roadside and canal bank to mangrove and hammock.

Initially, the Council described four categories of plants, ranging from those already established and harming native communities to plants with potential to do so. Recently, the Council reduced its list to three groups. Category 1 includes those plants widespread in Florida that already have established a potential to invade and disrupt native plant communities. Category 2 is composed of plants expanding rapidly on a local level, or that show a potential to invade and disrupt native communities. Category 3 is the group that can form dense, monotypic populations, mostly on disturbed sites, such as roadsides, agricultural lands, and canal banks.

Here are the plants from the most recent ranking, which is updated on a regular basis. The list is not without controversy, as not all horticulturalists agree about the potential threat of many of the plants included.

Category 1

Abrus precatorius, rosary pea
Acacia auriculiformis, earleaf acacia
Ardisia elliptica, shoebutton ardisia
Casuarina equisetifolia, Australian pine
Casuarina glauca, suckering Australian pine
Cinnamomum camphora, camphor-tree
Colubrina asiatica, lather leaf
Cupaniopsis anacardioides, carrotwood
Dioscorea bulbifera, air potato
Ficus microcarpa (*F. nitida, F. retusa* var. *nitida*), laurel fig
Jasminum dichotomum, Gold Coast jasmine
Lantana camara, lantana
Lonicera japonica, Japanese honeysuckle
Lygodium microphyllum, Old World climbing fern
Melaleuca quinquenervia, melaleuca
Melia azedarach, China berry
Mimosa pigra, catclaw mimosa
Neyraudia reynaudiana, Burma reed, cane grass
Paederia foetida, skunk vine
Panicum repens, torpedo grass
Pueraria montana, kudzu
Rhodomyrtus tomentosa, downy-myrtle
Sapium sebiferum, Chinese tallow tree
Scaevola taccada var. *sericea* (*S. frutescens*), scaevola, half-flower
Schefflera actinophylla (*Brassaia actinophylla*), schefflera
Schinus terebinthifolius, Brazilian pepper
Solanum viarum, tropical soda apple

Category 2

Adenanthera pavonina, red sandlewood
Agave sisalina, sisal hemp

Albizia lebbeck, woman's tongue tree
Antigonon leptopus, coral vine
Asparagus densiflorus, asparagus fern
Asystasia gangetica, Ganges primrose
Bauhinia variegata, orchid tree
Bischofia javanica, bischofia
Callisia fragrans, inch plant
Calophyllum calaba, mast wood
Casuarina cunninghamiana, Australian pine
Cereus undatus, night-blooming cereus
Cestrum diurnum, day jasmine
Colocasia esculenta, taro
Cryptostegia grandiflora, Malay rubber vine
Dalbergia sissoo, Indian dalbergia, sissoo, India rosewood
Enterolobium contortisiliquum, earpod tree
Epipremnum pinnatum cv. *Aureum*, pothos
Eugenia uniflora, Surinam cherry
Ficus altissima, banyan tree
Ficus benjamina, weeping fig
Ficus elastica, India rubber tree
Flacourtia indica, governor's plum
Fleuggea virosa, fleuggea
Hibiscus tiliaceus, mahoe
Hyptage benghalensis, hyptage
Imperata brasiliensis, cogon grass
Imperata cylindrica, cogon grass
Jasminum fluminense, jasmine
Leucaena leucocephala, lead tree
Ligustrum sinense, privet
Lygodium japonicum, Japanese climbing fern
Macfadyena unguis-cati, cat's claw
Manilkara zapota, sapodilla
Melinis minutiflora, molasses grass

Merremia tuberosa, wood rose
Murraya paniculata, orange jessamine
Nephrolepis multiflora, Asian sword fern
Ochrosia paviflora (*O. elliptica*), kopsia
Oeceoclades maculata, ground orchid
Oryza rufipogon, red rice
Paspalum notatum, Bahia grass
Pennisetum purpureum, Napier grass
Pittosporum pentandrum, pittosporum
Pouteria campechiana, canistel
Psidium guajava, guava
Psidium littorale (*P. cattleianum*), strawberry guava
Rhoeo spathacea (*R. discolor*), oysterplant
Sansevieria hyacinthoides (*S. trifasciata*), bowstring hemp
Solanum toryum, turkey berry
Syngonium podophyllum, arrowhead vine
Syzygium cumini, jambolan, Java plum
Syzygium jambos, rose apple
Tectaria incisa, incised halberd fern
Terminalia catappa, tropical almond
Thespesia populnea, seaside mahoe
Triphasia trifolia, limeberry
Wedelia trilobata, wedelia

Category 3
Achyranthes indica, Devil's horsewhip
Brachiaria mutica, para grass

Cassia coluteoides (*Senna pendula*), climbing cassia
Catharanthus roseus, Madagascar periwinkle
Cynodon dactylon, Bermuda grass
Dactyloctenium aegyptium, crowfoot grass
Eremochloa ophiuroides, centipede grass
Eucalyptus camaldulensis, Murray red gum
Furcraea cabuya, Central American sisal
Hyparrhenia rufa, jaragua
Indigofera spicata, creeping indigo
Kalanchoe pinnata, life plant
Mucuna pruriens, cow itch
Nephrolepis hirsutula cv. *superba,* petticoat fern
Panicum maximum, Guinea grass
Rhynchelytrum repens, Natal grass
Ricinus communis, castor bean
Rottboellia cochinchinensis (*R. exaltata*), itch grass
Russelia equisetiformis, firecracker plant
Selaginella willdenovii, peacock fern
Sesbania emerus (*S. exaltata*) bequilla
Solanum diphyllum, solanum
Solanum tampicense, Tampico soda apple
Spathodea campanulata, African tulip tree
Spermacoce verticillata
Sporobolus jacquemontii, smut grass
Stenotaphrum secundatum, St. Augustine grass
Urena lobata, Caesar's weed
Zebrina pendula, zebrina

SELECTED BIBLIOGRAPHY

Amranand, Pimsai. *Gardening in Bangkok.* Bangkok: The Siam Society, 1970.

Barbour, Thomas. *That Vanishing Eden: A Naturalist's Florida.* Boston: Little, Brown and Co., 1945.

Barnett, Michael R., and David W. Crewz, eds. *An Introduction to Planting and Maintaining Selected Common Coastal Plants in Florida.* Gainesville, Fla.: Sea Grant Extension Program.

Bell, C. Ritchie, and Byron J. Taylor. *Florida Wild Flowers and Roadside Plants.* Chapel Hill, N.C.: Laurel Hill Press, 1982.

Berry, Fred, and W. John Kress. *Heliconia, An Identification Guide.* Washington and London: Smithsonian Institution Press, 1991.

Blombery, Alec, and Tony Todd. *Palms.* London, Sydney, Melbourne: Angus & Robertson, 1982.

Broschat, Timothy K., and Alan W. Meerow. *Betrock's Reference Guide to Florida Landscape Plants.* Cooper City, Fla.: Betrock Information Systems, Inc., 1991.

Burch, Derek, Daniel B. Ward, and David W. Hall. *Checklist of the Woody Cultivated Plants of Florida.* Gainesville, Fla.: University of Florida Press, 1988.

Bush, Charles S., and Julia F. Morton. *Native Trees and Plants for Florida Landscaping.* Gainesville, Fla.: Florida Department of Agriculture and Consumer Services.

Campbell, Richard J., ed. *Mangos: A Guide to Mangos in Florida.* Miami: Fairchild Tropical Garden, 1992.

Carr, Archie, and the editors of Time-Life Books. *The Everglades.* New York: Time Life Books, 1973.

Carson, Rachel Louise. *Silent Spring.* Boston: Houghton Mifflin, 1962.

Chellman, Charles W. *Insects, Diseases and Other Problems of Florida Trees.* Gainesville, Fla.: Florida Department of Agriculture and Consumer Services, 1975.

Courtright, Gordon. *Tropicals.* Portland, Oreg.: Timber Press, 1988.

Davidson, Alan, and Charlotte Knox. *Fruit: A Connoisseur's Guide and Cookbook.* New York: Simon and Schuster, 1991.

Dillard, Annie. *Pilgrim at Tinker Creek.* New York: Harper's, 1974.

Dorn, Mabel. *Under the Coconuts in Florida.* South Miami: South Florida Publishing Co., 1946.

Dorn, Mabel White, and Marjory Stoneman Douglas. *The Book of Twelve for South Florida Gardens.* South Miami: The South Florida Publishing Co., 1928; reprinted by South Florida Horticultural Society, 1988; Magazine Press, 1974.

Douglas, Marjory Stoneman. *The Everglades: River of Grass.* St. Simons Island, Ga.: Mockingbird Books, 1974.

Ellefson, Connie Lockhart, Thomas L. Stephens, and Doug Welsh. *Xeriscape Gardening.* New York: Macmillan Publishing Co., 1992.

Graf, Alfred Byrd. *Tropica.* East Rutherford, N.J.: Roehrs Co., 1978.

Hoshizaki, Barbara Joe. *Fern Growers Manual.* New York: Alfred A. Knopf, 1979.

Janzen, Daniel H., ed. *Costa Rican Natural History.* Chicago and London: The University of Chicago Press, 1983.

Jaworski, Henry. *Orchids Simplified.* Shelburne, Vt.: Chapters Publishing, 1992.

Kale, Herbert W., II, and David S. Maehr. *Florida's Birds*. Sarasota, Fla.: Pineapple Press, 1990.

Kilmer, Anne. *Gardening for Butterflies and Children in South Florida*. West Palm Beach: The Palm Beach Post. 1992.

Lessard, W.O. *The Complete Book of Bananas*. Miami: 1992.

Mathias, Mildred E., ed. *Flowering Plants in the Landscape*. Berkeley, Los Angeles, London: University of California Press, 1982.

Meerow, Alan W. *Betrock's Guide to Landscape Palms*. Cooper City, Fla.: Betrock Information Systems, Inc., 1992.

Meerow, Alan W. *Native Ground Cover for South Florida*. Gainesville, Fla.: University of Florida, Institute of Food and Agricultural Sciences, 1990.

Meerow, Alan W. *Native Shrubs for South Florida*. Gainesville, Fla.: University of Florida, Institute of Food and Agricultural Sciences, 1990.

Meerow, Alan W., Henry M. Donselman, and Timothy K. Broschat. *Native Trees for South Florida*. Gainesville, Fla.: University of Florida, Institute of Food and Agricultural Sciences, 1992.

Menninger, Edwin A. *Flowering Trees of the World for Tropics and Warm Climates*. New York: Hearthside Press, Inc., 1962.

Morton, Julia F. *Exotic Plants for House and Garden*. Racine, Wis.: Golden Press, 1971.

Morton, Julia F. *500 Plants of South Florida*. Miami: E.A. Seemann Publishing Inc., 1974.

Myers, Ronald L., and John J. Ewel, eds. *Ecosystems of Florida*. Orlando: University of Central Florida Press, 1990.

Neal, Marie. *In Gardens of Hawaii*. Honolulu: Bishop Museum Press, 1965.

Northern, Henry T. *Introductory Plant Science*. 3rd ed. New York: The Ronald Press Co., 1953.

Olkowski, William, Sheila Daar, and Helga Olkowski. *Common-Sense Pest Control*. Newtown, Conn.: The Taunton Press, 1991.

Parks, Arva Moore. *Miami, The Magic City*. Revised edition. Miami: Centennial Press, 1991.

Pickering, Charles. *Chronological History of Plants*. Boston: Little, Brown and Co., 1879.

Popenoe, Wilson. *Manual of Tropical and Subtropical Fruits*. New York: Macmillan Co., 1920; facsimile of the 1920 edition, Hafner Press, 1974.

Rawlings, Marjorie Kinnan. *Cross Creek*. St. Simons Island, Ga.: Mockingbird Books, 1942.

Salisbury, Frank B., and Cleon W. Ross. *Plant Physiology*. 2nd ed. Belmont, Calif.: Wadsworth Publishing Co., Inc., 1978.

Scurlock, J. Paul. *Native Trees & Shrubs of the Florida Keys*. Pittsburgh, Pa. : Laurel Press, 1987.

Shuttleworth, Floyd S., Herbert S. Zim, and Gordon W. Dillon. *Orchids*. Racine, Wis.: Golden Press, 1970.

Simpson, Charles Torrey. *In Lower Florida Wilds*. New York: Putnam, 1920.

Smiley, Nixon. *Florida Gardening Month by Month*. 3rd ed. Coral Gables, .Fla: University of Miami Press, 1986.

Stresau, Frederic B. *Florida My Eden*. Port Salerno, Fla.: Florida Classics Library, 1986.

Stevenson, George B. *Palms of South Florida*. Miami: Fairchild Tropical Garden, 1974.

———*Trees of the Everglades National Park and the Florida Keys*. Miami: Banyan Books, 1969.

Stilig, Peter D. *Florida Butterflies and Other Insects*. Sarasota, Fla.: Pineapple Press, 1989.

Sturrock, David. *Fruits for Southern Florida*. Stuart, Fla.: Southeastern Printing Co., Inc., 1959; reprint by Horticultural Books, Inc., 1980.

Tasker, Georgia. *Wild Things, The Return of Native Plants*. Winter Park, Fla.: The Florida Native Plant Society, 1984.

Tomlinson, P.B. *The Biology of Trees Native to Tropical Florida*. Allston, Mass.: Harvard University, 1980.

Walcott, Derek. *Omeros*. New York: Farrar Straus Giroux, 1990.

Watkins, John V., and Thomas J. Sheehan. *Florida Landscape Plants, Native and Exotic*. Revised edition. Gainesville, Fla.: The University Presses of Florida, 1975.

Wilson, Edward O. *The Diversity of Life*. Cambridge, Mass.: The Belknap Press of Harvard University Press, 1992.

Workman, Richard W. *Growing Native*. Sanibel, Fla.: The Sanibel–Captiva Conservation Foundation, Inc., 1980.

GARDENS TO VISIT

BOTANICAL GARDENS in South Florida are excellent places to begin planning your own garden. You will find plants beautifully displayed and fully labeled, along with knowledgeable horticulturists who can answer your questions. Admission fees vary.

Butterfly World in Tradewinds Park, 3600 W. Sample Road, Coconut Creek. Tropical gardens, vine pergolas, and a butterfly museum, as well as a plant shop and gift shop, make this one of the world's largest butterfly farms. Classes on butterfly gardening are held monthly. Hours are 9 A.M. to 5 P.M. Monday through Saturday and 1 to 5 P.M. Sunday.

Fairchild Tropical Garden, 10901 Old Cutler Rd., Miami, is 83 acres, the largest tropical botanical garden in the continental United States. One of the world's finest collections of palms and cycads along with flowering trees, shrubs, and vines. Designed by William Lyman Phillips. Hours are 9:30 A.M to 4:30 P.M. every day.

Flamingo Gardens and Arboretum, 3750 Flamingo Rd., Davie. Sixty acres in what once was an orange grove. Heliconias are a specialty. Beautiful strolling garden and aviary. Hours are 9 A.M. to 5 P.M. daily.

Fruit and Spice Park, 24801 SW 187th Ave., Homestead. A collection of hundreds of tropical fruit trees and vegetables. Tasting is always on the docket during a garden tour. Hours: 10 A.M. to 5 P.M. daily.

The Kampong of the National Tropical Botanical Garden, 4013 Douglas Rd., Coconut Grove. Former home of famous plant explorer David Fairchild, this estate has rare fruit plant-ings, an ethnobotanical collection, and flowering trees from around the tropical world. Tours by appointment.

Marie Selby Botanical Gardens, 811 S. Palm Ave., Sarasota, off U.S. 41. Eleven acres open to the public, with a glorious tropical display house, food garden, strolling grounds, and a botany museum. Hours: 10 A.M. to 5 P.M. every day except Christmas.

Mounts Botanical Garden, 531 N. Military Trail, West Palm Beach, behind the Palm Beach Cooperative Extension Service offices. Features landscape plantings for homeowner comparison, tropical fruits, annual display gardens, and water gardens. Hours: 8 A.M. to 5 P.M. daily.

In addition, check out the county and state parks in your area for nature trails, pamphlets on native plants, and to see subtropical Florida at its best. Do not forget Everglades National Park in Dade County, Big Cypress National Preserve and the Fakahatchee Strand in Collier County, and Corkscrew Swamp Sanctuary, an Audubon Society preserve near Naples.

Other Resources

The University of Florida's Institute of Food and Agricultural Sciences/Cooperative Extension Service has offices in every county in Florida. In South Florida, the addresses are:

Dade/IFAS Cooperative Extension Service
18710 SW 288th St.
Homestead, FL 33030

Broward/IFAS Cooperative Extension Service
3245 College Ave.
Davie, FL 33314.

Palm Beach/IFAS Cooperative Extension Service
531 N. Military Trail
West Palm Beach, FL 33406.

The South Florida Water Management District has an 800 number for information on xeriscape/water conservation. It is 1-800-662-8876. Or write:

South Florida Water Management District
P.O. Box 24680
West Palm Beach, FL 33416

INDEX

A

Abrus precatorius, 159
Acacia auriculiformis, 38, 159
   farnesiana, 74, 95
Acalypha, 25, 78
Acalypha hispida, 81
   wilkesiana, 81
Acer rubrum, 56-57
Achyranthes indica, 161
Acoelorrhaphe wrightii, 117, 123
Acrocromia aculeata, 123
Acrosticum danaeaefolium, 87
Adenanthera pavonina, 160
Aechmea, *83*, 100, 101
Aechmea blanchetiana, 93, 101
African bush daisy, 97
African tulip tree, 38, 71, 161
Agave, 77
Agave augustifolia, *126*
Agave sisalina, 160
Ageratum, 14
Aglaomorphas, 105
Aglaonemas, 43, 79, 88, 103
Aiphanes, 119
Aiphanes caryotifolia, 119
   erosa, 119
Air conditioning, energy conservation and, 56

Air layering, *28*, 28-29
Air potato vine, 89, 159, 160
Albizia lebbeck, 38, 160
Aliette, fungicide, 42, 43
Allamanda, 16, 79, 81, 89
Allamanda cathartica, 89
Alligator flags, 4
Alligator lily, 87
Alligator pear, 133
Allspice, 67, 96, 129
Alocasia, 103
Alocasia cuprea, 103
   sanderiana, 104
Alteramnus lucida, 96
Aluminum plant, 88
Alyssum, 14
Amaryllis, 29
Ambrosia beetle, 136
American beautyberry, 141
Amranand, Pimsai, 136
Amyris elemifera, 144
Anderson's Crape hibiscus, 80, 82
Andromeda Gardens, 107
Angel's trumpet, 81, 128
Angraecum sesquipedale, 109
Anhinga, 145
Annatto, 71, 81
Annonas, 136

Anthracnose, disease, 9, 133
Anthurium, 102
Anthurium clarinervium, 103, *112*
   crystallinum, 103
   hookeri, 43
   magnificum, 103
Antigonon leptopus, 160
Ants, 46, 140
Aphids, 45, 46, 49, 51, 82, 114
Apple banana, 135
Apple blossom cassia, 16, 68, *69*, 71
Aralia, 84
Ardisia ellipitica, 160
   escallonioides, 81
   paniculata, 146
Areca palm, 119
Arenga engleri, 123
   tremula, 123
Aristolochia grandiflora, 89
   ringens, 89
Aroids, 11, 41, 102-104, *111*
   cold-tolerant, 43
Arrowhead, wildflower, 143
Arrowhead vine, 161
Arrowroot, 124
Artillery fern, 85, 88
Asclepias currassavica, 143
   tuberosa, 143, 144

Ascocendas, 112
Ascocentrums, 112
Asian sword fern, 160
Asparagus densiflorus, 160
Asparagus fern, 160
Asplenium serratum, 105
Association of Florida Native Nurseries, 77
Aster caroliniensis, 144
Asystasia gangetica, 160
Atemoya, 136, 137
Ateramnus lucidus, 57, 144
Atlas of United States Trees: Vol. 5, Florida, The, 77
Australian pine, 2, 38, 160
Australian tree fern, 106
Autumn, 8
Averrhoa carambola, 65, 136
Avocado, *12*, 15, 38, 133-34, 137
   pruning, 22-23, 25
"Avocado, The," 134

B

Baccharis, 8
Baccharis halimifolia, 74
Bacillus thuringiensis (Bt), 9, 45
Bacterial disease, 51
Bactris major, 123

Bahama cassia, *4*, 74, 140, 141, 144
Bahama senna, 74
Bahia grass, 161
Bailey palm, 120, *125*
Bald cypress, 64
Bamboo, 81
Banana, 43, 134-36, *135*, 137
Banana with a Hundred Hands, 136
Banks, Sir Joseph, 107
Banyan tree, 160
Baobab, 68
Barbados cherry, 137, 147
Barbour, Thomas, xi-xii, 64
Barrier shrubs, 77
Bats, 145
Bauhin, Casper, 79
Bauhin, John, 79
Bauhinia galpinii, 68
    monandra, 68, 71
    punctata, 79
    purpurea, 13, 68, 71
    variegata, 68, 71, 79, 160
    x *blakeana*, 68, 95, 146
Bayberry, 73
Bay cedar, 79
Bayleton, fertilizer, 49
Beach lily, 157
Beach morning glory, 87
Beach sunflower, 86, 97, 142
Beach verbena, 87, 97, 143, 144
Beautyberry, 7, 73, 74, 97, 141, 146
Bees, 49, 110
Beetles, 48-49, 58, 130, 137, 146
    Ambrosia, 136
    Cuban May, 48-49, 137
    Euphoria, 49
    Ladybug, 47, 82
    May, 16-17
Befaria racemosa, 144

Beggar's tick, 144
Begonia, 29, 41
    Wax, 14, *15*
Bequilla, 161
Bermuda grass, 161
Betrock's Palms for the Landscape
    (Meerow), 122
Bidens alba, 143
Big Cypress National Preserve, 164
Big Cypress Swamp, 3, 128
Biology of Trees Native to Tropical Flor-
    ida, The (Tomlinson), 57, 62-63
Biosolids, as fertilizer, 32
Bird-of-paradise, 107
Birds, 4-5, 6, 8, 140, 145
    attracting, 73, 146-47, 156-57
Bird's-nest anthurium, 43, 102
Bird's-nest fern, 104-105
Bischofia, 38, 160
Bischofia javanica, 38, 160
Bismarckia nobilis, 119
Bismark palm, 119
Bixa orellana, 81
Blackbead, 76, 79, 144, 155
Blackburn, Linda, 156
Blackburn, Roger, 156
Black ironwood, 96, 156
Black olive, 23, 24, 25, 26, 57, 95, 146
    Spiny, 96
Black rot, 114
Black sapote, 137
Blanket flower, 86, 97
Blazing star, 144
Blechnum serrulatum, 104
Blechum brownei, 142, 144
Bliss, William, 134
Blister mites, 48
Block, Henry, 141, 142
Block, Kathy, 141

Blolly, 5, 96, 146, *148*, 155
Blood, as fertilizer, 32
Blue-eyed grass, 143
Blue flag iris, 143, 157
Blue-gray gnatcatcher, 145
Blue jays, 145, 146, 147
Blue lantan palm, 120
Blue porterweed, 141, 142, 143, 144,
    145, 147
Blue vanda, 113
Bok Tower Gardens, 87
Bombax, 68
Bombax ceiba, 68, 71
Borassus flabellifer, 123
Borrichia arborescens, 85-86
    frutescens, 79, 142
Boston fern, xiv, 87, 97, 106
Bottlebrush, 68, 71, 146
Bottle palm, 120
Bougainvillea, 21, 77, 97
Bower plant, 89
Bowstring hemp, 161
Boxthorn, 77
Brachiaria mutica, 161
Bracken, 141
Brahea brandegeei, 123
    dulcis, 123
Brassaia actinophylla, 160
Brazilian cloak, 82
Brazilian pepper, 2, 159, 160
Brazilian plume, 21, 82
Breynia disticha roseo-picta, 81
Bridal bouquet, 89
Brittle thatch, 118
Bromeliads, 2, 7, 11, *12*, 29, *52*, 79,
    83, *86*, 100-102
    dividing, 29
    fertilizing, 101

    freezes and, 43
    as groundcovers, 85, 88
    hurricane care, 41, 42
    pests, 101
Broward County Cooperative Exten-
    sion Service, 35
Brown-eyed susan, 143, 144
Brown thrashers, 145, 146, 147
Brugmansia, 128
Brunfelsia, 21, 77-78
Brunfelsia americana, 14, 81, *126*
    nitida, 81, 128
    pauciflora, 81
    undulata, 81
Buccaneer palm, 118
Bucida buceras, 57, 95
    spinosa, 96
Buddleja globosa, 81
    officinalis, 143
    variabilis, 81
    volvilei, 81
Bud rot, 123
Bugs, 9, 47
Bulbuls, 146
Bulnesia, 96
Bulnesia arborea, 68, 96
Bulrushes, 157
Buntings, 146, 157
Burch, Derek, 38
Bureau of Aquatic Plant Manage-
    ment, The, 157
Burma reed, cane grass, 159, 160
Bursera simaruba, 57, 96, 146, 155
Butea monosperma, 16, 68
Butterfly, 76, 124, *140*, 157
    gardens, *75*, 140-45
    pineland plantings for, 141-42
Butterfly bush, 81, 128, 143
Butterfly Gardening with Florida's

Native Plants (Huegel), 42
Butterfly milkweed, 144
Butterfly pea, 144
Butterfly World, 142, 164
Buttonwood, 79, 96
    Green, 65
    Silver, 67, 74, 75
Butt rot, 42, *48*, 50, 120, 123
Byrsonima lucida, 74, 146

C

Cabada palm, 119
Cabbage palm, 118, 146
Caesalpinia, 65
Caesalpinia mexicana, 65
    pulcherrima, 64
Caesar's weed, 161
Caladium, 16, *86*, 88, 103
Calamondin, 65, 131, 137
Calathea, 2, 29, 78, 81
Calathea grandiflora, 81
    insigni, 81
    loesener, 81
    warscewiczii, 81
Calcium, 30, 34
Calendula, 14
Calliandra, 79
Calliandra emarginata, 68
    haematocephala, 68, 143, 146
Callicarpa americana, 74, 97, 146
Callisia fragrans, 160
Callistemon citrinus, 68
    viminalis, 68
Calocarpum sapote, 137
Calophyllum calaba, 160
Calyptranthes pallens, 64, 74, 147
    zuzygium, 64
Campbell, Richard, 133
Camphor-tree, 160

Canaga odorata, 68
Canary Island date palm, *48*, 120
Candlestick tree, 69
Canistel, 161
Cape jessamine, 82
Capparis cynophallophora, 65, 96, 144
Carambola, 65, 136, 137
Carbon, 30
Cardinals, 145, 146, 147
Carica papaya, 65
Carissa, 77
Carissa macrocarpa, 77, 81, 128
Carribbean fruit fly, 61
Carrotwood, 160
Caryota mitis, 123
    rumphiana, 123
    urena, 123
Cassia, 69, 141, 145
Cassia alata, 14, 21, 69
    bahamensis, 71, 74
    chapmanii, 144
    coluteoides, 161
    fistula, 16, 69
    javanica, 16, 69, *69*
Castor bean, 161
Casuarina 38
Casuarina cunninghamiana, 160
    equisetifolia, 160
    glauca, 160
Catbirds, 146, 147
Catclaw mimosa, 160
Catharanthus roseus, 161
Cat's claw, 79, 144, 160
Cattley, William, 109
Cattleya, 110, 112, 114
    freezes and, 43
    repotting, 114-15
Cattleya labiata, 109

Cattley guava, 67-68
Cauliflory, 67
Cedar waxwings, 146, 147
Center for Plant Conservation, 139
Centipede grass, 161
Central American sisal, 161
Cereus undatus, 160
Cestrum diurnum, 160
    nocturnum, 82, 128
Chalcid fly, 136
Chalice vine, 16, 89
Chamaedorea elegans, 119
    ernesti-augusti, 119
    metallica, 119
Chamaedorea Palms, The Species and Their Cultivation (Hodel), 119
Chamaerops humilis, 77, 123
Charlemagne (rose), *129*
Charlotte Sophia, Queen, 107
Chemical insect control, 49
Chenille plant, *78*, 81
Cherry hedges, pruning, 25
Chicle, 61
China berry, 160
Chinese fan palm, 120, *121*
Chinese hat plant, 14, 21
Chinese privet, *83*, 84
Chinese tallow tree, 159, 160
Chives, 46
Chlorine, 30, 34
Chlorophytum comosum, 88
Chorisia, 13
Chorisia insignis, 69
    speciosa, 69-70, 96
Chrisalidocarpus cabadae, 123
Christmas candle tree, 14, 21
Christmas palm, 122
Chronological History of Plants (Pickering), 134

Chrysalidocarpus cabadae, 119, 123
    lutescens, 119, 123
Chrysobalanus icaco, 74-75, 147
Chrysophyllum oliviforme, 57-58, 146
Cigar orchid, 109
Cinnamomum camphora, 160
Citrus, 65, 128, 130-32, 137, 142, 144, 145, 157
    foot rot, 50
    pests, 131-32
    pruning, 24, 25, 131
    seeds, 26
    watering, 130, 131
Citrus aurantiifolia, 65
    latifolia, 65
    reticulata, 65
    sinensis, 65
    x *paradisi*, 65
    x *tangelo*, 65
City gardens, 8
Clamshell orchid, 109
Clerodendrums, 146
Climbing aster, 144
Climbing cassia, 161
Clitoria mariana, 144
Clock vine, 89
Coccoloba diversifolia, 58, 146
    uvifera, 58
Coccothrinax argentata, 117
    crinita, 119
Cocculus laurifolius, 82
Cockspur coral tree, 96
Coconut palm, 41, 111, 119-20
Cocoplum, 74-75, 79, 147, 151
Cocos nucifera, 119-20, 123
Codiaeum variegatum, 82
Cogon grass, 160
Cold, protecting plants from, 14-15, 43, 114

Coleus, 16
Colocasia, *86*, 103
Colocasia esculenta, 160
Colubrina asiatica, 160
Commelina erecta, 7
Common-Sense Pest Control (Olkowski, Daar, and Olkowski), 49
Complete Book of Bananas, The, (Lessard), 135
Compost, 9, 31, 34-35, 56
Congea tomentosa, *80*
Conocarpus erectus, 65, 67, 75, 96
Conservation
    energy, 8, 54-56
    water, 11, 44, 91-97
Coontie, 87, 141, 144, 152, 156
Cooperative Extension Service, 44, 164
Copernicia baileyana, 120, 125
    curtisii, 123
Copper, 34, 44, 135
Copper leaf, 81
Copper-pod, 70
Coral bean, 71, 76, 79
Coral honeysuckle vine, 145
Coral vine, 160
Cordgrass, 157
Cordia, 140, 143, 144
    globosa, 75
Cordia boissieri, 67, 96
    globosa, 143, 144, 145
    sebestena, 58, 67, 146
Cordyline fruiticosa, 79
Coreopsis, 142
Coreopsis leavenworthii, 142
Corkscrew palmetto, 118
Corkscrew Swamp Sanctuary, 3, 53, 63, 164
Corypha elata, 123

Costa Rican Natural History (Hartshorn), 61
Courtright, Gordon, 67
Cow itch, 161
Cow's horn, 109
Crabwood, 57, 96, 144, *148*, 155
Crape jessamine, 84
Crape myrtle, 71, 82, 84
    Queen's, 70
Creeping indigo, 161
Crescentia alata, 96
Crinum americanum, 86, 128
    asiaticum, 86, 128
Crinum lily, 85
Crossandra, 16, 82
Cross Creek (Rawlings), 5
Crossopetalum ilicifolium, 86
Crotalaria pumila, 144
    rotundifolia, 144
Croton, 25, 78, 82
    Pineland, 144, 156
Croton linearis, 144
Crowfoot grass, 161
Crown-of-thorns, 77
Cryptostegia grandiflora, 160
Cuban May beetle, 48, 137
Cupaniopsis anacardioides, 160
Cuphea hyssopifolia, 82
Cup-o-gold, 89
Curtis's milkweed, 7
Custard apple, 136, 137
Cuthbertia ornata, 7
Cuttings, 26-27
Cutworms, 48
Cycads, 124-25, 152
Cycas revoluta, 125, *125*
Cygon, insecticide, 49, 101, 114
Cymbidium pascelis, 113
Cynodon dactylon, 161

Cypress, 4, 5, 16, 63, 64, 150, 157
Cyrtopodium punctatum, 109
Cyrtostachy renda, 117

D

Daar, Shelia, 49
Daconil, fungicide, 44
Dactylifera, 120
Dactyloctenium aegyptium, 161
Dade County pine, 96, 151
Dahoon holly, 4, 59, *60*, 63, 146, 150, 157
Dalbergia sissoo, 160
Damsel bugs, 47
Darwin, Charles, 109
Datura, 128
Davallias, 105
Day jasmine, 160
Day lily, 88, 128
Dead rat tree, 68
Deering, Charles, estate of, 155
Delonix regia, 70, 96
Dendrobium, 113, 114, 115
Dendrobium nobile, 113
    phalaenopsis, 113
Devil's horsewhip, 161
Dianthus, 14
Dictyosperma album, 120, 123
Dieffenbachia, 43, 79, 103
Dillard, Annie, 139
Dioon, 77
Dioon edule, 77
Dioscorea bulbifera, 160
Dipel, insecticide, 49
Diseases, plant, 50-51
Dividing plants, 29-30
Dodonaea viscosa, 75
Dodson, Calaway, 110
Dogwood, Jamaica, 61, 64, 96

Dorn, Mabel, 61
Doves, 146
Downy-myrtle, 2, 160
Downy woodpecker, 145
Dragonflies, 146
Drought, 5, 44
    plants tolerant to, 94, 95-97, 142
Drupes, 67, 75
Dune sunflower, 144
Duranta repens, 76, 143
Dusting, 49
Dutchman's pipe, 89
Dwarf ixora, 79
Dwarf lantana, 97, 144
Dwarf palmetto, 118
Dwarf pentas, 142
Dwarf poinciana, 64-65
Dwarf rhoeo, 97
Dwarf tree fern, 104
Dwarf twinflower, 143
Dyschoriste oblongifolia, 143

E

Earleaf acacia, 38, 159
Earpod tree, 160
Ear tree, 38
Edison, Thomas, home of, 78
8-4-12 fertilizer, 137
8-3-9-3 fertilizer, 132
8-2-10-3 fertilizer, 65, 131, 136
Elderberry, 73, 145, 146, 147
Elkhorn fern, 106
Ellefson, Connie Lockhart, 92
Encephalartos horridus, 124
Encyclia cochleata, 109
    cordigera, 110
Energy conservation, 8, 54-56
Enterolobium contortisiliquum, 160
    cyclocarpum, 38

Epipremnum pinnatum, 160
Epsom salts, 113, 125
Equitant oncidiums, 113
Eranthemum, 82
Eremochloa ophiuroides, 161
Erigeron quercifolius, 143
Ernodia littoralis, 86, 97
Erythrina, 15
Erythrina caffra, 70
   crista-galli, 70, 96
   herbacea, 70, 76
Eucalyptus, 38
Eucalyptus camaldulensis, 161
Eugenia axillaris, 64
   confusa, 64
   foetida, 64
   rhombea, 64
   uniflora, 82, 160
Euphorbia, 14, 82
Euphorbia milii, 77
Euphoria beetle, 49
Everglades, 149, 157
Everglades National Park, *2, 4,* 66,164
Exothea paniculata, 59
Exotic Pest Plant Council, 67, 68, 74
   most invasive plant list, 110, 160-
   61

F

Fairchild, David, 47, 68
Fairchild Tropical Garden, 14, 34, *36,*
   42, 43, 88, 101, 118, *121,* 123, 124,
   125, 164
Fakahatchee grass, 145, *153*
Fakahatchee Strand, 128, 164
Ferns, 11, 41, 42, 85, 104-106, 155
   dividing footed, 30
   fertilizing, 106
   as ground covers, 87

Fertilizer, 30-32, 122,
   applying, 31-32
   chemical, 11
   granular, 31-32, 34
   liquid, 21, 31
   organic, 32
   slow-release, 20, 32
Fertilizing, 15, 21, *31,* 41
   bananas, 135
   bromeliads, 101
   citrus, 130-31
   cycads, 125
   ferns, 106
   mangoes, 132-33
   orchids, 110
   roses, 130
Ficus, *55*
   altissima, 160
   aurea, 144, 146
   benjamina, 74, 160
   citrifolia, 59, 144, 146
   elastica, 160
   microcarpa, 47, 160
   niitida, 160
   retusa, 160
Fig, 137
Firebush, 76, 97, 140, 142, 144, 145,
   146, 147, *148*
Firecracker flower, 82
Firecracker plant, 161
Firethorn, 147
Fish meal, as fertilizer, 32
Flacourtia indica, 160
Flame-of-the-forest, 68
Flame vine, 89
Flamingo Gardens and Arboretum,
   21, 107, 164
Flamingo plant, 82
Flaveria linearis, 143

Fleabane, 143
Fleuggea, 160
Fleuggea virosa, 160
Flickers, 147
Florida Bay, 6
Florida Cooperative Extension Ser-
   vice, 26, 32, 47
Florida Landscape Plants (Watkins
   and Sheehan), 70
Florida Native Plant Society, 77
Florida orange Geiger, 67
Florida privet, 76, 79, 145
*Florida's Birds, A Handbook and Ref-
   erence* (Kale and Maehr), 147
Florida Solar Energy Center, 56
Florida thatch palm, 118
Floss-silk tree, 13, 14, 69-70, 96, 146
Flower beds, 11, 14, 20-21
Flowering shrubs, 79
   trees, 23, 68-71
Flycatchers, 146, 147, 157
Foliar spray, 135
Fondeur, Joseph, 107
Forestiera segregata, 76
4-6-8 fertilizer, 41, 43
14-14-14 fertilizer, 20
Foxtail palm, 122
Fragrance in the garden, 128-29
   orchids, 110
   shrubs for, 77-78
Frangipani, 16, 96
Fraxinum caroliniana, 144
   pennsylvanica, 144
Freezes, 42-44
Freshwater wetland, 157
Frizzle top, 121
Frogs, 47
Fruit and Spice Park, 26, 164
Fruit flies, 61, 65

Fruiting date palm, 120
Fruit trees, 23, 128, 130-37
Fungicides, 15, 130. *See also* brand
   names
Fungus, 51, 134
Furcraea cabuya, 161

G

Gaillardia, 86, 142, 143, 144
Gaillardia pulchella, 86, 97, 143, 144
Galphimia glauca, 82
Gamolepis chrysanthemoides, 97
Ganges primrose, 160
Gann-Matzen, George, 151, 156
Ganoderma, 42, 50, 120
Ganoderma zonatum, 48, 123
Gardenia, 77-78, 82
Gardenia jasminoides, 82, 128
   thunbergia, 78, 82
Gardening, 2-3
   seasons, 3-8, 13-17
   tools, 19-20, 51, 114
   urbanization, xi
   water-conserving, 91-97
*Gardening for Butterflies and Children
   in South Florida* (Kilmer), 144
Gardening in Bangkok (Amranand),
   136
Gardens
   attracting birds, 145
   butterfly, 140-45
   city, 8
   natural, 150
   pleasure, 127-28
   xeriscape, 91
Garlic, 46
Gastrococós crispa, 123
Geiger tree, 46, 58, 67, 71, 146
George III, King, 107

Geranium, 14
Gerbera daisy, 14
Gesneriads, 42
Ghost orchid, 109
Giant leather fern, 79
Giant sword fern, 87
Ginger, 41, 43
Glory bush, 84
Gold Coast jasmine, 160
Golden creeper, 86, 97
Golden dewdrop, 76, 143, 145
Golden leather fern, 79
Golden Malayan coconut, 120
Golden orb weaver, 138
Golden rain tree, 13, 71
Goldenrod, 143, 144
Golden shower tree, 16, 71, 69
Gopher apple, 156
Governor's plum, 137, 156, 160
Grackles, 145, 146
Grapefruit, 14, 65, 131
Grass, 85, 92, 95
Grasshoppers, 17, 45, 48, 86
Green ash, 144
Green buttonwood, 65
Green shrimp plant, 142, 144
Grevilla robusta, 38
Ground cherry, 156
Ground covers, 56, 85-88
    drought-tolerant, 97
Ground orchid, 161
Grubs, 48
Guaiacum sanctum, 67, 96
Guapira discolor, 96, 146
Guava, 67, 137 161
Guettarda scabra, 76, 97, 140
Guiana chestnut, 16
Guide to the Natural Communities of
    Florida, A, 77

Guinea grass, 161
Gumbo-limbo, 5, *5*, 57, 63, 64, *146*,
    148, 155, 156
Guzmania, 100, 101

H

Habitat restoration, 149-57
Hamelia, 142
Hamelia patens, 76, 97, 144, 145, 147
Hammer, Roger, 145
Hammock, 7, *148*, 150, *151*, 152,
    155-56
Hand fern, 104
Harms, Bill, 156-57
Harms, Jean, 156-57
Harpullia arborea, 96
Hartshorn, Gary, 61
Hatracking, *24*, 40
Hawaiian tree fern, 106
Hawks, 145, 157
Heavenly bamboo, 84
Hedychium coronarium, 128
    gardnerianum, *102*
Helianthus debilis, 86, 97, 144
Heliconia, 29, 41, 43, 80, 106-109
Heliconia, An Identification Guide
    (Fondeur), 107
Heliconia caribaea, *17*, 43, 107
    psittacorum, 107
    rostrata, 107
    stricta, 107
    wagneriana, 107
Heliconia Society International, 107
Hemerocallis, 128
Herbs, 128
Hercules club, 144
Hibiscus, 16, 79-80, 82, 147
    pruning, 25, 80
    pests, 80, 82

Hibiscus coccineus, 144
    rosa-sinensis, 82, 147
    tiliaceus, 160
Hodel, Don, 119
Hollies, 4, 59, 63, 82, 84, 146, 150,
    157
Holly-leaf malpighia, 84
Homalomena, 103
Home Orchid Growing (Northern),
    115
Honduran mahogany, 63
Honeysuckle vine, 145
Hong Kong orchid, 68, 71, 79, 95,
    146
Horticultural oil, 47
Howea fosterana, 120
Hubbuch, Chuck, 42, 124
Huegel, Craig, 142
Hummingbirds, 76, 145, 146, 147,
    157
Hurricane Andrew, 7, *23*, *36*, 37, *39*,
    40, 41, 42, 49, 58, 71, 88-89, 101,
    121, 133, 134, 155, 156
Hurricane Donna, 7
Hurricane palm, 120
Hurricanes, 37-42
    care of gardens after, 38
    precautions, 17, 37
    pruning, 17
    season, 7, 13, 17
Hymenocallis floridana, 86
    latifolia, 87
    palmeri, 87
Hyophorbe lagenicaulis, 120
    verschaffeltii, 120, 123
Hyparrhenia rufa, 161
Hyptage, 160
Hyptage benghalensis, 160

I

Ilex cassine, 59, 146
    krugiana, 59
    vomitoria, 82
Impatiens, 14, 44, *105*
Imperata brasiliensis, 160
    cylindrica, 160
Inch plant, 160
Incised halberd fern, 161
India-hawthorn, 97
Indian dalbergia, 160
India rosewood, 160
India rubber tree, 160
Indigo bunting, 146
Indigofera spicata, 161
In Gardens of Hawaii (Neal), 134
Ingram, Dewayne, 26
Inkberry, 76, 79
Inkwood, 59, 63
Insecticidal soap, 46, 48, 131-32
Insecticides, 49. *See also* brand names
Insects, 9, 17, 44-49, 51, 135
    chemical control of, 49
    non-chemical control of, 9, 46-48
International Palm Society, 116, 119,
    122
Invasive plants, 110, 160-61
Ipomoea microdactyla, 143
    pes-caprae, 87
    stolonifera, 87
Iris virginica, 143
Iron, 30, *33*, 34, 134
Ironweed, 143, 144
Irrigation, 92
Itch grass, 161
Ixora, 25, 79

J

Jaboticaba, 67, 136, 137

Jacaranda, 16, 70, 71, 96
Jacaranda mimosifolia, 70, 96
Jacobinia, 82
Jade vine, 16, 89
Jamaica caper, 65, 71, 96, 144, 155
Jamaica dogwood, 61, 64, 96
Jambolan, 161
Japanese climbing fern, 160
Japanese honeysuckle, 160
Jaragua, 161
Jardin Botanicao Robert y Catherine
    Wilson, 107
Jasmine, 89, 159, 160
Jasminum dichotomum, 160
    fluminense, 160
    officinale, 128
Jatropha, 82
Jatropha integerrima, 82
Java plum, 161
Jaworski, Henry, 115
Jefferson, Thomas, 129
Jerusalem thorn, 71, 96
Joewood, 79
Joyner, Gene, 130
Juniper, 97
Juniperus conferta, 97
Jurong BirdPark, 107
Justicia brandegeana, 82
    carnea, 21

K

Kalanchoe, 14, 97, *126*
Kalanchoe pinnata, 161
Kale, Herbert W., II, 147
Kampong of the National Tropical
    Botanical Garden, 70, 164
Kapok, 68
Kentia palm, 120
Kestrels, 145

Key lime, 65, 131, 137
Key thatch, 118
Kigelia pinnata, 70
Kilmer, Anne, 144
Kingbirds, 157
King Sago, 125
King's mantle, 79
Kissimmee River restoration, 149
Knapp, Ethyle, 113
Knight, Robert, Jr., 136
Kocide, fungicide, 15, 42, 114
Kopsia, 67, 161
Kress, John, 106
Krugiodendron ferreum, 96
Krug's holly, 59
Kudzu, 160
Kumquat, 65, 131, 137

L

Lacewings, 47, *47*
Ladybug beetle, 47, 82
Lady of the night, 81
Lady palm, *116*, 121
Lady slippers, 115
Lagerstroemia indica, 82, 84
    speciosa, 70, 96
Lance-pod, 70
Lancewood, 61, 64, 146, 151
Land restoration, 149-57
Landscape palms, 119-22
Landscaping, conservation
    energy, 54-56
    water (xeric), 91, 92
Langlois, Arthur and Margaret, 116
Lantana, *86*, 128, 141, 142, 144, 160
    Dwarf, 97, 144
    Pineland, 87, 97, 152
    Weeping, 97
Lantana camara, 160

depressa, 87, 97
ovatifolia, 97, 144
montevidensis, 97
Larval plants, butterfly-attracting,
    144
Latania loddigesii, 120
    lontaroides, 120
    verscheffeltii, 120
Lantan palm, 120
Lather leaf, 160
Laurel fig, 160
Laurel oak, 62, 144
Lead tree, 160
Leaf-spotting disease, 123
Leather fern, *9*, 79, 87, 157
Leea coccinea, 84
Lemon, 131
Lessard, Bill, 135
Lethal yellowing disease, 51, 119, 120
    palms susceptible to, 123
Leucaena leucocephala, 160
Leucophyllum frutescens, 97
Liana, 88-89
Liatris, 141, 144
Lichen, 7
Licuala grandis, 111
Life plant, 161
Lignum vitae, 5, *66*, 67, 71, 96
Ligustrum, 25, 74, 84
Ligustrum japonicum, 84
    sinense, 84, 160
Lilies, 7, 86, 87, 88, 157
Lily turf, 88
Limber caper, 145
Lime, 131
    Key, 65, 131, 137
    Persian, 65, 137
Limeberry, 77, 84, 161
Lipstick plant, 81

Liquid Green, 125
Liriope, 29
Liriope muscari, 88
Litchi chinensis, 136
Live oak, 22, 23, *52*, 62, 142, 146, 151
    Southern, 96, 144, 153
Liverwort, 7
Livistona chinensis, 120, *121*, 123
    rotundifolia, 123
Lizards, 7, 145, 146
Locustberry, 74, 146
Lonchocarpus violaceus, 70
Longan, 137
Lonicera japonica, 160
Lopper, 20
Loquat, 137
Luker, Robin, 23
Lupine, 7
Lychee, 26, 136-37
Lygodium japonicum, 160
    microphyllum, 160
Lyon Arboretum, 107
Lysiloma, 152
Lysiloma latisiliqua, 60, 128, 146, 152

M

Macadamia, 137
Macfadyena unguis-cati, 160
Madagascar jasmine, 129
Madagascar periwinkle, 161
Maehr, David S., 147
Magnesium, 30, *33*, 34
Magnolia, sweet bay, 5, 60-61, 71,
    128, 144
Magnolia virginiana, 60, 128, 144
Mahoe, 160
Mahogany, 4, 46, 62-63, 97, 146, 151
Maidenbush, 76, 79
Maidencane, 157

Maidenhair fern, 104, *105*
Malathion, insecticide, 49, 80, 82, 114
Malay rubber vine, 160
Malpighia coccigera, 84
    glabra, 147
Malvaviscus arboreus, 147
Mamey sapote, 136, 137
Mancozeb, fungicide, 15, 42, 123
Maneb, 15
Manganese, 30, 34, 135
    deficiency, *32*, 125
Mangifera indica, 132
Mango, 9, 24, 25, 26, *132*, 132-33, 137
*Mangos: A Guide to Mangos in
    Florida* (Campbell), 133
Mangrove, 6, 7
Manilkara bahameensis, 61
    zapota, 61, 96, 160
Man-in-the-ground, 143
*Manual of Tropical and Subtropical
    Fruits* (Popenoe), 63, 137
Manure, 32, 135
Manzate, fungicide, 42, 44, 114
Maple, red, 4, 5, 56-57, 64, 150, 157
Marantas, 78
Marie Selby Botanical Gardens, 104,
    164
Marigold, 16
Marlberry, 81, 146
Marsh rabbit, *147*
Mastic, 5, 64
Mast wood, 160
Matheson Hammock, *55*
May beetle, 16-17
Mealybugs, 46, 49
Medinilla, 84
Medinilla magnifica, 84
Mediterranean fan palm, 77
Meerow, Alan, 87, 122

Melaleuca, 2, 159, 160
Melaleuca quinquenervia, 160
Melia azedarach, 160
Melinis minutiflora, 160
Merremia tuberosa, 161
Metasystox R, insecticide, 49
Mexican breadfruit, 103
Mexican calabash, 96
Mexican heather, 82
Miami: The Magic City (Parks), 124
Miami Orchid Show, 16
Microsorium scolopendria, 88
Milk pea, 144
Milkweed, 26, 142, 143, 145
    Curtis's, 7
Mimosa pigra, 160
Miniature powder-puff, 68
Mint, 7
Mist bed, 27
Mites, 49, 50, 134
    Blister, 48
    Rust, 48
    Spider, 15, 16, 47-48, 49, 130, 137
Miticides, 49
Mockingbirds, 145, 146, 147
Mohammed, 134
Molasses grass, 160
Molybdenum, 31, 34
Mondo grass, 88
Monrovia Nursery, 69
Monstera, 41
Monstera deliciosa, 43, 103, 137
Morinda, 7
Morton, Julia, 76
Morus rubra, 146
Mosquitoes, 101
Moths, 48, 110, 140
Mounts Botanical Garden, 164
Mourning doves, 145

Mucuna pruriens, 161
Mulberry, 73, 146
Mulch, 11, 31, 56, 94
Murraya paniculata, 84, 147, 161
Murray red gum, 161
Musa balbisana, 134
    paradisiaca, 134
Mushroom root rot, 50
Mussaenda, 43, 84
Mussaenda erythrophylla, 84
Myrcianthes fragrans, 64, 147
Myrciaria cauliflora, 67
    jaboticaba, 136
Myrica cerifera, 67, 76, 96, 128, 144,
    146
Myrsine, 8, 141, 156
Myrtle-of-the-river, 64
Mysore raspberry, 137

N

Nandina domestica, 84
Nannorrhops ritchiana, 123
Napier grass, 161
Nasturtium, 14
Nasturtium bauhinia, 68
Natal grass, 161
Natal plum, 77, 81, 128
National Arborist Association, 40-41
National Tropical Botanical Garden
    (Coconut Grove), 47, 70, 164
National Tropical Botanical Garden
    (Kauai), 107
National Xeriscape Council, 92
"Native Ground Covers for South
    Florida" (Meerow), 87
Native plants, xi
    palms, 117-18
    shrubs, 74-77
    trees, 56-71

*Native Trees and Shrubs of the Florida
    Keys* (Scurlock), 76
Natural gardens, 150
Neal, Marie, 134
Necklace pod, 76, 79, 97, 140, 141,
    144, 145, 147
Nectandra coriacea, 61, 146
Nectar plants, butterfly-attracting,
    143-44
Needle palm, 118
Nematodes, 20, 50, 82, 130, 135, 137
Neodypsis decaryi, 120
Neoregelia, 101
Neoregelia spectabilis, 101
Nephrolepis biserrata, 87
    cordifolia, 87, 97
    exaltata, 87
    hirsutula, 161
    multiflora, 161
Nerium oleander, 84
Neyraudia reynaudiana, 160
Nicholas I, Czar, 109
Nicolson, Dan, 102
Nicotiana, 128
Night spider, 44
Night-blooming cereus, 160
Night-blooming jessamine, 82, 128
Nitrogen, 30, *33*, 34
Non-chemical insect control, 46
Norstog, Knut, 124
Northern, Rebecca Tyson, 115
Nutrient deficiencies, 34

O

Oak, 5, 16, 62, 141, 152, 153
    Laurel, 62, 144
    Live, 22, *52*, 62, 142, 146, 151
    Scrub, 7
    Silk, 38

Southern live, 96, 144, 152
Turkey, 62
Ochrosia elliptica, 67
  paviflora, 161
Oeceoclades maculata, 110, 161
Old man palm, 119
Old World climbing fern, 160
Oleander, 15, 84
Olkowski, Helag, 49
Olkowski, William, 49
Omeros (Walcott), 37
Oncidium, *16*, 113
Ophiopogon japonicus, 88
Orange jasmine, 74
Orange jessamine, 74, 77, 84, 147,
  160
Orange, 65, 131
*Orchid Flowers: Their Pollination and
  Evolution* (Dodson and van der
  Pijl), 110
Orchids, 2, 11, 14, 15, 16, 42, 51, *108*,
  109-15, 129, 130
  diseases, 114
  dividing, 29
  fertilizer, 110
  fragrant, 110
  freezes and, 44
  growing, 110
  repotting, 114-15
  seeds, 26
Orchids Simplified (Jaworski), 115
Orchid tree, 160
Orioles, 147
Orthene, insecticide, 80, 82
Oryza rufipogon, 161
Osmocote, fertilizer, 20
Oven birds, 145
Oxhorn Bucida, 57
Oysterplant, 88, 97, 161

P
Paederia foetida, 160
Painted bunting, 146, 147
Palmetto, 141
  Corkscrew, 118
  Dwarf, 118
  Saw, 87, 97, 118, 140-41, 152, 156
  Scrub, 118
Palms, 2, 117-23
  butt rot, 42, *48*, 50, 120, 123
  care of, 122-23
  diseases of, 123
  fertilizer, 122-23
  freezes and, 43-44
  hurricane care, 41-42
  landscape, 119-22
  lethal yellowing, 51, 119, 120, 123
  native, 117-18
  planting, 22
  potassium deficiency in, 34, 122
  seeds, 26
  wrapping, 14-15
Palms of South Florida (Stevenson), 122
Panama disease, 135
Pandorea jasminoides, 89
  ricasoliana, 89
Panicum maximum, 161
  repens, 160
Pansy, 14
Papaya, 65, 137
Paphiopedilum, 113, 115
Paphiopedilum concolor, 113
Paradise tree, 62, 96, 146, 155, 156
Para grass, 161
Parakeets, 146
Parker, Jack, 56
Parkinsonia aculeata, 96
Parks, Arva, 124
Parrots, 146

Parsley, 142, 145
Parthenocissus quinquefolia, 147
Pascuita, 14, 82
Paspalum notatum, 161
Passiflora, 142
Passiflora, 129, 144
  edulis, 89, 137
  laurifolia, 137
  suberosa, 89, 145
Passion flower, 89
Passion fruit, 136, 137
Passion vine, 144, 145
Paurotis palm, *3*, *9*, 64, 117, 157
Peacock fern, 161
Pelican flower, 89
Peltophorum pterocarpum, 71
Pennisetum purpureum, 161
Pentas, 16, *86*, 88, *90*, 142, 144, *150*
  cuttings, 26-27
  dwarf, 142, *150*
Pentas lanceolata, 88, 144
Peperomia, 87
Peperomia obtusifolia, 87
Pepper grass, 144
Perfume tree, 68
Periphyton, 4
Persea americana, 38, 133
  borbonia, 134, 144
  palustris, 144
Persian lime, 65, 137
Petrea volubilis, 89
Petticoat fern, 161
Petunia, 14
Phalaenopsis, 16, 112-13, 114, 115
Philodendron, 88, 102
Philodendron bipinnatifidum, 103
  evansii, 43, 103
  giganteum x. *P. eichieri*, *102*
  hastatum, 43, 103

  lacerum, 43
  pinnatifidum, 43
  selloum, 43, 102
Phoenix canariensis, 120, 123
  dactylifera, 120, 123
  reclinata, 123
  roebelenii, 121, 123
Phoenix palm, 121
Phosphorus, 30, 34
Pickerelweed, 7, 143, 157
Pickering, Charles, 134
Pigeon plum, 5, 22, 58, 63, 146, 155,
  156
Pilea (aluminum plant), 88
Pilea cadierei, 88
  microphylla, 88
  serpyllacea, 85
Pilgrim at Tinker Creek (Dillard), 139
Pimenta dioica, 67, 96, 129
Pine, 14, 128, 156
  Australian, 2, 38, 160
  Dade County, 96, 151
  Sand, 7
  Slash, 61, 146
Pine bark beetle, 49
Pineapple, 137
Pineland croton, 144, 156
Pineland lantana, 87, 97, 152
Pineland moss rose, 143
Pinelands, 7, 151, 156
  butterflies, 141-42
  restoration, 141-42
  shrubs, 152
Pink porterweed, 142
Pink tab, 71
Pinus elliottii, 61, 96, 146, 151
Piscidia piscipula, 61
Pithecellobium guadalupense, 76, 144
  unguis-cati, 144

Pittosporum, 74, 161
Pittosporum pentandrum, 161
Planting, 8, 21-22
    Cycads, 125
    seeds, 25-26
    shrubs, 84-85
    trees, 21-22
Plants
    animal interactions, 140-41
    attracting birds, 146-47, 156-57
    care after hurricane, 41
    cuttings, 26-27
    diseases, 49-51
    dividing, 29
    fragrant, 128-29
    nutrient deficiencies, 34
    protecting from cold, 14, 43, 114
    tropical, 99-115
Pleasure gardens, 127-28
Plumbago, 84
Plumbago auriculata, 84
Plumeria rubra, 96
Podocarpus, 74
Poinsettia, 14, 82
Poisonwood, 5, *5*, 152
Polo, Marco, 63
Polypodium, 105
Polypodium polypodioides, 105
    scolopendrium, 105
Polypodium scolopendria, 88
Polyrrhiza lindenii, 109
Ponce de Leon, Juan, xi
Pond apple, 64, 157
Pond cypress, 64
Pongam, 96
Pongamia pinnata, 96
Pontederia cordata, 143
Pop ash, 144, 157
Popenoe, Wilson, 63, 137

Porterweed, blue, 141, 142 143, 144,
    145, 147
    Pink, 142
Portulaca, 14, 16
Portulaca pilosa, 143
Potassium, 30, *32*, 34, 42
    deficiency in palms, 122
Pothos, 2, 89, 160
Potting mix for flower beds, 20-21
Pouteria campechiana, 161
Powder-puff, 68, 79, 81, 143, 146
Powdery mildew, 15, 50, 133
Praying mantis, 47
Prickly pear, 141
Princess palm, 120
Pritchardia, 123
Privet, 84, 160
    Chinese, 84
    Florida, 76, 79, 145
"Propagation of Landscape Plants"
    (Ingram and Yeager), 26
Pruning, 11, 15-16, *23*, *24*, 43, 141
    after a hurricane, 38-40
    citrus, 131
    energy conservation and, 56
    rejuvenation, 25
    multi-trunked trees, 24
    paint, 25
    shrubs, 25, 85
    tools, 19-20
    trees, 22-25
Prunus myrtifolia, 62, 129
Pseudobombax ellipticum, 70
Pseudophoenix sargentii, 118
Psidium littorale, 67-68, 161
Psittacorum, 107
Psychotria, 147
    ligustrifolia, 76
    nervosa, 76

    sulzneri, 76, 151
Ptychosperma, 41
Ptychosperma elegans, 121
    macarthurii, 123
Pueraria montana, 160
Purple martins, 146
Purple orchid tree, 13
Purple passion flower, 89
Purple queen, 88, 97
Pygmy date palm, 41, 121
Pygmy fringe tree, 7
Pyracantha coccinea, 147
Pyrostegia venustra, 89

Q

Quailberry, 86
Queen palm, 42, 121
Queen's Crape myrtle, 70, 96
Queen's wreath vine, 16, 89
Quercus laevis, 62
    laurifolia, 62
    virginiana, 62, 96, 144, 146, 153

R

Rabbit bells, 144
Railroad vine, 87
Rainy season, 6, 7, 13, 17
Ramble, 119
Randia aculeata, 76, 97
Rattlesnake plant, 81
Rawlings, Marjorie Kinnan, 5
Red bay, 5, *9*, 134, 144, 145, 157
Red-bellied woodpecker, 145, 157
Redberry stopper, 64
Red cattleya, 113
Red-headed woodpecker, 146
Red kapok, 68
Red latan palm, 120
Red maple, 4, 5, 56-57, 63, 150

Red rice, 161
Red sandlewood, 160
Red stopper, 64
Red-tail hawk, 145
Red-wing blackbird, 145
Rejuvenation pruning, 25
Restoration, land, 149-57
Rhaphiolepsis indica, 97
Rhapidophyllum hystrix, 118
Rhapis excelsa, 121
Rhodomyrtus tomentosa, 160
Rhoeo spathacea, 161
    discolor, 97
Rhus copallina, 147
Rhynchelytrum repens, 161
Rhyncostyliis gigantea, 110
Ricinus communis, 161
Roaches, 114
Robins, 146, 147
Rodents, 46, 146
Rollins, Chris, 28
Rosa nitida, 129
Rosary pea, 159
Rose apple, 161
Rosemary shrubs, 7
Roses, 77, 128, *129*, 129-30
    fertilizer, 130
Rot, 114
    Black, 114
    Bud, 123
    Butt, 42, *48*
    Root, 50, 134
Rottboellia cochinchinensis, 161
Rough velvet seed, 76, 97
Roundup, herbicide, 85
Royal Botanic Gardens, 107
Royal palm, 5, 64, 41, *116*, 118
Royal poinciana, 16, 25, *40*, 70, 71, 96
Roystonea oleraccae, 123

regia, 123
Rudbeckia hirta, 143, 144
Ruellia, 82
Ruellia caroliniensis, 143, 144
Russelia equisetiformis, 161
Rust disease, 50
Rust mites, 48
Ryan, Cathy, 34

S

Sabal causiarum, 123
   etonia, 118
   miamienses, 118
   minor, 118
   palmetto, 118, 123
Sabal palm, 41, 118, 141
Sagittaria, 7, 157
Sagittaria lancifolia, 143
St. Augustine grass, 161
Salix caroliniana, 144
Saltbush, 4, 74
Saltmarsh willow, 79
Salvia, 14, 144
Salvia coccinea, 144
Samara, 56, 62
Sambucus canadensis, 147
Sanchezia, 78
Sander's List of Orchid Hybrids, 109
Sand pine, 7
Sanservieria hyacinthoides, 161
Sapium sebiferum, 160
Sapodilla, 61, 96, 137, 160
Sargent cherry palm, 118
Satin leaf, 57-58, 146, *148*, 155, 156
Sausage tree, 70
Savia bahamensis, 76
Sawgrass, *3*, 6
Saw palmetto, 87, 97, 118, 140-41,
   151-152, 156

Scaevola, 6
   half-flower, 160
Scaevola plumieri, 76, 79
   taccada, 160
Scale insects, 46-47, 49, 61, 80, 82,
   101
Scarlet hibiscus, 144
Scheelea, 123
Schefflera, 160
Schefflera actinophylla, 160
Schinus terebinthifolius, 160
Scrub, 7
Scrub dayflower, 7
Scrub oak, 7
Scrub palmetto, 118
Scurlock, Paul, 76
Scutellaria havanensis, 143
Sea-grape, 58, 63, 79, 127, 137
Sealing wax palm, 117
Sea oats, 6
Sea oxeye daisy, 79, 85-86, 142
Seaside goldenrod, 143
Seaside mahoe, 38, 161
Seasons, 3-8, 13-17
Seed meal, as fertilizer, 32
Seeds, planting, 25-26
Selaginella willdenovii, 161
Selby mix, 104
Serenoa repens, 87, 97, 118, 123
Servinia buxifolia, 77
Sesbania emmerus, 161
Setcreasea pallida, 88, 97
7-3-7 fertilizer, 32, 130
Sevin, insecticide, 49
Sewage sludge, as fertilizer, 32
Sewer vine, 89
Seymeria, 7
Seymeria pectinata, 7
Shade house, 43, 114

Shaving brush, 16, 70
Sheehan, Thomas J., 70
Shoebutton ardisia, 160
Shoestring fern, 105
Short-leaf fig, 59, 64, 142, 144, 146
Shrikes, 157
Shrimp plant, 16, 82
Shrubs, 73-85
   attracting birds, 146-47
   barrier, 77
   beds, 21
   care after a hurricane, 41
   colorful, 78-79
   drought-tolerant, 97
   exotic, 81-85
   flowering, 79
   fragrant, 77-78
   native, 74-77
   pineland, 152
   planting, 84-85
   pruning, 25, 56, 85
   seaside, 79
Sida acuta, 144
Sigatoka disease, 135
Silk oak, 38
Silver buttonwood, 65, 74, 75
Silver palm, *117*, 141
Silver trumpet tree, 71
Simaruba glauca, 62, 96, 146
Simpson, Charles Torrey, vi, xii, 62
Simpson stopper, 64, 147
Sisal hemp, 160
Sissoo, 160
Sisyrinchium miamiense, 143
6-6-6 fertilizer, 32, 130, 132
Skullcap, 143
Skunk vine, 160
Slash pine, 61, 146
Slow-release fertilizer, 32

Slugs, 45, 48, 114
Smilax, 8
Smut grass, 161
Snails, 45, 48, 101, 114
Snailseed, 82
Snapdragon, 14
Snowberry, 8
Snow bush, 81
Soap and water, insect control with,
   46, 87
Soapberry, 127
Soft rush, 157
Soil improvement, 92, 94
Solandra guttata, 89
Solanum, 161
Solanum diphyllum, 161
   tampicense, 161
   toryum, 161
   viarum, 160
Solidago sempervirens, 143
   stricta, 143
Solitaire palm, 121
Sooty mold, 131
Sophora tomentosa, 76, 97, 144, 147
Sophronitis coccinea, 113
Soursop, 137
South Florida Palm Society, 122
South Florida Water Management
   District, 11, 91, 92, 164
Southern live oak, 96, 144, 153
Southern sumac, 147
Southwest Florida Water Manage-
   ment District, 92
Spanish bayonet, 79, 144
Spanish moss, 101
Spanish needle, 142, 143
Spanish stopper, 64, 156
Sparrows, 147
Spartina, 157

Spathodea campanulata, 38, 161
Spatterdock, 157
Spermacoce verticillata, 161
Spicewood, 64, 74, 146, 147
Spider lily, 86
Spider mites, 16, 48, 49, 130, 137
Spider plant, 88
Spiderwort, 143
Spindle palm, 120
Spiny black olive, 96
Sporobolus jacquemontii, 161
Spot-breasted oriole, 146
Spring, 4-6, 16
Stachytarpheta fruiticosa, 147
    jamaicensis, 143, 144
Staghorn fern, 106
Staking trees, 40-41
Star apple, 137
Star fruit, 136
Statice, 14
Stenotaphrum secundatum, 161
Stephanotis floribunda, 89, 129
Stephens, Thomas L., 92
Stevenson, George, 122
Stewart Orchids, 110
Stinkbugs, 47
Stoppers, 64, 96, 155, 156
Strangler fig, *10*, 63, 64, 142, 144, 146
Strawberry guava, 161
Strelitzia nicolai, 109
    reginae, 109
Strelkow, Peter, 141, 156
String fern, 104
Strongylodon macrobotrys, 89
Subdue, fungicide, 42
Suckering Australian pine, 160
Sugar apple, 136, 137
Sulfur, 30, *33*, 34, 50
Sulser, Judy, 145

Summer, 6-7, 16-17
Sunflower, 14, 86, 97, 142, 144
Surinam cherry, 74, 82, 160
Swallows, 67, 157
Swamp, 1
Swamp bay, 144
Swamp lily, 86, 128
Swamp rose, 129
Sweet acacia, 74, 95
Sweet bay magnolia, 5, 60-61, 71, 128, 144
Sweet viburnum, 84, 129
Swietenia macrophylla, 63
    mahagoni, 62-63, 97, 146
Sword fern, 104
Syagrus amara, 122
    coronata, 122
    oleracea, 123
    romanoffzianum, 121, 123
    schizophylla, 123
Syngonium podophyllum, 161
Syzygium cumini, 161
    jambos, 161

T

Tabebuia, 15, 71, 97
Tabebuia caraiba, 71, 97
    chrysotricha, 71
    heterophylla, 71
Tabernaemontana divaricata, 84
Tamarind, 63, 137
Tamarindus indica, 63
Tampico soda apple, 161
Tangelo, 65
Tangerine, 65, 131
Tarflower, 144
Taro, 160
Tawnyberry holly, 59
Taxodium, 63

Taxodium ascenndens, 63
    distichum, 63
Tectaria incisa, 161
10-5-10 fertilizer, 122
10-10-10 fertilizer, 32, 132
Terminalia catappa, 38, 161
Tersan, fungicide, 114
Tetrazygia, 7, 147
Tetrazygia bicolor, 76, 147
Texas sage, 97
Texas wild olive, 67
Thespesia populnea, 38, 161
30-10-10 fertilizer, 104
Thomas, Thelma, 156
Thornbugs, 47
3-1-9 fertilizer, 135
3-1-6 fertilizer, 135
Three-seeded mercury, 156
Thrinax morrisii, *95*, 118
    radiata, 118
Thrips, 47, 48, 49, 114, 134
Thrushes, 146
Thryallis, 82
Thunbergia, 82
Thunbergia erecta, 79
    grandiflora, 89
Tibouchina urvilleana, 84
Tickseed, 142
Tillandsia, 101
Tillandsia cyanea, 101
Ti plant, 79
Tomatoes, 130
Tomlinson, Barry, 56-57, 62-63
Tools, gardening, 19-20
    cleaning, 51, 114
Torchwood, 79, 144
Torpedo grass, 160
Trachycarpus fortunei, 123
Tradescantia ohiensis, 143

Tree crinum lily, 128
Trees, 53-71
    attracting birds, 146
    brittle limb, 38
    care after a hurricane, 38-41
    energy conservation and, 54-56
    fast growing, 64
    flowering, 68-71
    freezes and, 43-44
    fruit, 23, 128, 130-37
    monoecious, 63
    native, 56-71
    planting, 21-22
    pruning, 22-25
    selection of, 54
    shallow root, 38
    small, 64-68
    staking, 40-41
    use on fill, 63
    wet areas, 64
Tree Tops Park, 157
Triangle palm, 120
Trimenzia martinicensis, 88
Triphasia trifolia, 77, 84, 161
Tropical almond, 38, 161
Tropical blue sage, 82
Tropical plants, 99-115
Tropical soda apple, 160
Tropicals (Courtright), 67
Trumpet tree, 71
Tuber sword fern, 87
Tulipwood, 96
Turkey berry, 161
Turkey oak, 62
Turk's cap, 147
Turtle grass, 6
12-4-12-4 fertilizer, 122
12-6-8 fertilizer, 78
12-6-10 fertilizer, 78

20-20-20 fertilizer, 41, 101, 106, 113
Twinflowers, 141

U

Under the Coconuts in Florida
    (Dorn), 61
University of Florida Institute of Food
    and Agricultural Sciences/Cooper-
    ative Extension Service, 164
Urbanization, xi, 139
Urena lobata, 161

V

Vanda, 14, 112, 114
    dividing, 115
    freezes and, 43
Vanda coerulea, 113
    tessellata, 113
van der Pijl, L., 110
Vanilla, 109
Vanilla planifolia, 109
    pompona, 109
    tahitensis, 109
Varnish leaf, 75, 152
Veeries, 146
Veitchia, 41, 122
Veitchia joannis, 122
    mcdanielsii, 122
    merrillii, 122, 123
    montgomeryana, 122, 123
    winnin, 122
Velvet-leaved coffee, 151
Velvet seed, 140, 152
Verbena, 141
Verbena maritima, 87, 97, 143
Vermiculite, 21
Vernonia blodgettii, 143

Viburnum, sweet, 74, 77, 84, 129
Viburnum odoratissimum, 84, 129
Vines, 88-89
    birds-attracting, 147
    garden, 89
    invasive, 89, 160
    wildlife-attracting, 89, 145
Vireos, 67, 146
Virginia creeper, 89, 147
Viruses, 51
Vitis species, 147
Vizcaya Museum hammock, 58, 89,
    155
Vresias, 101

W

Walcott, Derek, 37
Walking iris, 88
Wandering jew, 88
Warblers, 67, 145, 146, 147
Washingtonia robusta, 123
Wasps, 47, 49, 59, 140
Water, 2, 9
    for butterflies, 142
    conservation, 11, 44, 91-97
    supply, 2, 5, 13
    for wildlife, 4, 156-57
Waterholes, 4
Watering, 11, 15, 44, 51, 92
    after a hurricane, 38, 41
Water lily, 7, 157
Watkins, John V., 70
Wax begonia, 14, *15*
Wax jambu, 137
Wax myrtle, 4, 5, 7, 8, 22, 67, 76, 79,
    96, 127, 128, 141, 144, 146, 152,
    157

Webworms, 63
Wedelia, 88, 161
Wedelia trilobata, 161
Weeping fig, 160
Weeping lantana, 97
Welsh, Doug, 92
West Indian cherry, 62, 129, 156
West Indian holly, 84
West Indian lilac, 76, 147, 156
West Indies mahogany, 62-63
Wet feet, 63
White bauhinia, 16
White cordia, 71, 96
Whiteflies, 45-46, 49, 131
White Geiger, 67
White indigo berry, 76, 79, 97, 127,
    141
White lace euphorbia, 14
White stopper, 64, 156
Wild coffee, 8, *72*, 73, 76, 141, 145,
    147, 155, 156
Wild dilly, 61
Wildflowers, 7, 142-43, 155
Wild grape, 89, 147
Wildlife, 4-5, 6, 7, 139-40, 145,
    156-57
Wild lime, 63, 97, 144, 145
Wild petunia, 8, 143, 144
Wildscapes, 8-11
Wild tamarind, 60, 64, 145, 146,
    148, 152, 155,
William Prince's Long Island
    Nursery, 129
Willow, 3, 144, 157
Winter, 3-4, 14-15
Wire weed, 144
Wodyetia bifurcata, 122

Woman's tongue, 38, 160
Wood rose, 89, 160
Woodpeckers, 145, 147, 157
Wrens, 147

X

"Xeric Landscaping with Florida
    Native Plants," 77
Xeriscape Gardening (Ellefson,
    Stephens and Welsh), 92
xeriscapes, 91, 164

Y

Yaupon holly, 82
Yeager, Thomas, 26
Yellow-bellied sapsucker, 146
Yellow flame, 71
Yellow lantan palm, 120
Yellow poinciana, 71
Yellow tab, 71
Yellowtop, 143
Ylang-ylang, 68, 71
Yucca, 144
Yucca aloifolia, 144
    filamentosa, 144

Z

Zamia, 83, 124-125
Zamia furfuracea, 83, 125
    pumila, 87, 124, 144, 152
Zanthoxylum clava-herculis, 144
    fagara, 97, 144
Zebra longwing, *75, 140*
Zebrina, 161
Zebrina pendula, 161
Zinc, 31, *33*, 34, 135
Zinnia, 14